REWORKING MODERNITY

W9-CJW-932

Hegemony and Experience:
Critical Studies in Anthropology and History
A series edited by William Roseberry
and Hermann Rebel

REWORKING MODERNITY

*Capitalisms
and Symbolic
Discontent*

*Allan Pred and
Michael John Watts*

RUTGERS UNIVERSITY PRESS

New Brunswick, New Jersey

Library of Congress Cataloging-in-Publication Data

Pred, Allan Richard, 1936–
    Reworking modernity : capitalisms and symbolic discontent / Allan
Pred and Michael John Watts.
        p.   cm. — (Hegemony and experience)
    Includes bibliographical references and index.
    ISBN 0-8135-1831-8 (cloth) — ISBN 0-8135-1832-6 (pbk.)
    1. Discontent—Social aspects. 2. Capitalism. 3. Civilization,
Modern—20th century. I. Watts, Michael. II. Title. III. Series.
HM291.P699   1992
306.3′42—dc20   91-42894
                                                                  CIP

British Cataloging-in-Publication information available

Copyright © 1992 by Rutgers, The State University
All rights reserved
Manufactured in the United States of America

To our graduate students, past and present

Such awareness is the result of our constantly having to take into account the simultaneity and extension of events and possibilities. . . . There are many reasons why this should be the case: the scale of modern power: the degree of personal responsibility that must be accepted for events all over the world: the fact that the world has become indivisible: the unevenness of economic development within that world: the scale of exploitation. All these play a part. Prophecy now involves a geographical rather than an historical projection: it is space not time that hides consequences from us.

John Berger

A society cannot exist, suggested Marx, without forging a representation of its unity. While this unity is attested to by the reciprocal interdependence of social agents, it is constantly threatened by the separation of their activities and the temporal mutability of social relations. The representation of unity in the context of restricted and mutable social relations thus implies the projection of "an imaginary community" by means of which "real" distinctions are portrayed as "natural", the particular is disguised in the universal, the historical is effaced in the atemporality of essence.

Claude Lefort

Contents

List of Figures and Tables

All photographs except Fig. 2.3 were taken by Michael Watts.

Acknowledgments

REWORKING MODERNITY is in large measure a product of some rather striking affinities and confluences over the last twenty years. On the one hand, we have been colleagues in the same department for well over a decade, teaching graduate seminars together, jointly benefiting from a rather extraordinary group of students, and from the wisdom and criticisms of some like-minded faculty. On the other, we have both had long associations with Gunnar Olsson, who, in different ways, has served as a mentor, friend, and intellectual beacon with respect to much of what we have both written over the last two decades. And not least there have been the chance meetings, unexpected associations, and reading groups that have come from being members of a Berkeley campus and a wider Bay Area community.

Michael Watts would like to acknowledge the generous support of the Social Science Research Council, the MacArthur Foundation, the National Science Foundation, and the Institute of International and Area Studies at the University of California, Berkeley, which has supported much of the fieldwork on which Chapters 2 and 3 are based. Insofar as much of what we do is a complex sort of collective undertaking, I would also want to thank the long-standing intellectual and personal support provided by Jane Guyer, Ivan Karp, Gill Hart, Paul Lubeck, Mick Taussig, John Broughton, and Michael Burawoy. The chapter on Nigeria is very much a product of talking to and learning from Paul Lubeck; the chapter on The Gambia, of some joint research and writing with Judy Carney, whose excellent studies I draw upon. Along the way Sara Berry, Pauline Peters, Allen Isaacman, Henry Bernstein, Diane Wolf, Frank Hirtz, Nancy Scheper-Hughes, Alain de Janvry, Paul Rabinow, Philippe Vaillancourt, Janet Roitman, Louise Lennihan, and Piotr Dutkiewicz have been the best of comrades. More recently a Berkeley reading group on the labor process, including Michael Burawoy, Dick Walker, Anno Saxenian, Harley Shaiken, Louise Lamphere, Gill Hart, Michael Johns, and Peter Evans, has been a real treat. Natalia Vonnegut performed her usual administrative and stenographic wizardry, and Cherie Seamans transformed my hopeless graphics. I would like to thank Susan Vogel, Executive Director of the Center for African Art in New York, who granted permission to use an illustration from the *Africa Explores* exhibition, and most especially I wish to thank the Congolese artist Trigo Piula who kindly granted permission to reproduce his astonishing 1988 canvas *Ta Tele* on the cover of the book. His work is a sort of monument to the reworking of modernity. And the editors of this series, Bill Roseberry and Hermann Rebel, both provided substantial comments on Chapters 2 and 3. Mary Beth has always been my best critic and my best friend. And without John Berger to read, and John Coltrane to listen to, I probably wouldn't have written anything.

Allan Pred would like to acknowledge the generous support provided by the Swedish Collegium for Advanced Studies in the Social Sciences, where I was a fellow while writing Chapter 4 and reworking Chapters 5 and 6. While there I repeatedly benefited from exchanges with Hilary Rose, Tinne Vammen, Björn Wittrock, Bo Gustafsson, Uskeli Mäki, and my other colleagues as well as from contacts with Roger Andersson and the entire group of critical human geographers associated with Uppsala University. As my existence for more than three decades has been bi-modal, split between Berkeley and Sweden, I have long-standing intellectual debts in the latter that extend beyond both Gunnar Olsson and my recent sojourn at SCASSS. I am especially thankful for the stimulation and challenges provided over the years by Torsten Hägerstrand, Orvar Löfgren, Ulf Hannerz, and, not least of all, my close friend Sven Nordlund. Moreover, the researching of Chapter 5 would not have been possible without the enormously kind assistance of Lasse Johansson and the entire staff of the archives at the City Museum of Stockholm. (Chapter 5 is derived largely from Chapter 4 of my *Lost Words and Lost Worlds: Modernity and the Language of Everyday Life in Late Nineteenth-Century Stockholm* [1990]. I am grateful to Cambridge University Press for permission to reuse the material in this book). At Berkeley, I have been uplifted, repeatedly recharged, and kept intellectually honest not only by the long train of remarkable graduate students that has passed through my formal seminars and informal reading groups, but also by a lengthy list of colleagues inside and ouside the Department of Geography, the most important of whom have been Dick Walker and Paul Rabinow. All too infrequent contacts with non-Berkeleyans Derek Gregory and Chuck Tilly have also left their imprint on my portions of the book. As always, Hjördis, Erik, and Michele have lovingly remoored my creative flights. And without the brilliant reworkings of modernity fashioned by Walter Benjamin and James Joyce, I probably would have never had either the wit or the courage to take off in the first place.

Prefactory Articulations

FROM THE INCEPTION OF modern industrial technology to the present, the history of capital accumulation has been synonymous with processes of uneven development, with the constant emergence, realigned interaction, and transformation of local capitalisms. The local appearance, modification, and eventual disappearance of specific forms of modern(izing) capital have always been one with the transformation of physical articulations between the local and the extralocal, or "global"; with the transformation of economic linkages between local and nonlocal units at other locations; with transformations in the movement of inputs, outputs, money, information, and people between local and more or less geographically distant sites. But the articulations resulting from the local appearance and transformation of new forms of capital—from the making of new investments and the implementation of new technologies and labor processes—are never restricted to the realm of physical flows. These resulting articulations are also given voice in cultural forms. For the workplace practices and social relations associated with new forms of capital cannot be confined to the abstract, cannot avoid being directly lived and experienced, cannot escape being given meaning-filled expression by thinking and feeling women and men.

The cultural articulations associated with new forms of capital may involve terms and expressions denoting the new itself; denoting newly erected facilities and newly altered local landscapes; denoting new types of technology and equipment; denoting the organization, details, and moments of new labor processes; denoting the new social relations of those processes. More important, from our vantage point, they are likely to assume some form of symbolic discontent, some form of cultural contestation, some form of struggle over meaning deriving from the experience of new material circumstances and new power-relation-embedded rules, from the experience of disjunction and discontinuity, from the experience of the "modern" shockingly displacing the "traditional," in a word, from the experience of modernity.

This book is about the cultural articulations that accompany processes of capital accumulation as they unfold under geographically and historically specific circumstances. It is about the context-dependent, geographically and historically contingent forms of contestation that develop in response to the inner contradictions of the capital-labor relation. It is about the symbolic discontent that emerges as new forms of capital make their local appearance; as the agents and actions of capital intersect with already existing—more or less deeply sedimented—everyday practices, power relations, and forms of consciousness; as local residents simultaneously experience modernity and hegemony in new guises. What we seek to do is to critically analyze such cultural confrontations both in general conceptual terms and in terms of specific case studies that stretch from the late-nineteenth-century period of competitive industrial capitalism to the present era of "flexible accumulation" and crisis, while extending geographically from rural West Africa to the densely urbanized San Francisco Bay Area.

The revolutionary capacity of capital, its ability repeatedly to reinvent itself in the face of overinvestment and overcapacity crises, its remarkable ability to self-mutate, has not only resulted in uneven development and a multiplicity of capitalisms, but precipitated a multiplicity of experienced modernities. It has also yielded a multiplicity of simultaneous modernisms—an array of cultural, ideological, and reflective reactions to modernization within the realms of art, literature, science, and philosophy. As intellectuals committed to a critical interpretation of the world and as individuals whose pre-Berkeley biographies have taken shape in different places, in the context of different everyday practices and power relations, in the context of different capitalisms, we possess the potential to deploy rather different modernisms, different modernisms that are intertwined with the very phenomena we are attempting to address. In order to make our representations in a manner that is forcefully consistent with the message of our book as a whole, we have chosen to exploit that potential by using somewhat different approaches and stylistic modes, both in giving parallel conceptualizations of the interplay of capitalism, modernity, and symbolic discontent and in telling our empirically diverse (geographical-hi)stories.

In choosing to employ an unconventional textual strategy, in choosing a textual strategy that at one and the same time places the book's parts in tension with one another and emphasizes their unity, we are self-consciously and unashamedly choosing to make the p(r)o(s)etics of our textual strategy the politics of our textual strategy. We believe that innovative social theory cannot be truly innovative, that a critical social science cannot be truly critical or counterhegemonic, unless it allows room for representational practices that attempt to break out of the taken-for-granted while simultaneously striving for clarity of expression, unless it allows room for efforts that move outside the confines of deeply sedimented, largely unexamined, and unreflectingly reproduced representational practices. After all, if "the word is the ideological phenomenon par excellence" (Volosinov [1929]1986:13) and is thereby saturated with power relations, then this is no less true of the conventional academic word, of the taken-for-granted logics embedded in the conventional writing styles of both mainstream and critical social science. What we have in mind is less the deconstruction of conventional writing practices than their occasional radical reconstruction—especially since those practices are at odds with the world we are trying to capture and make critical sense of. If the worlds of capitalism and modernity are complexly multi-linear rather than straightforwardly unilinear, and if those worlds are characterized not only by temporality but also by spatiality—by simultaneous diversity—must we restrict ourselves to the convention of strictly unilinear sentences that wittingly or unwittingly deny the spatial and emphasize neat temporal sequence? If the worlds of symbolic discontent are polyphonous, must we restrict ourselves to univocal modes of expression? These questions aside, the politics of our textual strategy also can be put in terms that directly speak to you. We choose an unconventional textual strategy because we do not wish your author-ized reading of our tales to go uncolored by our partial formulations, because we wish somehow to make you understand and mentally hear what you otherwise might not understand or mentally hear, because we wish somehow to break through the filter of preconceptions and predispositions deeply rooted in your social, biographical, and disciplinary past, because we wish somehow to subvert the taken-for-granted (idea-logical) intertextual framework that you bring to bear upon our text—even if in so doing, we unavoidably alienate or make uncomfortable some who might otherwise be sympathetic.

The most extreme element of our textual strategy is Allan Pred's version of "Capitalisms, Crises, and Cultures" (Chapter 4), which takes the form of a verbal montage of aphorisms and propositions. Each one of these highly distilled aphorisms and propositions is to be mentally heard and reheard—eyed and re-eyed—not as a freestanding verbal fragment but as a conceptual fragment whose meaning is repeatedly enhanced and shifted by virtue of its juxtaposition with, its resonance with, succeeding and preceding fragments. These are aphorisms and propositions whose chameleonlike (mis)spellings, hyphenations, and word couplings are designed and re-signed to trigger previously unmade associations. These are aphorisms and propositions whose repetitive devices are intended to counteract the ill-suitedness of conventional linear sentences for representing the concurrent diversity and complexity of the world. For in returning and re-returning to a central word or phrase, we move about in a cubist manner, rotating around the coexisting face(t)s of the object or subject in question, viewing each face(t) from a different location, but in effect from the same point in time. These are aphorisms and propositions whose exploitation of the physicality of the text is meant to make the comprehensible (discursively taken for granted) appear strange and the strange (that which has not been integrated into existing discourse) appear comprehensible.

These are aphorisms and propositions whose seemingly poetic form
is a form of brute punctuation,
a means of forcing the reader
    to a brief reflective halt,
    to a momentary stop and ponder,

and then another,
    and another,
in order to suggest meaning,
    to emphasize and focus,
    to shed white on (what) matters.
No wordplay for the sake of wordplay here.

Having said all this, it should be emphasized that we regard our project and our textual strategy as modernist rather than "postmodernist." The condition of the world we are dealing with—marked as it is by the transitory and the fragmented, by the incessant spectacle of the new, by an all-pervasive commodity fetishism and bureaucratic rationality—is "hyper-modern" rather than "postmodern." And our preoccupation with textual strategy is not merely a postmodernist turn toward language, as we insist upon the unbreakable links among language, power relations, *and* the materiality of everyday life.

Finally, it must be underscored that our focus on the complex articulations of capitalism, culture, and modernity is not to suggest that the experiences of modernity are *all* situated within this nexus. Localized experiences of modernity also derive from, among other things, new incursions of bureaucratic rationality. However, the intricate, context-dependent articulations that emerge among specific bureaucratic rationalities, culture, and modernity are beyond our purview, deserving a lengthy treatment of their own.

REWORKING MODERNITY

CHAPTER 1

Capitalisms, Crises, and Cultures I: Notes toward a Totality of Fragments

What is modernity? It is, first of all, an ambiguous term; there are as many types of modernity as there are societies. Each society has its own. . . . Since 1850 [modernity] has been our goddess and our demoness. In recent years there has been an attempt to exorcise her, and there has been much talk of "postmodernism." But what is postmodernism if not an even more modern modernity?

Octavio Paz, *In Search of the Present*

Culture is the constant process of producing meanings of and from our social experience and such meanings necessarily produce a social identity for the people involved.

John Fiske, *Understanding Popular Culture*

The symbolic struggle . . . over the power to produce and to impose the legitimate vision of the world [is central because] . . . classification . . . the words, the names which construct social reality as much as they express it . . . [are] the stake par excellence of political struggle.

Pierre Bourdieu, "Social Space and Symbolic Power"

Preview

FROM WHAT VANTAGE POINTS are we to understand the various guises, metamorphoses and reconfigurations of historical and contemporary capitalisms? How might we simultaneously apprehend both the global and transnational forms of capitalist accumulation *and* the symbolic forms, the local discourses and practices, through which capitalism's handmaidens—commodification, massification, and exploitation—are experienced, interpreted, and contested? How are the multiple modernities referred to by Octavio Paz (1990) worked and reworked, fashioned and refashioned, against a backdrop of global, transnational forces?

According to anthropologist Clifford Geertz, these questions call for "a continual dialectical tacking between the most local of local detail and the most global of global structure in such a way as to bring them into simultaneous view" (1984:69).¹ It is precisely this dialectical tacking, how the "outside" is an integral part of the constitution and construction of the "inside"—how society as a constitutive process is expressed powerfully in political, economic, and cultural formations and simultaneously "internalized [to] become individual wills" (Williams 1977:87)—that we seek to address in this book. We seek to unravel, in other words, the various historical configurations and reconfigurations of capitalism in an effort to understand how difference, connectedness, and structure are produced and reproduced within some sort of contradictory global system, within a totality of fragments. And yet we endeavor to do so without becoming mired in the vastness of particularisms and without incarcerating complex and contradictory social experiences within the prisonhouse of "unproblematic and simplistic class or epochal labels" (Roseberry 1988:14).

Prisms, or How the Local Becomes the Global Becomes the Local Becomes . . .

Difference is now encountered in the adjoining neighborhood, the familiar turns up at the ends of the earth. . . . The world is increasingly connected, though not unified, economically and culturally. Local particularism offers no escape from these involvements. Indeed, modern ethnographic histories are perhaps condemned to oscillate between two metanarratives: one of homogenization, the other of emergence; one of loss, the other of invention. . . . Everywhere in the world distinctions are being destroyed and created. . . .
James Clifford, *The Predicament of Culture*

Cities find themselves caught in a contradictory logic of globalization and localization.
Margit Mayer, "Politics in the Post-Fordist City"

Not too far from where we live and teach lies the Santa Clara Valley, an icon of "postindustrial" America, the microchip Mecca of the new information age.² In popular representations of high-tech growth, the Silicon Valley is the midwife to the microelectronics industry, a sort of entrepreneurial hothouse, which gave birth to a generation of computer wizards, programmers, and hackers, who converted backlot garage enterprises into multibillion-dollar companies (Malone 1985). Rarely has one place been so rapidly, and so uncritically, mythologized in the course of its own genesis and development. Innovative venture capital, a university brains trust, and the discipline of the market were brought together, so the story goes, in an unorthodox West Coast business culture, spawning what Walter Benjamin called a "wish image of the collective," a dream of the epoch to follow: "To the form of the new means of production that in the beginning is still dominated by the old one (Marx), there correspond in the societal superstructure wish images in which the new is intermingled with the old in fantastic ways" (cited in Buck-Morss 1989:115). Silicon Valley is a late-twentieth-century Schumpeterian miracle, standing as a vivid counterpoint to a chronically outmoded, geriatric rust belt crushed by the weight of foreign competition and ultimately crippled by the burden of traditional and outmoded labor arrangements and technologies. It has become the place "everyone seeks to imitate" (Walker 1989:9): Silicon Glen in Scotland, Silicon Desert in New Mexico. The wish images are duplicated endlessly.

In a remarkably brief period of time, former orchards along the southwestern shore of the San Francisco Bay were transformed into the leading center of technical innovation in computer hardware and software, in electronic chips and microprocessors, and, not least, in missile guidance systems. By the mid-1980s, Sunnyvale, in the heart of the Valley, had more millionaires per capita than any other city of its size in the world. In a couple of decades, prime agricultural land around San Jose, Campbell, and Santa Clara came to house the hub of a *world* industry. Seemingly overnight, the local had become the global.

The genesis of Silicon Valley has been extraordinary by any measure. The county population lept from 290,000 in 1950 to almost 1.3 million in 1980; employment grew at close to 6 percent per annum between 1964 and 1984. Across the region, the nature of work, employment and labor market structures, ethnic composition, and social structure underwent a quite stunning metamorphosis. In many respects, the Silicon Valley stands in the vanguard of what has been seen as a major reconfiguration, a "restructuring," to employ the current lexicon, of postwar U.S. capitalism, specifically, the partial replacement of so-called Fordist systems of production, which dominated the golden years of U.S. economic growth between 1945 and the Vietnam War. At the very least, the Valley led the nation in new employment and work patterns: a highly segmented labor market, sharply stratified by gender, race, and ethnicity, and temporary or flexible employment four times higher than the U.S. average. According to the Immigration and Naturalization Service, at least 25 percent of the Silicon Valley workforce is undocumented. The ethnic complexity associated with the demographic and employment booms of the 1970s, particularly in cities such as San Jose, is simply bewildering. Perhaps only as bewildering as the landscape itself is a topography reminiscent of Thomas Pynchon's description of the fictional Californian city of San Narciso in the novel *The Crying of Lot 49:* "Like many named places in California, San Narciso was less an identifiable city than a grouping of concepts—census tracts, special purpose bond-issue districts, shopping nucleii all overlaid with access roads . . . a vast sprawl of houses which had grown up all together" (1966:12).

Contrary to expectations, the economic growth and dynamism of the 1970s had turned to disillusionment and recession by the middle of the 1980s as the good ship *Santa Clara* ran aground on the treacherous reefs of world competition. The computer boom was cut short quite abruptly in 1985 by the crisis in the microchip industry. A confluence of massive overproduction, Japanese competition, and proliferation of offshore assemblage, testing, and wafer fabrication triggered a major recession and substantial redundancies in an industry already characterized by high turnover and volatility. By mid-1986 layoffs had reached 1,000 per month, and the industrial vacancy rate in the Valley was 40 percent, the highest in the country (Hayes 1989:18–19).

While the boom-and-bust character of the Valley is widely appreciated, the extent to which its silicon revolution turned a particular local world upside down is rarely appreciated. The transformation of the Santa Clara Valley was an industrial revolution of sorts, encapsulating new forms of work, of employment, and, indeed, of family life and culture. Dennis Hayes captures this revolutionary upheaval in his book *Behind the Silicon Curtain:* "In Silicon Valley there occurred a confusing but inexorable transformation from apricot orchards, Main Street and ranch hospitality to 'smart' missile labs, theme malls, and residence hotels. It was reminiscent, in its thoroughness and abruptness, of the enclosures of the English commons and the rise of the urban 'manufactories' that thrust the industrial revolution upon the world" (1989:16).

Valley workers, overwhelmingly women and minorities in the electronics assembly sector, experienced these changes directly at the point of production, most especially in the so-called "clean rooms," where assemblage and testing were conducted. But the microelectronics revolution also unleashed important changes in the social and ideological environment, in what Scott and Storper (1989:22) fleetingly refer to as the "collective social and institutional order . . . appearing in the locales of flexible production." Judith Stacey (1987, 1990), for example, has written of the patterns of family turbulence and domestic changes associated with the rise of the Silicon Valley, a refashioning of the family that represents an exaggeration of national, even of Californian, trends. Divorce rates tripled between 1977 and 1985 while the national rate doubled; divorces in the Valley now significantly exceed marriages. At the same time, the percentage of "nonfamily households" grew much faster than the national average, and abortion levels exceeded by one and a half times the U.S. figure. Stacey shows how the crisis in the family, and notably for single women, has a material basis in the new production system and in the highly segmented labor markets, but it is a crisis spoken to less by feminism or class politics than by organized religion, especially evangelical groups, who attempt to reconstitute the family from the scattered domestic shards of postindustrialism. In a quite different ideological sphere—catering more to the white engineers and professionals employed in research and design—Hayes (1989:135–159) sees a "mass therapeutic culture" forged from the new holy trinity of work, shopping, and fitness.

Behind the silicon curtain is, of course, a vastly more complex international drama, the story of the changing geography of industrial complexes and regional development on a world scale (Storper and Walker 1989)—nothing less, in fact, than a redrawing of the contours of the postwar global economy, what has been designated a "new international division of labor" (NIDL).[3] Although we do not wish to exaggerate the growth of industrial mass production modeled on the Fordist assembly line in the newly industrializing countries, the 1960s did witness nonetheless an important shift in the economic geography of the world system. Export processing zones (EPZs), typically dominated by textiles and electronics, emerged during the 1960s as state strategies to entice increasingly mobile capital in search of relatively cheap and unorganized labor. EPZs were the peripheral manifestations of the same forces that had given birth to the Silicon Valley. Their specific location reflected not only international competition within certain key industries but also key developments elsewhere: the capacity of multinational companies to separate physically various firm functions, technical innovations in transportation and communication, and the genesis of a Third World proletariat, engendered in part as a consequence of agrarian changes and mobilized under the auspices of authoritarian states (Froebel et al. 1980; Lipietz 1985). The shunting-off of labor-intensive but mechanizable operations, a "delocalisation of precise and limited segments of sectors" (Lipietz 1987:31), was geared primarily to export markets and characterized by intense exploitation (notably of women). Spawned initially in Singapore, Taiwan, and Hong Kong, EPZs subsequently spread to outliers, such as Malaysia and the Philippines, and represented a sort of workplace deskilling on an international scale. These despotic and labor-intensive forms of industrialization, christened "bloody Taylorism" by the French regulationists (Lipietz 1987), have given rise to considerable debate over the relative weight of cheap labor versus market deepening in peripheral industrialization and to the relatively narrow and unidirectional vision of technical change associated with some NIDL theorists (Schoenberger 1989). But it seems clear, nonetheless, that some of these sites are no longer residual assembly points at the margins of the world system but are moving, rapidly so in the cases of Malaysia and South Korea, toward something like regionally or nationally integrated production complexes with their own sources of innovation, institutional linkages, and economic growth trajectories.[4] The local becomes the global becomes the local becomes . . . perhaps the global?

The general thrust of our argument here is quite simple. The creation of new industrial spaces in the United States, such as the Silicon Valley, are part and parcel of an unprecedented globalization of production in the postwar era. The extension of capitalist relations of production into the Third World has moved beyond the much-vaunted Newly Industrialising Countries (NICs), however, and the Taylorist frontier has advanced in the last decade to embrace the likes of the Philippines, Thailand, Mauritius, China, Bangladesh, and Sri Lanka. As a consequence, assembly and testing functions are sufficiently footloose that certain sorts of labor skills can be tapped in quite "backward" agrarian societies, and enterprises can accordingly be located even in relatively isolated rural locales, capturing the labor power of first-generation female workers, many of whom are drawn directly from peasant families.

Diane Wolf (1991) and Aihwa Ong (1987) have brilliantly charted this advancing frontier in their ethnographies of new capitalist work relations, and of the impact of electronics multinationals in particular on neophyte workers and local communities in Southeast Asia. Ong focuses on how the Malay women workers, while able to challenge male authority at home through the independence conferred by the wage, confront intense capitalist discipline imposed by the male-supervised work rhythms of the factory. In a Muslim and patriarchal society, this paradox is experienced by women workers as a sort of moral disorder, in which they are "alienated from their own bodies, the products of their work and their own culture" (Ong 1988:38). Ong sees spirit possession among the women workers as a language of protest mediating between the contradictory ideologies of Muslim patriarchy and modernity. Wolf conversely sees wage income among the village daughters in rural Indonesia as a catalyst for struggles and negotiations over female autonomy and over local forms of family obligation. Female workers, unlike their Malaysian sisters in the face of a much more rigid social structure and a patriarchal surveillance state, are able to manufacture a measure of consent within the family. To this extent, the arrival of global capital, and of industrial work discipline, no more imposes the dead hand of subordination or marginalization on women workers than the patriarchal authority of the "traditional" Javanese family always produces a passive capitulation by household members to its demands. Globality and locality are inextricably linked, but through complex mediations and reconfigurations of "traditional" society; the nonlocal processes driving capital mobility are always experienced, constituted, and mediated locally. An industrial and distinctively gendered working class is made; yet, through its own use of cultural and symbolic resources, it makes itself. In our language, a working and reworking of modernity.

It is striking, of course, how similar, and different, are the experiences and life histories at two geographically distant termini of the world electronics system. As Judith Stacey documents the ravages of the "postmodern family" in California, Ahiwa Ong and Diane Wolf describe families and gender identities also in flux thousands of miles distant in Malaysia and Java. Communities *separated* by massive physical, cultural, and economic distances, *linked* through the complex circuits of the global electronics industry, are *unified* and yet *differentiated* in their occupation of what Jameson (1984) calls a "hyperspace," a domain in which local experience no longer coincides with the place in which it takes place. Difference and connectedness, fragments and totalities.

The history of a small valley on the western side of San Francisco Bay contains, then, an important moral. Namely, the "inconstant geography of capitalism" (Storper and Walker 1989) that the Silicon Valley constitutes is one particular expression of the dynamic capacity of capitalism to periodically restructure itself, technically, institutionally, organizationally. These metamorphoses and upheavals, which provide the broad canvas for our detailed case studies, are simultaneously local and global, technical and spatial, cultural and economic. As Brecht pointed out long ago, it is capitalism as a totality, and not communism, which is thoroughly radical.

Any understanding of capitalism's many representations demands a constant tacking back and forth between spatial levels of analysis, between abstraction and concreteness, between structure and agency. Any treatment of the revolutionary capacities of capitalism must instantiate the economic in the social, the political, and the cultural.

Multiple Capitalisms

> What metamorphoses is capitalism capable of?
> Eric Alliez and Michel Feher, "The Luster of Capital"

If the intellectual landscape of the Western capitalist states during the past decade can be encapsulated by a broad sensibility, it is that we are in a period of momentous change, in which long-cherished political and economic practices have been jettisoned in the name of capitalist renewal, a period that in some British political circles has been called the onset of New Times.[5] Marxist critic Stuart Hall (1989) talks of a Janus-faced "Brave New World," encompassing both an economic and "a broader social cultural" visage. The new economy carries the marks of a shift to new information technologies and to more flexible, decentralized labor processes and work organization, and a decline of the old manufacturing base. The genesis of "sunrise" industries, conversely, heralds a shift to flexible labor markets, privatization through subcontracting, product differentiation geared toward a self-conscious targeting of lifestyle, taste, and culture, an explosion of service and white-collar occupations, the rapid feminization of wage work, and an unprecedented globalization of productive and financial capitals. In its sociocultural aspect, "New Times" is taken to embrace a plethora of sometimes ill-defined tendencies, including political fragmentation, pluralism, new identities, a weakening of older collective (class) solidarities, and the rise of so-called new social movements.

All of this intellectual heat has generated a substantial, and somewhat confusing, terminology for an equally diverse cast of changes: postindustrialism, disorganized capitalism, neo-Fordism, flexible accumulation, post-Fordism, just-in-time capitalism, to name but a few.[6] For some, this lexicon signals the final cataclysmic victory of a triumphant world capitalism and, as such, the eclipse of history. For others, it represents the waning of an *ancien régime*, of an old social order; the demise of the golden age of postwar capitalism. The first act of the Reagan administration in the United States, after all, was to break the air traffic controllers' strike; in Italy, wage indexation was weakened; in Britain, the crushing of the miners' strike signaled a massive, state-backed assault on organized labor; and in France, employee protections were rapidly dismantled. Welfare cutbacks, the privatization of services, and attacks on the contractual basis of the social wage signaled a certain sort of world on the wane. That world—of the right to work, of an essentially Keynesian project to ensure employment and steady wages—has been systematically dismantled in the name of deregulation, property-holding democracy, and, of course, freedom.

At the heart of "New Times," however, is an economic sea change, a fundamental shift—albeit still in train—from the old, mass production Fordist economy to a new, more flexible, post-Fordist order (Harvey 1991). By some accounts, the restructuring of the 1970s and 1980s can only be understood as a response to the social and spatial rigidities of "massification," of mass production and consumption (Alliez and Fehrer 1987:316). In this view, "the regime in which the worker is subjected to capital is fading and being replaced by a regime in which individuals are enslaved by, or rather, incorporated into, capital" (p. 317). "New Times" mark the end of the factory fortress (of confinement as such) and "the birth of a new figure, a production space charaterizable as a space of fluidity and mobility" (de Gaudemar 1987:285). The logic of this new paradigm is contained in certain patterns of industrial reorganization— for example, the vertical disintegration of large firms—and in its most exaggerated form as the dissolution of the factory, as in the apparel putting-out system in Mexico City or Barcelona, "which spreads out over the city as if the city were a huge factory" (Casals 1985:142).

Without endorsing some of the cruder and often hyperbolic visions of capitalist "restructuring," and without questioning the reality that commodity production for profit still remains the mainstay of economic life, it is clear that a genuine transformation of capitalist social relations is under way, associated with new, or nascent, structures of accumulation. The first thing that needs to be said about this transition is, of course, that it is not in any sense unusual (that is, historically unprecedented); indeed, it is a structural attribute of capitalism itself. Moreover, the history of capitalism is pockmarked with periods of quite revolutionary transformation, a sort of reconstruction from within, *but within limits set by the logic of capital itself.* One only need think of the debates at the turn of the century over the rise of monopoly capitalism, or the rise of Taylorism and "scientific capitalism."

Second, this rupture is not narrowly confined to the advanced capitalist states as such, but is intrinsically global in scope, embracing the complex differentiations within the Third World during the last three decades. The meteoric rise of the NICs (particularly the Four Asian Tigers) as centers of both export production and Fordist consumption has occurred coeval with a massive growth of Third World debt (over $1.3 trillion in 1988) and an extreme marginalization of some parts of the globe (Africa most notably). Long before the ascendancy of Gorbachev, sub-Saharan Africa had experienced a massive *perestroika* of its own—in the form of Draconian International Monetary Fund (IMF) and World Bank "stabilization" programs—suffering unthinkable hardship in the name of a return to the market (Watts 1990a). By the early 1970s, the postwar Bretton Woods financial and geopolitical order had essentially collapsed as a result of growing international competition, the declining hegemony of the United States (measured by its massive trade deficit and the dollar devaluation in the early 1970s), and the extraordinary, if contingent, impact of the Organization of Petroleum-Exporting Countries (OPEC). The new Thatcherite-model world order of the 1990s combines Bretton Woods globalism with the economic orthodoxy of the Versailles covenant of 1919 (Mead 1990): free global markets, chronic problems of oversupply and weak demand, trade rivalries, and a world order subject to speculative bubbles and financial collapses. The collapse of communism is simply the most dramatic political expression of this new topography of world capitalism.

In spite of a certain unanimity over the existence of some sort of shift *within* the boundaries of industrial capitalism, there is much acrimony and debate over the depth, character, and profundity of these realignments.[7] How flexible are the new machines? How unitary was/is Fordist production? How far has post-Fordism proceeded? Are we really witnessing an end to mass production? These legitimate questions have not been facilitated by the sort of epochal transitions anticipated by the spokespersons for the "Great Divide" or "New Times" or those who purport to document the vertiginous collapse of "old capitalism." Nevertheless, one can legitimately talk of a "restructuring" understood as "qualitative changes in the relations between constituent parts of a capitalist economy" (Lovering 1990:198). A large body of geographic scholarship, the so-called restructuring research program, has directed its attention to these qualitative changes, building upon a long-standing Marxist interest in uneven development and in what David Harvey (1982) sees as the "spatial fixes"—the geographic reconfigurations of capitalism—associated with structural crises induced by overinvestment and falling rates of profit.[8]

Implicit in this debate is, of course, the recognition that capitalism can, indeed must, be periodized and the institutional characteristics of capital and labor theorized as a basis for a more subtle rendering of the multi-headed hydra that is historical capitalism. As Storper puts it: "Capitalism itself—not only in fact but also in theory—can never be the same [in the] post-Fordist era as it was in the Fordist era, which in turn should have been different from capital as Marx theorized it. . . . In the course of historical geography, the nature of capital is revealed . . ." (1987:420). It is on this ground that the capitalist restructuring meets the French regulationists (Lipietz 1987; Aglietta 1979), for whom the current epoch is rendered distinctive by virtue of the dislodging of the domi-nant model of postwar growth, the Fordist "regime of accumulation."[9] The latter is understood as a system of production (the Fordist labor process) *and* as an institutional set of relations, or mode of regulation—in the postwar U.S. context, a Keynesian package of collective bargaining and international financial agreements—which constitutes a relatively stable means by which mass consumption and production provide for balanced growth. To this degree, those concerned with flexible accu-mulation, with restructuring, and with regulation share a concern with middle-level concepts that allow for geographic divergence, temporal rhythms, and institutional diversity in the development of capitalism rather than a monolithic, undifferentiated model of capitalist develop-ment (Walker 1989:6).

The phases of capitalist mutation are relatively stable but are always crisis-prone;[10] they are distinguished both by internal diversity (there are a variety of Fordisms, as Jessop [1988] observes) and by periods of what Schumpeter called "creative destruction," which mark off the periods of restructuring and transition. These watersheds are, of course, always technical in nature, involving a transformation in the forces of produc-tion, but are also, as Storper and Walker (1989) rightly emphasize, spa-tial and social revolutions. Industrial breakthroughs are often sector- or site-specific and typically involve innovations in labor relations and work organization. Periodizing capitalism is, then, at one with processes of uneven development; the geography of global accumulation is, by the same token, constituted through a spectrum of local capitalisms.

Several decades of capitalist restructuring in the advanced capitalist states brings home in a powerful way the centrality of time and space in grappling with historical capitalism. On the one hand, capitalism can be distinguished (that is, periodized) by its regimes of accumulation, which are bracketed, so to speak, by periods of instability and turmoil. And on the other hand, the dynamic and unstable logic of capitalism produces complex temporal rhythms *within* the relatively stable periods of regime growth. Innovation and profitability are always uneven between sectors and over space, and competition produces its own contingent market perturbations (mineral booms, for example), so one must be sensitive to the differential temporalities, pace, speed, and rhythms, of social and economic change within the overarching "stability" of a regime of accumulation (Aminzade 1989).

A similar sensitivity is demanded of space. Within the confines of a unified world market and a concomitant international division of labor, there are both national and local capitalisms, a spatial sensitivity that takes us back to Trotsky's ideas of combined and uneven development. The global reach of capitalism has transplanted capitalist relations onto foreign soils, whose different social structures produce different class configurations and different institutional forms of capital and labor.

To assert the local is in no sense to deny the *global* character of capitalism (both take place simultaneously, of course) or to obviate the need to theorize the *abstract* properties (for example, the crisis-proneness) of capitalism. Our (spatial) point is simply that how things develop depends in part on *where* they develop, on what has been historically sedimented there, on the social and spatial structures that are already in place there (Pred 1990a). A sensitivity to space, and to time, reveals that there are a *multiplicity of capitalisms* contained within the brittle edges of capitalist laws of motion and within the inner contradictions of the capital-labor relation (Soja 1989). The mutation of local, national, and historical capitalisms—what Burawoy (1985) calls difference within a structured totality—is the terrain on which our case studies are located.

Multiple Modernisms and the Shock of the New

Each era of accelerated modernization has been a fertile spawning ground for powerful new modernisms.

Edward Soja, *Postmodern Geographies*

How are space and time mediated by and expressed through the metamorphoses of capitalism? This important question is alluded to by Castells and Henderson (1987) in their treatment of the territorial transformations of global restructuring. In their language, one fundamental aspect of the "internationalization of techno-economic processes" is the tendency for "the space of flows to supersede the space of places" (p. 7). Deleuze and Guattari (1977) refer to this sort of phenomenon as "deterritorialization," in which the actual dynamics of a given location rely on, and are shaped by, activities and forces that are decidedly nonlocal. The logic and dynamics of territorial development are increasingly placeless. Yet at the same time, social relations, and much of what passes as everyday life, continue to operate according to a local, place-oriented logic (the "space of places"). If the dominant logic imposes a space of flows, the defense of specific interests and identities "takes the form of *irreducible local experience*" (Castells and Henderson, 1987:7 [emphasis added]). Local experience is opposed to abstract flow in such a way that the new territorial dynamics—urban, rural, and regional transformations linked to restructuring—are fundamentally shaped by the contradiction between "placeless power and powerless places" (p. 7).

It is precisely this contradiction—a contradiction rooted in the relentless drive for profit, in the speeding up and interconnectedness of social life—that strikes to the heart of contemporary debates over space, geography, and modernity (Berman 1982; Harvey 1989; Soja 1989; Jameson 1984). Marx and Engels commented quite specifically on these revolutionary capacities of capitalism, the "uninterrupted disturbances of all social relations," the "everlasting uncertainty and agitation" (1952:25) that distinguished the bourgeois epoch. In this fashion, the newly formed is swept away before it ossifies, a property of modernization that Berman sees as *the* definitive characteristic of modernity, the latter understood as "a mode of vital experience": "Modern environments and experiences cut across all boundaries of geography and ethnicity, of class and nationality, or religion and ideology; in this sense modernity can be said to unite all mankind. But it is a paradoxical unity . . ." ([for] it pours us all into a maelstrom of perpetual disintegration and renewal 1982:15). Modernity, then, captures "a broad mesh of sensibilities" (Soja 1989: 25), the most fundamental being the experience of space, time, and being within the maelstrom of capitalist modernization.

David Harvey (1985, 1989) has sought to root modernity in this sense in a theory of capital, and more precisely in a *mode of production of capitalist space*. In this view a particular regime of capitalist accumulation produces a landscape of accumulation whose fixity subsequently becomes a barrier to be overcome in the course of capitalism's perpetual efforts to annihilate space with time. Periods of capitalist restructuring engender the "creative destruction" of landscapes—what Berman calls the "pitiless destruction of everything and everyone it cannot use" (1982:121)—a devalorization that Harvey sees as a simultaneous moment of "space-time compression." In other words, each mutation of capitalism "constructs objective conditions of space and time sufficient unto its needs and purposes of material and social reproduction" (Harvey 1990:419). Periods of revolutionary change between regimes of capitalist accumulation ipso facto revolutionize these objective qualities producing an overwhelming "sense of compression of our spatial and temporal worlds" (Harvey 1989:240). In the contemporary epoch, it is the experience of this compression—what Jameson calls "hyperspace" and what Castells and Henderson (1987) call "powerless places and placeless power"[11]—that constitutes the lineaments of postmodernity. There is, of course, nothing "post" about this experience at all; rather, it is modernity speeded up, the experience and representation of speed and social elasticity associated with a sort of fast capitalism (Paz 1990; Virilio 1988; Aggar 1989).

What is true of capitalist mutations is equally true of modernity itself. Modernization is, as Soja says, "periodically accelerated to produce a significant recomposition of space-time-being" (1989:27); these systemic, wavelike restructurings of capitalism—the "age of revolution" between 1830 and 1851, the so-called "second industrial revolution" at the end of the nineteenth century—are inscribed within social formations as *multiple modernities,* and by extension *multiple modernisms,* the latter understood as an array of cultural, ideological, and reflective reactions to modernization within the realms of art, literature, science, and philosophy.

Lest we be accused of reductionism, it should be made clear that modernism is no more a simple mirroring of modernization than modernization is synonymous with capitalist logic (cf. Jameson 1989). But it is also imperative that these sets of realities not be ripped asunder. In this sense Jameson is quite right to link late-twentieth-century capitalism with "our insertion into radically discontinuous realities" (1988:351) and hence to identify our occupation of a hyperspace in which "the truth of experience no longer coincides with the place in which it takes place." Our task in this book is to address the multidimensionality of this process by pulling apart particular conjunctures in the course of historical capitalism—to grapple with the simultaneous production of connectedness and difference, of locality and globality, of the inside and the outside. In this way, we may begin to approach the "rich language of the commodity with all its intricate history of social and spatial relations stretching back from our dinner table into almost every niche of labor activity in the modern world" (Harvey 1990:32).

Postmodern Geographies or Maps of Meaning?

This latest mutation in space—postmodern hyperspace—has finally succeeded in transcending the capacities of the individual human body to locate itself, to organize its immediate surroundings perceptually, and cognitively to map its position in a mappable external world.
                                   Fredric Jameson, "Cognitive Mapping"

In part driven by the changing realities of contemporary capitalism, social theory has grown to appreciate the fundamental role of space in discussions of modernity. As Soja has shown in his *Postmodern Geographies,* the history of the social sciences contains a radical marginalization of the geographical imagination and conversely a powerful historicism according pride of place to history (Soja 1989). Soja claims that these concepts of history are so deeply etched into the stuff of modernism that space can only be reasserted in social theory in the name of postmodernism. It is in this sense that Soja and others have turned their attentions to so-called postmodern landscapes. Soja turns quite explicitly to Los Angeles, which he calls the "quintessential postmodern place" (p. 63), not because it is a blueprint for late capitalism, and hence to be duplicated elsewhere, but because "particular experiences of urban development and change occurring elsewhere in the world are being duplicated in Los Angeles" (p. 221). Soja's mandate is not only to reassert the significance of space but to do so by distancing himself from the crude materialism in which "capital is the crude and restless *auteur*" (p. 157) and by seeking to provide an alternative that deconstructs *the* most postmodern of places with a postmodern narrative.

We invoke Soja's work here because it is exemplary and because in several senses our text is woven from the same cloth. Like him, we believe that places have "distinctive historical geographies, [their] own time-place structuration" (p. 158); like him, we argue that one must never lose sight, amidst the welter of semiotic and cultural particularisms, of "the hard contours of capitalism's 'inner contradictions' and 'laws of motion'" (p. 158). In his experimental geography, Soja adopts a twofold strategy: first, by periodizing and regionalizing capitalism's metamorphoses—four modernizations that recompose the macrogeographic landscape (pp.164–187)—and second, by locating the city-region of Los Angeles in the "globalization of capitalism" (p.190). Soja can then turn his geographic imagination to Los Angeles, what Baudrillard calls the Galactic metropolis, in a spellbinding narrative, an exhilarating aerial foray across the military bases and the ramparts, compelling sweep around towers, freeways, and shopping malls, into the "compartmentalized corona of the inner city," through the "shattered sea of fragmented yet homogenized communities" (p. 244). This is urban morphology, travel writing, of a very high order and of a very different sort!

Yet there is paradox and irony in his postmodern geography of late capitalism. As a sort of geometry of the "epitomizing world-city," Soja provides a brilliant account. But amidst the "extraordinary crazy quilt ... [and] a dazzling ... patchwork mosaic" (p. 245) there is little in the way of people, communities, networks and struggles; in short, the socially differentiated experience of, and response to, globalization (Massey 1991). In a simpleminded sense, there is little in the way of ethnography, and hence (and more critically) equally little in the way of palpable experience, of how literally millions of people struggle to handle, deal with, represent, and interpret the Galactic metropolis. In a self-consciously postmodernist text, the absence of other voices is strikingly, and incongruously, absent.[12] There is no need to romanticize East Los Angeles or, indeed, to see resistance and tactics of antidiscipline in every act of consumption on Rodeo Drive or in every drive-by in Watts. But everyday life there is, and as Michael Davis (1985, 1987, 1990), Carlos Munoz, Jr. (1989), and others have shown, a vibrant terrain of new political spaces and struggles rooted in a cultural mosaic of staggering complexity—what Davis has aptly described as a "culture of Ragtime ... [rather than] the deathwish of postmodernity" (1987:75).

A seeming indifference to the embeddedness of material and cultural life—the reworking of modernity—is, in fact, an endemic and problematic absence in much of the ('New Times') debate, and even in some discussions of the culture of contemporary capitalism.[13] Even the locality studies in Britain have generally tended to see the community as an unproblematic entity subject to external forces (Lovering 1989) and failed to discuss how changing and multiple identities—debates over inclusion, exclusion, rights, and citizenship—are precisely at stake in the restructuring of community life. Perhaps this is not a claim that can be made of David Harvey's (1985) brilliant work on nineteenth-century Paris, but even in his latest discussion of postmodernity there is a danger, also seen in Jameson's analysis of the culture of late-twentieth-century capitalism, of "homogeniz[ing] the details of contemporary landscape" (Davis 1987:107). It should be said that much anthropological work rooted in ethnographic and cultural relations tends to be as weak in situating local knowledge and meanings on the grand map of capitalism[14] as geographers have been in struggles over meaning.

If the local is to be theorized, then this should be undertaken in such a way that the external determinations are articulated with internal agency, with locally shared knowledges and practices, with shared but socially differentiated meanings and experiences. Both Cooke (1990a, 1990b) and Lovering (1989) are right to note that the local has a "proactivity" expressed in struggles that either embody or contest what they call historically sedimented institutions.[15] Hence the realm of "tradition" or "custom" provides much of the symbolic raw material around which local communities, interest groups, and classes rework and refashion the modernizations of capitalist transformation. It is this complex cultural and symbolic topography, what Hebdige (1979:18) calls "maps of meaning," rather than the political and economy cartography of capitalism of the sort that Soja has provided, that is lacking in much of what passes for postmodern geography and contemporary social theory.

Ironically, one of the most impressive sorts of mediations among cultural, spatial, and symbolic forms and moments of radical disjuncture in the course of capitalist development is the work of a literary theorist. Kristin Ross (1988) discusses the Paris Commune, which she sees as not solely an uprising against the political practices of the Second Empire: "[I]t was also, and perhaps above all, a revolt against deep forms of social regimentation. In the realm of cultural production, for instance, divisions in place under the rigid censorship of the Second Empire and the constraints of the bourgeois market . . . were fiercely debated" (1988:5). Ross attempts to identify the common structures of everday life among the French oppositional cultures of the 1870s, and "the most condensed of fictions: poetry" (1988:3). The spine of her study links the Paris Commune and the seizing of government by workers in March 1871 with the poetry of Rimbaud. What mediates the two is space, what she calls, following Henri Lefebvre, "social space." Late-nineteenth-century France witnessed a series of spatial displacements associated with the growth and deepening of manufacture between the 1840s and the

1870s, and an ever more Draconian state. It was a period, according to Ross, of two spatial movements: one was the projection onto a global scale of Haussman's "fantasy of the straight line," reflected in new patterns of spatial integration and the emergence of French colonialism. The second was the first realization of urban space as revolutionary space. The Commune was imbricated in such spatial changes—many of the Communards, for example, were migrants to Paris—and its discourses bring into play the geographic, "horizontal" experience of French life.

For Ross, the Commune was a reaction to the social classification and policing of everday life, to the social space of the Second Empire; indeed, its organization represented the breakdown of a certain sort of spatial hierarchy. Rimbaud prefigured in his poetry a social space adjacent to the one activated by the insurgents. For Rimbaud space was "active and generative," and his poetry contained a vision of social space that mediates between the "discursive realm and the event" (Ross 1988:32).

Ross's study of the Paris Commune can be seen as a meditation on what we previously noted as placeless power and powerless places. On the one hand, there is the space-time compression of late-nineteenth-century society—the Haussmanization of Paris, the changing relations between Paris and the provinces, the rise of a colonial consciousness—and on the other, the social space of Rimbaud's poetry. In this sense, she examines the complex mediations between the discursive and the event—how it was that Rimbaud's poetry was "a creative response to the same objective situation in which the insurrection in Paris was another" (p. 32). Rimbaud conceived of space as "a specific form of operations and interactions" (p. 35) in a manner analogous to the way in which space and hierarchy "came to be contested in the social imagination of the Communards" (p. 4). There is, in short, a homology between the prose poem and the fashioning of the barricades.

These sorts of relations and configurations—what we see as mediations and articulations among capitalisms, crises, and cultures—seem to assume particular significance at certain historical moments. In any event, culture in an active sense is, in our view, a prerequisite for locating actors, for understanding everyday life, within the political and economic matrices of capitalism. Not all actors have, of course, an equal capacity to determine meanings, to nominate, to define symbolic forms and hence to act. Indeed, it is this circumscribed intersection of meaning and practice, the structured capacity of subjects (Callinicos 1987), that is at the heart of our case studies.

Space, Identity, Difference

But the shifting social construction of space and time as a result of the restless search for profit creates severe problems of identity: To what space do I as an individual belong? Do I express my citizenship in my neighborhood, city, region, nation or world?

David Harvey, "Flexibility: Threat or Opportunity?"

A new and historically original dilemma, one that involves our insertion as individual subjects into a multidimensional set of radically discontinuous realities, who[se] frames range from the still surviving spaces of bourgeois private life all the way to the unimaginable decentering of global capital itself. Not even Einsteinian relativity, or the multiple subjective worlds of the older modernists, is capable of giving any kind of adequate figuration of this process.

Fredric Jameson, "Cognitive Mapping"

In stressing the periodic reconfigurations of historical capitalism and the space-time compression associated with its mutations, we necessarily raise some important questions concerning the relationships between identity—whether personal or collective—and place. As Gupta and Ferguson (1992) note, representations of space tend to be associated with images of rupture, break, and disjunction. Nowhere is this clearer than in the simple mapping of divided space onto various sorts of national, social, and cultural identities. Take for example the following quote from Gellner:

[C]onsider two ethnographic maps, one drawn up before the age of nationalism, and the other after. . . . The first map resembles a painting of Kokoschka. The riot of diverse points of color is such that no clear pattern can be discerned. . . . [But] the ethnographic and political map of . . . the modern world . . . resembles not Kokoschka but, say, Modigliani. There is very little shading; neat flat surfaces clearly separated . . . little if any ambiguity or overlap. (1983:139–140)

The world of national spaces is precisely conceived as one of partitionings and discontinuities, which then become naturalized in such a way that people and place are permanently territorialized or rooted (Malkki 1990).

This simple mapping procedure is, of course, deeply problematic. It cannot readily account for those who occupy the borderlands or interstitial zones—the migrant worker, the diaspora community. Multiculturalism within one locale and the hybrid cultures of postcolonialism are equally resistant to this simple cartographic maneuver by which space and identity are unproblematically mapped. And Anderson has shown how nationalism itself must be aligned with processes of imagination and globality, with "the large cultural systems that preceded it out of which—as well as against—it came into being" (1983:19). The space-identity relations must, in other words, be understood in terms of the production of cultural difference within an increasingly interconnected global system of cultural, economic, and political relations (Gupta and

Ferguson 1992). This is a process of territorial inscription in which identities emerge at various sites (places) forged from within global political and economic realities. Nowhere is this clearer, for example, than in the case of the revisionist debate over the San-speaking !Kung (the "Bushmen") of Botswana. Rather than seeing this culture as a product of isolation, survival, and adaptation, Wilmsen (1989) has shown how those attributes are "recent products of a process that unfolded over two centuries" (p. 157). It is the *production of cultural difference within a structured system of global political economy* that is central to an understanding of both the territory-identity relation and to the reworking of modernity.

These relations are thrown into bold relief when one begins, as we do in this book, from the creative destruction of capitalism and its attendant reconfigurations of space. In the contemporary epoch, for example, the extent of mobility, displacement, and what Edward Said calls "generalized homelessness" is unprecedented. At the same time the processes of integration and connectedness, both through something like a transnational public sphere (Appadurai 1990) and through new forms of capitalist accumulation on a global scale, have torn asunder any sense of tightly bounded spaces. There is an implication here of the erasure or diminution of spatial relations and attachment to place (what geographers call a sense of place) but we wish to reiterate that space has not become marginal to lived experience. Rather, a central question seems to be how spatial meanings are worked, reworked, and fought over under these "postmodern" conditions, how space is "reterritorialized," and what sorts of identities and differences are produced with what sorts of cultural, symbolic, and other materials.

In the case studies that follow, the questions of space, identity, and difference surface with great regularity. We have chosen to couch them in terms of the large abstractions of capitalism, modernity, and symbolic discontent. Each of our four case studies refers to a specific site within a historically specific global capitalism in which space, identity, and difference are being reconfigured and reworked, and, indeed, contested, in new sorts of ways. Each narrative unveils shocks of modernity that are rather different in form, are experienced through distinctive sorts of local practices, and are expressed in contrasting "languages" (gender and property rights, religious identity, popular geographies, worker interests). In each case an understanding of the political economic restructuring of capitalism at a particular moment provides a critical building block upon, and out of which, the locally specific struggles over everyday life are constructed. We are concerned to identify both the particular issues and practices at stake, and the cultural and symbolic resources that are brought to bear in the production of the new, local modernities.

The first two cases studies are drawn from the contemporary period and from the Third World. In the first, I seek to account for a particular

Muslim reformist movement (the Maitatsine movement), which arose in the interstices of the Nigeria oil boom in the 1970s. The form of rapid industrialization associated with the influx of oil revenues provides the context within which a specific sort of peripheral capitalism developed. I link this "fast capitalism" associated with Nigeria's oil-based accumulation to the broad cultural context of debates in Islam, both inside Nigeria and within the world Muslim diaspora. The Maitatsine movement provides a compelling case of why and how a self-proclaimed prophet and his followers attempted to create both a distinctive sort of Muslim community and identity. The focus is simultaneously the local form of capitalist development, the class-based experience of it, and the cultural and symbolic resources that were employed, interpreted, and fought over as a means to construct difference—in this case, a different sense of Muslim community and identity.

The second case is agrarian and rural, focusing on the familiar case of technological change (the introduction of Green Revolution rice-growing technologies) in a West African peasant society. What is different about the irrigation tehnologies is that they radically transformed the nature of peasant work by introducing new relations of production, namely, contract farming. The broader political economic context is, therefore, the ways in which capital is taking hold of peasant production—new forms of the internationalization of agriculture—but the immediate focus addresses how new work relations are experienced, negotiated, and fought over within the farming household. Insofar as peasants are contracted to grow rice as households, struggles over work—who will work, under what conditions, for what return?—are primarily domestic, internalized within the household. I explore how the reshaping of the culture of work intensifies struggles within the household, which are fought out in terms of gender, property rights, and the customary conduct of familial obligation. Again, within one site in a globalized political economy, new forms of difference are being produced and fought over; in a sense, a sort of local modernity is at stake.

In the second part of the book, two quite different cases are introduced (see Chapter 4 for an introduction). Both are rooted in the economic and political restructuring of the advanced capitalist states. The first is the story of the "popular geography" of the Stockholm working classes at the end of the nineteenth century. The second charts the struggles over a South Korean steel plant located in northern California. What links these diverse circumstances, however, are cultural contestations that accompany the local insertion of forms of capital and the consequent transformations of everyday life—the reworking of modernity.

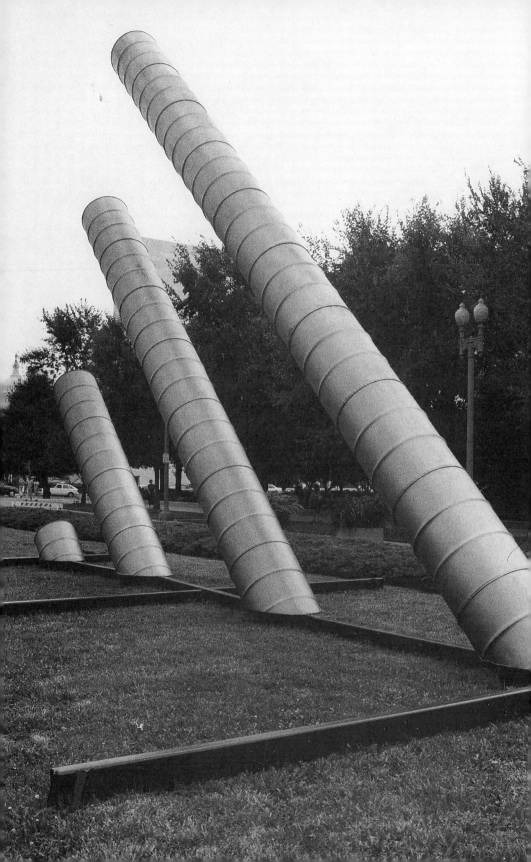

The Shock of Modernity: Petroleum, Protest, and Fast Capitalism in an Industrializing Society

His face is turned toward the past. Where we perceive a chain of events, he sees one single catastrophe which keeps piling wreckage upon wreckage and hurls it in front of his feet. The angel would like to stay, to awaken the dead, and make whole what has been smashed. But a storm is blowing from Paradise; it has got caught in his wings with such violence that the angel can no longer close them. The storm irresistibly propels him into the future to which his back is turned, while the debris before him grows skyward. This storm is what we call progress.
Walter Benjamin, *Illuminations*

Introduction

BORN INTO RURAL POVERTY in 1927 in northern Cameroon, Moham-medu Marwa (alias Mallam Maitatsine, alias Muhammedu Marwa, alias Muhammedu Mai tabsiri) left his birthplace when he was about sixteen years old. He attached himself to a local Muslim cleric and apparently displayed exceptional brilliance in the Qu'ranic science of exegesis (*tafsir*). His exegetical skills were acquired as an a student (*almajirai*) in local Muslim networks and nonformal schools (*makarantar allo*). Settling in the city of Kano, the mercantile capital of Nigeria, around 1945, he was a regular visitor at the preaching sessions around the Shahauci and Fagge grounds in the old quarters of the city, providing unorthodox interpretations of Qu'ranic verses read by his associate, Mallam Aminu Umar, recently returned from learning "in the East." Marwa insisted that the Qu'ran was the *only* valid guide to behavior and belief, and thus rejected both the sunna and the shari'a. The basis of his inflammatory reading of the Qu'ran involved stripping away the hidden meanings within the sacred text by rooting his analyses of verse in local West African conditions. In particular, by playing on the meanings and phonetic associations of certain Arabic and Hausa words, Marwa, or Maitatsine, as he became known locally, provided a powerful antimaterialist thrust to the

Qu'ran. His vehement denunciation of bicycles, apparel, cigarettes, buttons, cars, and so on brought him his name, Maitatsine, derived from the Hausa adage *Allah ta tsine* (God will curse). By 1962, Marwa had gained some local notoriety as a troublesome, charismatic, and unorthodox preacher, and Emir Sanusi of Kano actually brought him to trial. He was imprisoned for three months and promptly deported. Marwa's local stature grew substantially, however, following his prediction that Emir Sanusi would fall from power; he was, in fact, ousted several years later in the wake of the military coup.

Marwa returned to Kano shortly after his deportation—sustaining the popular belief that reactionary forces in high places supported his variety of militant Islam—and continued to live and preach in the city. He was arrested and imprisoned again in 1966–1967 and also in 1973–75 but was not deported. In the period following Marwa's return to Kano, the open spaces of 'Yan Awaki and Kofar Wombai provided a sort of beachhead, a sanctuary in which his students could be housed in makeshift dwellings and which by the late 1970s included urban gardens to sustain the growing numbers of followers. By 1979 there was something like a community (*tsangaya*) in place; Maitatsine's compound in 'Yan Awaki housed at least three thousand persons.[1] At the suggestion of Maitatsine, the followers carried little or no money—to sleep with more than one naira (equivalent to about seventy-five cents) was to exhibit a lack of trust in Allah—and dressed simply, characteristically begging for alms or working as transient laborers in occupations typically reserved for dry season migrants (*'yan cin-rani*), such as cart pushing, tea selling, and petty trade.

Maitatsine's followers (*'Yan Tatsine*) became increasingly visible around the old city, operating in small groups of three to five people, preaching at major junctions near the Sabon Gari mosque, around Koki, and at Kofar Wombai (see Figure 2.1). Through recitations and unorthodox interpretations of the Qu'ran, the students vigorously attacked materialism, modernity, unjust leaders, corrupt clerics (*ulema*), and all brotherhood followers.[2] Unorthodox behavior fueled rumor on a grand scale. Kano's wealthiest contractors and one of the most powerful voices of the northern oligarchy, popular opinion had it, materially supported the Maitatsine movement. In addition, hearsay had it that Maitatsine was lent support, and financial sustenance, both from luminaries within the ruling Nigerian federal party, the conservative and northern Muslim—dominated National Party of Nigeria (NPN), and from the incumbent Kano State administration, the populist People's Redemption Party (PRP). Rumor also fed the mystique of Maitatsine's magical powers. The government tribunal on the 'Yan Tatsine movement reported grotesque (but largely unsubstantiated) tales of cannibalism, human slaughter (a "human spare parts department," as the northern press referred to it), mass graves, drugged students, and brainwashed women. At the same time, there were reports of extraordinary bravery—Marwa certainly felt

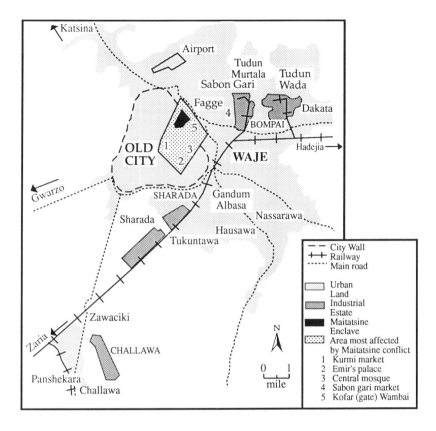

Fig. 2.1 The Geography of the Maitatsine Movement, Kano City, December 18–28, 1980

himself to be invulnerable—and impressive self-discipline by the 'Yan Tatsine. There was, in short, something like a moral economy within the tsangaya. Sometime in 1979, according to testimony by one of his wives, Marwa apparently declared his own prophethood.

On November 26, 1979, the governor of Kano State wrote to Marwa demanding that the quarter be vacated within two weeks. Originally intending to vacate 'Yan Awaki, Marwa apparently changed his mind, and promptly sent out a letter to his diaspora communities calling in reinforcements to fight the "infidels." The 'Yan Tatsine planned to overrun and take control of the Friday Mosques in Kano, NEPA (the national electricity utility), and the emir's palace; in their denunciation of the government and appropriation of "all land in the name of Allah," there was an allusion at least to some sort of seizure of power. On December 18, 1980, four police units were sent to the Shahauci playground, near the emir's palace, to arrest some of Maitatsine's preachers. Disorganized police forces were ambushed by "fanatics"—the language is taken from the popular press—armed with bows and arrows, daggers, and machetes. Arms were seized and police vehicles burned; by late afternoon, a huge plume of smoke hung over the city. Over the next few days, in a climate of growing chaos and popular fear, fighting spread and casualties were mounting. By December 21, with the police effectively unable to control the situation, vigilante groups (*'Yan Tauri*) entered the scene, and complex negotiations ensued between the Kano State governor, Abubakar Rimi (who feared the imposition of martial law by the federal government and hence for his own political survival), and local authorities concerning whether the army should be invited to intervene. On December 22, 'Yan Tatsine supporters were reportedly entering Kano to join the insurrection (six busloads of supporters from Sokoto were diverted en route), and trucks full of corpses were seen leaving the city.

After five days of stalemate, confusion, and escalating violence, the army intervened on December 29, with ten hours of mortar barrage, supported by air force bombardment. Incurring major losses, the 'Yan Tatsine escaped and marched out of the city into the western districts along the Gwarzo Road. Maitatsine led the exit from the 'Yan Awaki quarter after the ferocious bombardment by state security and military forces but was injured and died in the western districts outside the city walls (Figure 2.2). His body was later removed from a shallow grave, kept at a local mortuary for several days, and then cremated at the request of local au-

Fig. 2.2 The Old Quarter ("Old City") of Kano City

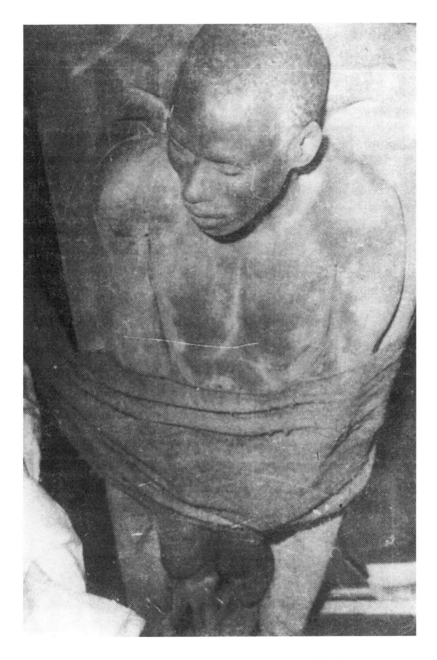

Fig. 2.3 The Body of Maitatsine on Display at Kano Central Police Station

thorities to obviate possible martyrdom among his converts and followers. Photographs of Maitatsine's body were hot-selling items in the aftermath of the insurrection (Figure 2.3), peddled by young boys at busy intersections in the city (Christelow 1985).

According to the official tribunal figures, 4,177 people died (excluding police and military), but the human toll was clearly much greater. Some quite reliable estimates range as high as 10,000 dead; 15,000 were injured and 100,000 rendered homeless. The physical damage was enormous. In Fagge, 82 houses and 249 shops were destroyed; in 'Yan Awaki 165 houses were destroyed and heavily scarred. Of the 917 people arrested, 12 percent were juveniles, and 185 were non-Nigerian. Many thousands of Maitatsine's supporters avoided arrest and scattered to various states in the north.[3] Between 1981 and 1985, four more incidents occurred between Maitatsine's followers and state authorities in urban and quasi-urban locations across northern Nigeria; perhaps four thousand to five thousand persons died in these conflagrations (see Appendix 2A).

Oil, Islam, and capitalism have, on occasion, made for an explosive mixture. Muhammed Reza, Iran's late Shah of Shahs, is simply the most infamous casualty—and Ayatollah Khomeini only the most vilified product—of just such an inflammable concoction of petrolic accumulation and Muslim sensibilities. There are, of course, other stories to tell of life on the petroleum roller coaster, stories at once more prosaic and less radical in character than Iran's Shi'ite revolution, but equally capable of throwing into dramatic relief the complex relations among culture, class, and community, indeed, of capturing what Robert Hughes (1980) calls "the shock of the new." This case study analyzes a Muslim millenarian movement in Kano city, in northern Nigeria, the so-called Maitatsine insurrection whose broad contours were described at the beginning of this chapter. A bustling, energetic city forged in the crucible of seventeenth- and eighteenth-century trans-Saharan trade, Kano has become the economic fulcrum of Nigeria's most populous state, a densely settled agricultural heartland of perhaps well over ten million people. In the course of sixty years of British colonial rule, Kano developed as West Africa's preeminent entrepôt, a city whose fortunes were organically linked to the vicissitudes of the world market in one commodity—peanut oil. But it was oil of an altogether different sort—petroleum—that ushered in the revolutionary changes of the last two decades.

Awash in petrodollars, urban Kano was transformed, seemingly overnight, from a traditional Muslim mercantile center of 400,000 at the end of the Civil War (ca. 1970) into a sprawling, anarchic metropolis of over 1.5 million, equipped with an industrial workforce of over 50,000. From its mercantile cocoon, Kano emerged as a full-fledged metropolitan industrial periphery, propelled by a radical deepening of capitalist social relations. At the zenith of the petroleum boom, new industrial estates sprung up at Challawa and Sharada in the city periphery (Figure 2.1), armies of migrants poured into the city, and the icons of modernity, the massive state-sponsored building projects, dotted the city. Kano became, on the one hand, an enormous construction site and, on the other, a theatre of orgiastic consumption.

The reconfigurations of urban life, community relations, and styles of consumption in urban Kano were, of course, part of an overarching transformation of Nigerian society wrought by OPEC and the oil boom. The Nigerian state banked $140 billion between 1970 and 1983 from its federally controlled petroleum industry. Government revenue grew at close to 40 percent per annum during the 1970s. Oil price hikes in 1973–1974 and in 1978–1979, the symbols of a restructuring of the world petroleum industry, unleashed a spasm of state-led investment and industrial development in Nigeria, reflected in the national index of manufacturing output, which almost tripled between 1972 and 1980. The absolute number of manufacturing establishments and of industrial wage workers, the Nigerianization of management, the scale of direct investment by multinationals, and the shares of federal and regional state capital in industrial output all witnessed positive growth rates throughout a halcyon boom period presided over by a succession of military governments (1972–1979). The luster of black gold promised, for the chosen few, the "dawn of prosperity and progress for the petroleum rich" (Amuzegar 1982:814).

Fifteen years after the euphoria of the first oil boom, Nigeria's economic future—and, indeed, the prospects for other oil producers, such as Mexico and Venezuela—appears by contrast to be quite bleak, if not austere. Spiraling debt, fueled by a seemingly infinite appetite for imports, the collapse of oil prices in the early 1980s, and the onslaught of Draconian IMF programs have prompted massive retrenchment and economic hardship. They are, in fact, the hallmarks of a roller coaster economy, which has fundamentally shaped the everyday life of all sectors of Nigerian society. In this sense, Sayre Schatz (1984) is quite mistaken to emphasize what he refers to as an "inert" Nigerian economy—the transition under oil from an economy with a weak engine of growth to one with no engine at all—since the scale of public sector activity and the growing commodification of many aspects of everyday life represented an important source of social change, however limited was self-sustaining capitalist growth.[4] These perturbations—what I, following Walter Benjamin, shall call the shock of modernity—were triggered by the frenzied consumption, investment, and construction of the oil boom era, and it is this world awash with money that provides the environment within which the Muslim insurrectional activity of the 1980s was incubated.

The ferocious, Muslim-inspired revolts that surfaced between 1980 and 1985 in several cities of northern Nigeria represent a particular political and cultural expression of the changing economic geography of Nigerian capitalism. Social protest in a newly industrializing state, such as Nigeria, must be rooted in the particular trajectory, the actually existing local configuration, of capitalist development (cf. Trotsky 1969,

1977). In this regard, the impact of oil on Nigeria, and its capacity to generate huge rents for the state throughout the 1970s, lent industrial development, and urban social processes more generally, a particularly intense, speedy, and yet, as I hope to show, quite anarchic quality. This phenomenon approximates in the abstract what Paul Virilio (1986:3) calls the "production of speed." It is this fast capitalism amidst Islam—an articulation of precapitalist and capitalist institutions, and of new material practices with deeply sedimented cultural forms—that provides the material and symbolic raw material upon which Maitatsine and his followers drew. In light of what David Harvey calls in his new book, *The Condition of Postmodernity*, "the progressive monetization of relations in social life transforms the qualities of time and space" (1988:228), the oil boom fashioned a period of "space-time compression," but in the Nigerian case it represented a specific articulation of two world-systemic processes: Islam and capitalism. It is the experience of this quite singular form of space-time compression that provides the context of the millenarian movements of northern Nigeria in the 1980s.

And what of the Muslim insurrections themselves? To what extent were they significant features of the social and political landscape of Nigeria's oil boom? Were these so-called "fanatics" and "disturbances," to use the official lexicon, structurally significant? What sort of meaning can they be given? Not surprisingly, in a context of fragile civilian government, debates over the role of sharī'a in a purportedly secular state, and deep-seated regional antagonisms animated by the 1979 Nigerian elections, the Maitatsine disturbances were invested with wildly different interpretations. Throughout the 1980s, *Maitatsine* was employed as a term of abuse and delegitimation; in the popular press, the 'Yan Tatsine were described as "fanatics"—and as "cult followers" by the *New York Times* (January 12, 1981, 4)—particularly in the pages of the influential northern newspapers, whose strong connections to the powerful brotherhoods and to the northern aristocracy predisposed them to conservative interpretations. For many Christians in Nigeria, Maitatsine represented a terrifying drift toward Muslim fundamentalism, of which the ongoing debate over sharī'a law was part, while for the northern clerics, Maitatsine was a heretic and as such denied any Muslim status whatsoever. Ahmed Beita Yusuf (1988), a member of the northern Muslim intelligentsia, describes Marwa as evil incarnate, "witchcraft married to cannibalism," a devil who indoctrinated "coconut skulls and scuttle brains." Conversely, for Western critics, such as Daniel Pipes (1980), the insurrection, like the Shi'ite revolution in Iran, was the unrefined by-product of oil, a commodity "primarily responsible for the surge in Islamic political activities." The official federal inquiry, the Aniagolu tribunal (Nigerian Federal Government 1981a), blamed Maitatsine's fanatical control of Qu'ranic students and a wider environment of religious intolerance, weakening of traditional authority, and acts of negligence by Kano State officials and the security forces (see Appendix 2B).

The Maitatsine followers, I shall argue, constituted a certain disenfranchised segment of the northern popular classes (the *talakawa* in Hausa) who experienced, handled, and resisted a particular form of capitalism through a particular reading of—a counterhegemonic discourse within—Islamic tradition. It is a truism that Islam is a text-based religion, but we need to grasp the relationships between texts and the meanings they are purported to provide, what Lambek calls local hermeneutics:

> The specific problems raised by the translation of objective meaning of written language into the personal act of speaking . . . [is an act of] appropriation. . . . The nature of texts and the knowledge to be drawn from them in any given historical context are shaped by a sociology or political economy of knowledge: how textual knowledge is reproduced . . . what social factors mediate access to texts, who is able to read and in what manner, who has the authority to represent . . . and how challenges to such authority are manifested. (1990:23–24)

Islam is a text-based religion that is made socially relevant through citation, reading, enunciation, and interpretation, and to this extent Islam does not prescribe wholly unambiguous action for its adherents (Fischer and Abedi 1990). Indeed, as Fischer and Abedi have brilliantly shown in their book, *Debating Muslims*, there is a dialogic and hermeneutical tradition within Islam rooted in the enigmatic, oral, performative, and esoteric qualities of the Qu'ran. The same religious symbols can therefore be infused with radically different meanings (Gilsenan 1980). Tradition itself is constantly negotiated, contested, and reinvented in the context of efforts by rulers and ulema to enforce other meanings in a world turned upside down by "modern" oil monies. Just as Gramsci once observed that every religion is in reality a multiplicity of distinct and contradictory religions (cited in Billings 1990:21), so, there is a multiplicity of Muslim voices, and this multivocality can be fueled by the heteronomy, difference, and fragmentation propagated by commodity booms. That is to say, capitalism of a particular sort threw these religious multiplicities into bold relief, generating struggles over meanings.[5] Such symbolic contests escalated, for conjunctural reasons that I shall describe, into violent insurrection.

This chapter also speaks to a second matter, namely, the construction of a collectivity, or more properly, the imagination of a community and the capacity of its members to act—in short, the common identity shared by a self-consciously Muslim community, the nature of belief associated with its insurrectional activities, and the historical conditions of modernity within which the community is forged (Cook 1990). Here, I take note of William Roseberry's prescient observation that proletarianization is an uneven process, creating a heterogeneous, fractioned popular class; hence the question is "How is the feeling of community or homogeneity created within social relations that are neither communal nor homogeneous?" (1989:224). The Maitatsine movement in Nigeria was creative in at least two senses. First, the community was an act of imagination distinguished, as Ben Anderson (1983) has observed more generally, by the style in which it was imagined. And second, within a historical context of more embracing communities of class and nation, the Maitatsine community built a local alternative, a counterhegemonic image of community imagined from within Islam itself. Central to this process were the cultural and symbolic forms—the selected tradition, as Raymond Williams (1977) calls it—by which an alternative image and a counterdiscourse were built, fought for, and struggled over. These images are both products of, and responses to, particular forces, events, and structures in Nigerian society, but they also involve a particular reading of the past to shape the present. Walter Benjamin, in his great study of Baudelaire, spoke directly to this tradition of the oppressed:

To the form of the means of production, which to begin with is still dominated by the old (Marx), there correspond images in the collective consciousness in which the new and the old are intermingled. These images are ideals, and in them the collective seeks not only to transfigure, but also to transcend, the immaturity of the social product and the deficiencies of the social order of production. In these ideals there also emerges a vigorous aspiration to break with what is outdated—which means, however, with the most recent past. These tendencies turn the fantasy, which gains its initial stimulus from the new, back upon a primal past. In the dream in which every epoch sees in images the epoch which is to succeed it, the latter appears coupled with elements of prehistory—that is to say of a classless society. The experiences of this society, which have their store-place in the collective unconscious, interact with the new to give birth to the Utopias which leave their traces in a thousand configurations. . . .[6]

The fantastic intermingling of the old and new is central to the Maitatsine insurrection and to its utopian vision (cf. Marx 1963, 1972). These utopias are often contradictory of course, reflecting the contradictory experience of past and present and a contradictory consciousness among the agents—peasants, workers, and so on—themselves. But as the case of Maitatsine reveals, these contradictions need not inhibit the capacity of subaltern classes to act in strategically significant ways, and rework in unorthodox ways a modernity of their own.

On the Precipice:
Regions, Class, and Accumulation before Oil

The [newly independent Nigerian] state was dominated by a "class" that was inherently incapable of ruling or giving coherent economic direction to state and society. It sought to inherit the state not subdue it. Having fought the colonial "ruling class" to a democratic outcome . . . the political class, once independence was achieved, fought against itself most of the time.

Sam Nolutshungu, *Fragments of a Democracy*

[B]ehind the liberal facade of formal political institutions and debate [1960–1966] lay a series of vicious struggles over the allocation and distribution of political offices, the award of contracts . . . and the distribution of social and economic benefits.

Robin Cohen, *Labour and Politics in Nigeria*

The contradictory nature of the petroleum boom can be best grasped by situating petroleum revenues on the larger canvas of the political character of Nigeria's fledgling state in the post-colonial period. At Independence in 1960, Nigeria's First Republic (1960–1964) operated under a democratic federal constitution. The three regions, Eastern, Western, and Northern (see Figure 2.4), products of quite different colonial and precolonial histories, exhibited distinctive relations between their ruling classes and other social forces (the peasantry, the colonial state, European merchants, and so on) in society at large. While the democratic period was short-lived, ending in a bloody coup in 1964, it did solidify the regional and ethnic basis of Nigerian politics. It was the era of Bello, Awolowo, and Azikwe, party bosses whose very names invoke the specter of ethnic party politics and "tribalism." Parties were, as Sam Nolutshungu (1990:89) observed, deliberate creations, "rather like regions only more so." Indeed, the collapse of the Republican constitution and the drift into civil strife and communal violence is typically seen as a product of the growing antagonisms among geographically rooted political, cultural, and religious identities, tensions that ultimately generated a profound legitimacy crisis for Nigerian federalism. The immediate cause of the collapse was the refusal of northern political leaders to follow established political procedures in the Western Region. In the context of mounting ethnic animosity, the inability to conduct a national census, and widespread political corruption, the deterioration of inter- and intra-party conduct led to a coup led by radical army officers. The intercession by the military prompted a series of chaotic struggles and countercoups, in which high-ranking civilian and military leaders were assassinated, and a rapid slide into civil war, marked by the secession of the Eastern Region, which came to be known as the Biafra war.[7]

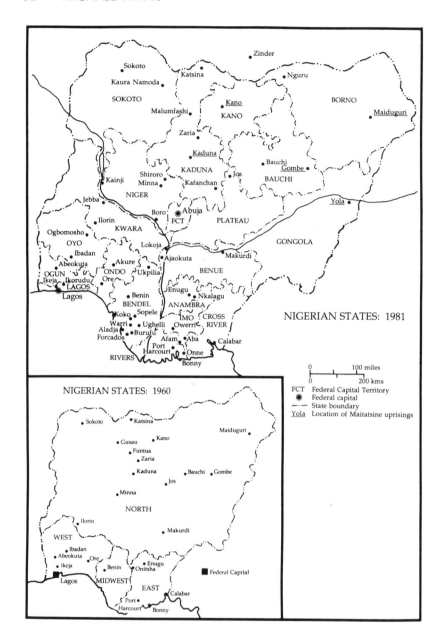

Fig. 2.4 Nigerian State Structure, 1960 and 1981

This crisis of legitimacy arose from a particular sort of colonial political economy in Nigeria, and specifically a marked geographic configuration of regimes of accumulation and modes of social regulation. The internal political geography of British colonialism in Nigeria had always expressed itself as a "cultural" geography, "emphasizing the distinctiveness of peoples, their cultures and needs" (Nolutshungu 1990:89).[8] British imperialism contained no notion of citizenship for colonial subjects but imagined particular traditions and customs whose ideological subject was the "native" or "tribalist," an individual defined by primordial ties to his or her local territory. The three semiautonomous regions exhibited certain structural similarities insofar as each was associated with a particular commodity and a statutory Marketing Board, which extracted, through classic price squeezes, peasant surpluses to finance party loyalists, administrators, and a nascent bourgeoisie. The Northern Region was, of course, the groundnut economy par excellence, and overwhelmingly Hausa-Fulani and Muslim. In the South, the Eastern Region was a Christian and predominantly Ibo (but this designated a multitude of local identities) area whose economic lifeblood was palm oil, and the Western Region was a cocoa region, a largely Yoruba-Benin constituency of both Christian and Muslim affiliations.

The intense regional forms of accumulation, politics, and ethnic identity were the creations of colonialism and of the differential incorporation of the north and south into a growing world economy. The south had been drawn into the world system through slavery, palm oil, and cocoa at various periods since the sixteenth century. Conversely, the Muslim north remained largely peripheral to global capitalism until the twentieth century but an integral part of an Islamic diaspora, which helped shape a distinctive cultural and legal tradition. The north had been powerfully shaped by the Sokoto caliphate—a product of the jihad of the early nineteenth century—which sustained a versatile Muslim mercantile capitalism and a prebendal, authoritarian form of patrimonial rule, presided over by a ruling class initially resistant to British colonialism.

As David Laitin, Paul Lubeck, Bala Usman, and others have shown, the impact of colonialism was to strengthen, indeed, in some cases to create, robust regional, ethnic, and religious identities.[9] British indirect rule in Nigeria generally privileged the northern ruling classes, however, with whom the British cemented a class alliance against those they took to be radical, and uppity, educated southern nationalists. The population of the Northern Region exceeded that of the entire south, and the Muslim elites were able to expand their class prerogatives, extracting surpluses from a subordinated peasantry. Northern hegemony took the form, in other words, of a specific sort of mercantile accumulation, in which indigenous merchants and ruling-class bureaucrats, in a class alliance with the colonial state, were sustained by export-led growth of cheap agricultural commodities. In order for the northern elites to preserve their authoritarian prebendal rule—and hence their regime of accumulation—they had to control the relatively weak federal center at Independence. The educated and "Westernized" southern populations, conversely, expected the rights and privileges of a bourgeois democratic state. With the growth of postwar nationalism, the British created (in spite of substantial opposition) a federation in which their northern conservative allies held a fragile hegemony and maintained an essentially mercantile capitalist, neocolonial regime. These intense regional and class contradictions in the context of the deepening of ethnic and religious affiliations naturally made for a structurally unstable situation at Independence.

It needs to be said of course that the regions were themselves somewhat fissiparous. The Northern Region was certainly not culturally or politically homogeneous, and within the regional elites there were competing criteria for access to power and resources. In this context, ethnicity and regionalism became the images employed by the first generation of independent leaders, such as Ahmadu Bello, Sardauna of Sokoto, to unite the region and to establish their hegemony over potential challenges from within the regional ranks. Equally, the regional ruling classes were in a sense quite similar; they were all unmistakably petit-bourgeois and constrained by colonial mercantilism. All the regional elites made appeal to something called tradition and to local territorial ties. The differences lay more in the articulation of tradition with modernity, conservatism, and radicalism and in regional class alliances "between those (in the South) that had a significant working class and salaried middle-class populations and those (in the North) that did not; those where a degree of elite political unification had been achieved around more or less centralising traditional structures (in the North) and the more fragmented ones (in the South)" (Nolutshungu 1990:91). In the final analysis, however, federalism had a regional and ethnic connotation, and the state purse emerged as the much-sought-after prize of party politics.

The construction of Nigeria's unique political economy was irreducibly spatial. Regional forms of accumulation and class formation coupled with limited geographic integration between regions bred both a weak federal center and a powerful rhetoric of collective identity based on geography. These contradictions fractured any national integrity that the First Republic may have had, and inexorably pushed the nation toward conflict, at the very moment, coincidentally, that oil production emerged as a powerful centralizing force in the mid-1960s. Regionalism and the vicious struggles over political office, contracts, and state benefits were not, of course, substantially changed by a bloody war, by the proliferation of states in its aftermath, or by the rise of a Christian northerner—Jack Gowon—as head of the military government (1966–1975). As the angel of history, oil profits fell upon a polity cross-cut by weak federalism, strong regionalism, and a complex, delicate coalition of military, senior civil servants, and high-ranking politicians, many of whom were creatures of the First Republic.

On the Roller Coaster:
Black Gold and Fast Capitalism

Oil creates the illusion of a completely changed life, life without work, life for free. Oil is a resource that anesthetizes thought, blurs visions, corrupts. . . . In this sense oil is a fairy tale, and, like every fairy tale, is a bit of a lie. . . . Oil, though powerful, has its defects.

Ryszard Kapuscinski, *Shah of Shahs*

A bubble of oil flows through the arteries which converge into the electoral heart.

Pablo Neruda, "Venezuela"

The 1970s were the decade of oil and of bristling petrolic nationalism. Twenty-eight Third World states were exporters of petroleum; each experienced, in varying measure, a huge influx of oil rents leveraged from a petroleum-dependent world by OPEC's successful cartelization.[10] Oil producers are, of course, a heterogeneous lot; lilliputian city-states, such as Qatar, with limited absorptive capacity[11] stand in sharp contrast to populous high absorbers, such as Indonesia, Venezuela, and Mexico. They also differ in their dependence on—and hence in the transformative power of—petroleum. Among OPEC members, for example, petroleum represented on average a whopping 78 percent of national export earnings in 1980. Nigeria stands, in this regard, as an archetypical high absorber since its domestic petroleum output in the 1970s—roughly 1.3 million barrels per day—was sufficient to sustain growth rates in state revenue of over 100 percent per annum. By 1980 Nigeria was, in fact, a monoculture, more so than it had ever been in the colonial era; 95.3 percent of total export revenues derived from oil, and over 55 percent of government revenue derived from the petroleum sector. Average annual growth rates for credit, money supply, and state expenditures were, respectively, 45 percent, 66 percent, and 91 percent between 1973 and 1980.[12]

How, then, can we begin to grasp, to use the language of the French regulationists (Lipietz 1987), the social character of the oil-based regime of accumulation? Let us note two rather obvious points at the outset. The first is that oil, as a global, highly internationalized commodity, necessarily projects oil producers into international circuits of capital. To this extent, one might talk of an *internationalization* of the state (Watts 1984). The second is that the enclave character of the oil industry, combined with the fact that oil revenues typically flow directly into national treasuries, has profound implications for state centralization and autonomy, and for what Albert Hirschmann (1976) calls fiscal linkages.[13] In this sense, the disposition of oil acts as a powerful centralizing force at the level of the state, which is accordingly projected into civil society (that is, "*domesticated*") via expanded forms of public ownership and investment. The oil boom initiated (1) an ostensibly new relationship with the world economy; (2) a new strategy of capital accumulation, as oil earnings overwhelmed previous sources of state surplus; and (3) a process of state centralization, growth, and enhanced autonomy, which generated the "problem of [the state] simultaneously managing capital accumulation and legitimizing itself and the accumulation process in civil society" (Mogahadam 1987:229).

The genesis of an enlarged and autonomous state as the mediator of the oil boom appears with particular clarity in Nigeria in the aftermath of the first oil shock (Watts and Lubeck 1983). State centralization had commenced, of course, with the exigencies of civil war, but it proceeded apace after 1973. The creation of new regional states (nineteen states from four semiautonomous regions; see Figure 2.4) deepened the fiscal dependency on a federal purse through statutory revenue allocation procedures. At the same time, it vastly expanded, in a simple quantitative sense, the bureaucratic strata at all levels of government. This *etatization* is seen in a multiplicity of guises: capital expenditures at the federal level increased by 800 percent in real terms between 1973 and 1980; the number of parastatals mushroomed to 800 by 1980; and the number of federal employees leapt to 280,000 (see Figure 2.5). The period after 1975 under the Murtala and Obasanjo military administrations (1975–1979) saw the high-water mark of state-bureaucratic growth and the consolidation of a state-capitalist sector. The federal government encouraged auto-assembly and initiated an ambitious capital and intermediate goods program, including an iron and steel sector, petrochemicals, and light engineering.[14] A series of indigenization decrees (beginning in 1972) unquestionably strengthened the position of, and expanded the financial base of, indigenous capital vis-à-vis foreign multinationals.[15]

The rise of a centralized, bureaucratic petrostate, with earnings in 1980 in excess of twenty-five billion U.S. dollars, transformed the material basis, if not the political character, of class rule in Nigeria. The regional elites no longer depended on access to surpluses generated by peasant producers but on oil rents redistributed through the state apparatuses.[16] Indeed, while the military–civil servant alliance maintained its precarious northern political hegemony, the vastly expanded oil revenues bankrolled a huge rent-seeking edifice, what Bardhan (1988:82) in describing India has referred to as a "flabby and heterogeneous dominant coalition preoccupied with a grabbing of public resources . . . through an elaborate network of patronage and subsidies." Not only did the state embark upon a massive program of infrastructural and industrial investment—attempting to lay the groundwork for systematic capitalist accumulation—but these expenditures became the means by which pet-

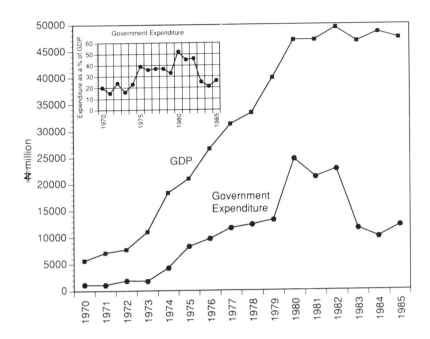

Fig. 2.5 The Growth of the Nigerian Public Sector (at current factor cost), 1970–1985

Source: Central Bank of Nigeria, *Economic and Financial Review*, 1970–1990.

rodollars were diverted to create pacts and coalitions within a divided national polity. Patronage, contracting, and subsidies were part of what Claude Ake (1981) describes as the desparate struggle to win control of the state. The state was privatized in unprecedented ways. Public office became, to employ Max Weber's language, a prebend.[17] Corruption on a gargantuan scale, hugely inflated contracts, and large state-sector subsidies abounded at all levels of the political hierarchy. The bureaucratic environment was characterised by astonishing indiscipline, chaos, and venality.[18]

In the wake of the return to civilian rule in 1979 these pathologies of the state reached new levels of venality. Government was more than ever, as Chinua Achebe (1988) observed in his novel, *Anthills of the Savannas*, a "crummy family business." Corruption contributed to a degeneration of state authority. According to Nolutshungu (1990:96), effective control of every tier of government became impossible; sporadic efforts to impose bureaucratic discipline "resulted in farce (for example, government buildings being set alight . . . with total impugnity . . . to destroy incriminating documents)." To the extent that the bureaucracy generally expanded—by 1980, the state wage bill was U.S. $1.5 billion, 35 percent of recurrent expenditures—the state siphoned off oil revenues to irrigate civil society, by fair means or foul, creating what Chatelus and Schemeil (1984) call a "circulation economy."

I have concentrated here on the growth and centralization of a state whose relative autonomy was cross-cut by the social-structural preconditions, by the inherited struggles, of the First Republic. A sort of spoils politics developed at the same moment that the state redistributed petrodollars to manufacture some sort of political consensus and simultaneously endeavored to assume the mantle of a developmental state. What transpired was a classic rentier state, crippled not simply by virtue of its rapid, and largely unplanned, growth but by endemic corruption and bureaucratic indiscipline.[19] A culture of corruption and extreme privatization of the state (an administrative crisis, in James O'Connor's [1984] language) was, of course, incompatible with an ambitious state capitalist program (that is, the accumulation functions of the state). In sum, a petrostate, in its efforts to perform enterpreneurial functions and simultaneously negotiate political alliances, had become both *the instrument for, and obstacle to, systematic capitalist accumulation*. Insofar as petroleum-based accumulation in Nigeria encouraged administrative failure (less generously, absolute chaos and a total lack of political accountability) and a flabby sort of industrial growth, it was inevitable that the state manufactured little in the way of popular legitimacy in civil society.

Four related facets of the oil boom fundamentally shaped the environment in which Maitatsine emerged. The first was the extraordinary commodity boom unleashed by the state. Nigerian merchandise imports increased from N1.1 billion in 1973 to N14.6 billion in 1981. Fueled by the explosion of federal and state bureaucracies and the infusion of money ushered in by the Udoji Commission salary increases in 1975, the oil boom wrought a spending frenzy. The proliferation of everything from stallions to stereos, a world apparently awash in money, produced a sort of commodity fetishism, what one commentator called Nigerian cargo cultism (Freund 1978).[20] The second was an urban construction boom of Stalinist proportions, spawned by public investment. The construction industry (roads, office construction, industrial plant) grew at 20 percent in the 1970s, sucking rural labor into mushrooming and hopelessly unplanned cities.[21] Third, the boom in oil led to the so-called Dutch disease, producing a lagged sector, notably in agriculture. Labor drawn from the rural sector, combined with escalating input costs, created a profit squeeze for many peasant producers and hence a sluggish agrarian economy (Roemer 1983; Watts 1987). Nigeria's classic agrarian exports (cocoa, groundnuts, palm oil) collapsed completely. Food imports exploded—wheat in particular—prompting a series of expensive state schemes (large-scale irrigation perimeters in the north) to import-subsititute.[22] Expensive, badly planned, and socially disruptive, these agrar-

TABLE 2.1. *Public Debt Service Charges in Nigeria, 1951–1986*

million billion Period	Average per year	% of GDP	Debt service ratio (%)
1951–1960	N3.2 million	0.2	n.a.
1961–1970	N53.3 million	1.8	n.a.
1971–1975	N75.6 million	3.0	0.9
1976–1980	N2,74.0 million	1.2	1.6
1981–1986	N1.9 billion	3.0	18.0

SOURCES: Ihimodu 1983; World Bank 1988; Economist Intelligence Unit 1981–1988.

ian interventions contributed to the growth of land speculation and quite dramatic social differentiation in some rural communities associated with the rise of so-called overnight farmers and large farmer-traders.[23] All of this contributed to rural-urban drift, to social dislocation in the countryside, and to the growing sense of state corruption and violence. And fourth, the appreciation of the exchange rate in a period of intractable inflation produced a classic "overshooting." A relatively rigid and inflexible growth of public sector imports (especially the expensive capital goods sector required to sustain the industrial sector) accounted for substantial balance-of-payments deficits by the mid-1970s and an escalation of external debt underwritten by chaotic and unregulated federal and local-state borrowing (see Table 2.1).[24] The good ship oil prosperity was, as a consequence, already heading for the reefs of austerity even in the halcyon period. The ship ran aground completely, however, in the early 1980s with the "discovery" of a massive external debt and the downturn in oil prices.[25]

Even with the second oil price hike in 1979, Nigeria's petro-euphoria and spending spree was already turning to pessimism and dissillusion. At best the oil revenues had lubricated the return to civilan rule. Less generously, the oil roller coaster also permitted substantial political continuity within the hegemonic bloc. On balance, the oil windfall proved to be an unmitigated disaster. By the early 1980s the civilian government was publicly talking of the "end of the boom" and of impending Draconian measures (Othman 1984; Awojobi 1982). The terrible vulnerability of an extreme dependence on one commodity had materialized with a vengeance. In this regard the comments of Dudley Seers over a twenty-year period are especially prescient. In 1964 he noted that petroleum economies, by virtue of the boom-and-bust cycle, possessed a "potentially explosive character." As head of the ILO mission to Nigeria in 1981, he concluded that the oil boom had almost certainly produced a deterioration in income distribution and, in the face of copious evidence of growing absolute rural and urban poverty, the conspicuous failure to meet "the basic needs of the people."[26]

Experiencing Petrolic Modernization: Poverty and Morality, and Culture and Class among the Kano Poor (Talakawa)

At the gates of the city, dispossessed of his land, deprived of his cultural identity and social framework, subject to uncertainty and harassment for the whole of his life, he arrived, demoralised and exhausted looking for streets paved with oil. And he was turned into a disguised beggar.

Hamza Katouzian, *The Political Economy of Modern Iran*

I call petroleum the devil's excrement. It brings trouble . . . look at this *locura*—waste, corruption, consumption, our services falling apart . . . and debt we shall have for years. . . . We are drowning in the devil's excrement.

Juan Pablo Alfonzo, Venezeulan diplomat, founder of OPEC

How was the peculiar conflation of surplus money, commodification, industrialization, and rapid material change "experienced," and quite specifically experienced by the urban poor (the *talakawa*)—the social basis of the 'Yan Tatsine recruits—in Kano?[27] I want to suggest that the question of experience contains two dimensions. The first is that the oil boom was experienced in class terms but that the social character of this class in Kano was, to use Marx's language, inherited from the past—this is the second aspect, the lived traditions, of Hall's (1980) definition. The central concept here is the self-conscious popular strata in Hausa-Fulani society identified locally as talakawa. The second is that the roller coaster of fast capitalism was experienced explicitly in terms of what Hall calls "meanings and values" (1980:26), and the central frame of reference here is, of course, Islam.

To begin with the question of class experience, according to a World Bank study in the early 1980s (cited in Lubeck 1985:379), 52–67 percent of Kano's urban population existed at the "absolute poverty level." This amorphous subaltern class, embracing small traders, workers, informal sector workers, the unemployed, and so on, had a social unity, however, in terms of a popular self-identity in Hausa society as commoners, or talakawa. According to Bargery's Hausa dictionary (1934:983), a *talaka* is "a person who holds no official position . . . a man in the street . . . a poor person." As an indigenous social category, it is of considerable antiquity, emerging from the social division of labor between town and countryside associated with the genesis of political kingdoms (the *sarauta* system) in the fifteenth century, and subsequently the emirate system under the Sokoto caliphate (1806–1902), in which a lineage-based officeholding class (*masu sarauta*) exercised political authority over subject populations (see Watts 1983; Lubeck 1981). *Talakawa* refers, then, to a class relationship of a precapitalist sort but also a political relationship among status honor-groups with distinctive cultural identities and lifestyles. Naturally, the talakawa have been differentiated in all sorts of complex ways through the unevenness of proletarianization—the industrial working class (*leburori*), for example, constituting an important social segment of the talakawa as such (Lubeck 1986).

While there is a generic sort of subalternity embodied in the notion of the talaka, I wish to identify two distinctive social segments from it, which represent the building blocks of the Maitatsine movement. Both are of some antiquity and were fashioned by locally distinctive social and cultural processes. The first are dry season migrants ('*Yan cin-rani*), who circulate through the urban economy during the long dry season, relieving pressures on domestic grain reserves in the countryside; they may generate limited savings, which are typically of great value to dependent sons preparing for marriage. I would include in this category migrants who are, strictly speaking, not participants in seasonal circulatory networks but as a consequence of the urban construction boom and the collapse of agriculture were drawn into the urban labor market in huge numbers. Almost wholly male, single, and young, and typically drawn from the densely settled and land-scarce northern provinces, they became semipermanent city residents, characteristically working in the construction sector, and as cart pushers, refuse collectors, itinerant laborers, and so on.[28] This floating population expanded dramatically in the 1970s, not only because of the construction boom, but because of the devastating impact of drought and food shortages in the early 1970s, and because of the dispossession of peasants associated with land speculation, fraudulent land claims, and inadequate state compensations in the periurban areas and in the vicinity of the huge state irrigation schemes.[29] In any event, the '*Yan cin-rani* were shuttled into the northern cities, such as Kano, during the oil boom, filling niches in the secondary labor market, constituting a sort of lumpenproletariat.

The second talakawa social stratum is rooted in the informal Muslim schooling system (*makarantar allo*), what Lubeck (1985) calls "koranic networks." These networks long predate the jihad and refer to a peripatetic tradition, rooted in the human ecology of the Sahel, in which students study with lay clerics (*mallams*) during the dry season. Students (*almajirai*) migrated to centers of Muslim learning and typically studied the Qu'ranic science of exegesis at the feet of notable scholars, often living in the entryways (*zaure*) of influential merchants and notables. Maitatsine was himself a product of this system. These networks were sustained by a sort of urban moral economy—begging and almsgiving as part of a normative set of relations between rich and poor—which served both to extend Islam into the countryside and to provide a measure of social and ideological integration for Hausa society as a whole. The students themselves often worked and as Shea (1975) has observed in his work on the nineteenth-century Kano textile industry, they acquired important commercial and craft skills. In Kano these students are referred to as *gardawa,* although, as Hiskett (1987) points out, this is a semantically dense term and also refers to adult Muslim students, aspirant mallams of sorts, who are not seasonal migrants as such, but longer-term urban residents.[30] As an ancient center of learning, of vigorous brotherhood activity, and of enormous mercantile wealth, Kano was quite naturally a major center of gardawa activity in spite of the fact that the colonial state had endeavored to systematically regulate Qu'ranic education, in the course of which the gardawa were increasing marginalized from, and became aggressively hostile to, Nigerian society.

If the talakawa as a class category (and the 'Yan cin-rani and gardawa as segments of it) represent the structural preconditions through which the oil boom was experienced by Maitatsine followers, then what are the immediate, proximate qualities of that experience in urban Kano? I shall focus on three sets of social relations: state mediation in the form of corruption and violent but undisciplined security forces, urban social processes (cf. Lubeck 1986), and the return to civilian party politics in 1979. I have already referred to the growing presence of the local and federal states in social and economic life. Kano State revenues for example grew from N33.3 million in 1971–1972 to N133.2 million in 1975–1976, and urban growth rates averaged 7–8 percent throughout the boom years. To this extent, the state was rendered much more "visible" in society by virtue of its expanded activities, including road and office construction and contracting of various sorts. This visibility was synonymous, however, with a shocking lack of political responsibility and state accountability. In popular discourse, the state and government meant corruption on a truely Hobbesian scale. Graft through local contracts, import speculation, foreign exchange dealings, drug smuggling, hoarding of food, and so on abounded at all levels of local and federal officialdom (Usman 1980, 1982). It was commonplace to hear the governor refered to as a thief, or hear that *Nigeriya ta lalachi* ("Nigeria has been ruined"). State indigenization even implicated the Muslim brotherhoods who owned shares in companies; the government was also centrally involved in the annual migration of one hundred thousand pilgrims who participated in the hadj, a sacred event that became synonymous with corruption and commodification. In the return to civilian rule, state corruption reached unprecedented levels; as the talakawa put it, *siyasa ta bata duniya*—"politics has spoiled the world." When the home of the governor was searched in Kano in 1983, U.S. $5.1 million was found stacked up in cardboard boxes—primitive accumulation of another sort. Ten percent of the Nigerian GDP was "discovered" in an unnamed private bank account in Switzerland; U.S. $15.0 billion of oil revenues "disappeared" in the civilian period.

In other words, the state mediated the oil boom in terms of corruption, chaos, and bureaucratic indiscipline. The talakawa were systematically excluded from access to the state, which they experienced as morally bankrupt, illegitimate, and incompetent. The police, who had been placed under federal jurisdiction, and the internal security forces were widely held to be particularly corrupt, disorganized, and violent; they embodied the moral and political decay of state authority and legitimacy (Usman 1982). In the context of rising urban crime, it was the police who appeared to be the trigger for all sorts of community violence; they were uniformly feared and loathed by Kano's urban poor. Indeed, it was the antiriot police who perpetrated the hideous slaughter of at least fourteen peasants at the Bakalori irrigation project, in a conflict over land compensation, six months prior to the Maitatsine insurrection. In the popular imagination, the police were feared and were explicitly refered to as *daggal*—literally, "the devil."

The second experience has been refered to by Paul Lubeck (1986) as "urban social processes," which operate at the level of the community in a manner analagous to the labor process for the individual worker at the point of production. The central issue here is not simply the anarchic and chaotic growth of Kano itself—how so much wealth could engender so much chaos, as the *London Economist* put it in 1982—but the changing material basis of talakawa reproduction and the assault on the community itself. First, urban land became a source of speculation for Kano merchants and civil merchants, reflected in the fact that the price of urban plots in the working-class Tudun Wada neighborhood increased twenty times between 1970 and 1978. Land records invariably disappeared (usually through mysterious fires), and compensation for land appropriated by the state was extremely corrupt and a source of recurrent conflict. Second, the escalation of food prices, typically in the context of price rigging, hoarding, and licensing scandals, far outstripped the growth of urban wages (see Table 2.2).[31] The inflationary spiral in wages and goods went hand in hand, of course, with an extraordinary internationalization of consumption by Kano's elites—car ownership grew by 700 percent in six years—and with the erosion of many of the traditional occupations within the secondary labor market taken by gardawa and 'Yan cin-rani. Nigerian novelist Chinua Achebe put it acutely: "[T]he peasant scratching out a living . . . the petty trader with all his wares on his head, the beggar under the fly over. . . . Twenty of these would be glad any day to be able to share *one* minimum wage packet" (1983:22–24).

And third, the state-funded Universal Primary Education (UPE) program represented both an ideological attack by proponents of "Western education" on its Qu'ranic counterpart and a practical assault on the mallams and the almajirai system. In Kano State, enrollment increased by 491 percent between 1973 and 1977; in the emirate of Hadejia, for

TABLE 2.2. *Food Prices and Wages in Kano during the Oil Boom, 1972–1980*

Year	Minimum urban wages in Kano City (N per year)	Rural wages in Kano State (N per day)	Food prices in Kano City Market (N per measure) Rice	Millet	Composite CPI (1975 = 100)	Rate of inflation (%)
1972	276	80K–N1	83K	17K	n.a.	n.a.
1973	276	—	—	—	66.3	6.1
1974	276	60K	—	—	75.2	13.4
1975	720	N1–2	N1.60	50K	100.0	33.0
1976	720	N1.20–1.60	—	—	123.9	23.9
1977	768	—	—	—	143.0	15.4
1978	768	N2	N2.50	N1.10	166.7	16.5
1979	846	N3	—	—	186.3	11.8
1980	1,200	N4	N5.50	N1.20	204.8	9.9
Percent increase (1972–1980)	435%	444%	662%	705%	309%	Average = 13.3% (1973–1980)

SOURCES: Williams 1980; World Bank 1979, 1981, 1985; Bienen 1983; Berry 1985; Collier 1983; Watts 1987; Lubeck 1987.
NOTES: One naira (N) or 100 Kobo (K) up until 1986 was equivalent to U.S. $1.34. As of 1989, the exchange rate was N1 = U.S. $6.70. The composite CPI (Consumer Price Index) is an aggregate of rural and urban prices for all items of consumption.

example, the number of primary schools lept from 36 in 1970 to 392 in 1980 (Stock 1985). With the return to civilian rule in 1979 and the subsequent fiscal crisis, primary education has, in fact, collapsed but the general point holds that in the 1970s the mallams in particular were vigorous critics of UPE and this is suggestive of a broader crisis in the gardawa system itself, which, as I suggested earlier, had been systematically marginalized by colonial rule.

The last aspect of the experience of modernity in Kano is explicitly political, namely, the return to civilan rule in 1979. In spite of the fact that the (NPN)—the party of the conservative northern oligarchy—was victorious at the federal level and dominated several state legislatures, a populist/socialist party—the PRP—swept to power in Kano State. The local government reforms of the 1970s had virtually eliminated the once-powerful Native Authority officials, who were replaced by university-educated administrators, but the triumph of PRP on a strong anti-aristocratic platform marked a qualitatively new political environment for the talakawa.[32] Much could be said about the PRP—not least its political split between "radical" and "conservative" factions—but in essence the assertion of a populist, procommoner administration provided a political space in which the Maitatsine movement could operate and indeed flourish. A militantly populist rhetoric by the PRP certainly spoke to all talakawa in a way that previous political discourses had not, and there is some evidence—to which I shall return—that the Maitatsine movements, as a déclassé segment of northern Muslim society, was tolerated by virtue of its antielitism, and perhaps actually coddled by the governor's office.[33]

The Moral Economy of Islam and Struggles over Meaning

I, too, like all migrants am a fantacist. I build imaginary countries and try to impose them on the ones that exist. I, too, face, the problem of history: what to retain, what to dump, how to hold onto what memory insists on relinquishing, how to deal with change.

Salman Rushdie, *Shame*

Every religion is in reality a multiplicity of distinct and contradictory religions.
Antonio Gramsci, *Prison Notebooks*

Let me, then, turn to the other aspect of the experience of modernity, which starts from the presumption that culture, in this instance, Islam, is a field of material and symbolic struggle. Naturally an enormous amount could be, and has been, said about the Muslim diaspora, of which northern Nigeria is an important part. I shall simplify, but hopefully not caricature, a complex historical narrative. In doing so, my concern is both to root Maitatsine's interpretations in a corpus of texts and discourses generally and to situate the Maitatsine movement on the changing map of the social organization of Islam in northern Nigeria during the oil boom years (Figure 2.6). One can only assess the particular meanings rendered to certain intellectual traditions and religious texts by Marwa and his drift toward violence and militancy against this broader canvas.

I begin with two generalizations. The first is that extraordinary ferment throughout the Muslim world in the 1970s and 1980s must be seen as part of a much longer reformist debate over Muslim interpretations of modernization and European dominance, dating back to the eighteenth century (Christelow 1985; Lapidus 1983; Roff 1987; Burke and Lapidus 1988). The context for these debates is, of course, the transformation of everyday life wrought by the incorporation of the Muslim world into a growing capitalist economy as well as the experience of European hegemony. How, in other words, would the intersection of two world processes, Islam and capitalism, be decoded through a shared symbolic matrix—the blueprint provided by the early Islamic *umma* (religious

Fig. 2.6 Muslims at Friday Prayer, Kano City

community) that flourished at Medina in the Prophet's lifetime and during the reign of the first four Rashidun caliphs that followed? Burke
(1986) has traced these movements of ferment in the Arab world in the
record of social protest between 1750 and the fundamentalism of the
1980s, but one might as readily examine the revivalist ferment at the end
of the eighteenth century and in the nineteenth century as an example of
these longer-term cycles of renewal. The resurgence of Muslim politics in
the era of petroleum should, in this sense, be seen as part and parcel of
long-standing tensions within Islam itself.

The second general point is that, like other great traditions, Islam is
paradigmatic in a cultural sense, and its origins provide the normative
basis of Muslim governance (Fischer and Abedi 1990). At the heart of
this paradigm, insofar as it shapes attitudes toward state, society, wealth,
and poverty, is the concept of justice. As Burke and Lubeck note, "popular Islamic ideas of justice . . . inhibit the flaunting of wealth and the
taking of interest, and encourage charity. The scripturalist tradition . . .
thus constrain[s] the choices open to Muslim actors . . . and also provide[s] repertoires of popular action and cultural vocabularies for their
expression" (1987:649). Of course, these abstractions derived from texts
and scripturalist discourses are filtered through local experiences and
through quite contrary models of the Islamic polity. In the Sunni tradi-

tion that concerns us here, Burke (1986) distinguishes between the Rashidun model, which roots justice and moral virtue in the early Muslim umma and the strict application of the sharī'a, and the imperial model of the later Arab caliphate, which has been typically invoked by incumbent Islamic govenments to justify *raison d'etat* policies. One might say that despite the distinctions and historical differences in political practice within the Sunni tradition, there is a thread—a patrimonial thread, embedded in a morally grounded social compact—that runs through the great tradition. The search for justice in an unjust world in the Muslim diaspora is, as Burke notes, analogous to the Western European notion of a moral economy. One could by way of an illustration point, for example, to the widely held belief that the Muslim state ensured the supply of grain at reasonable prices. As E. P.Thompson (1963) shows in his elaboration of the moral economy, these obligations are part of a patrimonial order, which was manipulated by the plebs and gentry alike.[34] Like its European counterpart, the Islamic moral economy was a configuration of symbols and traditions to be interpreted, struggled over, and fought for. Whatever its historical veracity, the moral economy is invoked to debate the present; if it is historical, the moral economy is also an ideological product of the present (Roseberry 1989:223).

What, then, was the local and historically specific Muslim environment in northern Nigeria that existed the 1970s in the wake of the jihad, and after a century of caliphal rule and sixty years of colonialism? I want to draw together three distinctive Islamic phenomena. The first speaks to the powerful Sufi brotherhoods (*tariqas*), most especially the Qadriyya, which is associated with the jihad of Usman dan Fodio in the early nineteenth century and more generally with the northern Hausa-Fulani aristocracy, and the Tijaniyya, founded by El-Hadj Omar Tall. Tahir (1975) and Paden (1974) show how the Tijaniyya transformed ritual and social practice in the colonial period and how the brotherhood grew and flourished in the fertile soil of colonial politics and merchant-capitalism. Unlike the Qadriyya, which was part of a class alliance between the sarauta and the colonial state, the Tijaniyya contained specific Mahdist, anticolonial and promercantile beliefs, which provided an apt cultural and social organization for a hegemonic northern bourgeoisie. As a direct counterweight to the tariqas, however, the 1970s witnessed the genesis of popular reformist sects in northern Nigeria—notably the 'Yan Izalas, founded in 1973 by Mallam Idris—whose aim is to abolish innovation and to practice Islam in strict accordance with the Qu'ran and the Sunna. Most closely associated with Sheikh Abubakar Gumi, the 'Yan Izala movement has a politically conservative and veiled anti-Western thrust, but it is widely suported by northern intelligentsia (Christelow 1987).[35] It is especially critical of Tijaniyya and of the influential Niassene branch, which spread in Nigeria in the 1940s, and it boasts President Babangida as one of its most illustrious members.[36]

The second dimension concerns the mallams and the institutional structures and networks, which may or may not be subsumed by the Sufi brotherhoods.[37] Many mallams are, of course, spokespersons for the tariqas and, to the extent that they are affiliated with state patronage, can be seen as proestablishment. There is nonethless a relatively independent laity (*malamin soro*), associated in particular with the indigenous Qu'ranic schools. There are three different forms of these schools: the traditional primary and higher schools and the so-called Islamiyya schools. In the primary schools (*makarantar allo*) for the almajirai, the Qu'ran is the main (and sometimes the only) text, typically learned by rote at a seminary. The 'Yan Tatsine were often products of this system, and the gardawa mallams are typically independent and usually sustained through alms. The higher schools (*makarantar ilimi*) range widely over theological and legal matters, including interpretation of the *hadith* (sayings attributed to God) and the Qu'ran. Most of the ilimi mallams are members of the brotherhood orders, participate in the *darikat* rituals, and are paid for their instructional activities. The Islamiyya schools are primary and secondary; they were set up in the 1930s (and expanded in the 1950s) with a syllabus comparable to Western forms of education but focusing on Arabic and Islamic studies. The Islamiyya schools are accredited (that is, recognized by the state—indeed, state-funded in part); graduates are typically employed as judges and scribes in the northern emirates and normally can gain entry into Nigerian universities. Many of the 'Yan Izalas are, in fact, products of the Islamiyya system, and Sheikh Gumi is perhaps its most distinguished and influential graduate.[38]

The critical point here, of course, is the tension between, and contradictory locations of, each system and its mallams, reflected in the struggles over the centrality of the Qu'ran, differing exegetical interpretations, and distinctive religious practices. This social organization of Islam has been changing through time and, indeed, has been reciprocally·engaged with the political economy of Nigeria, not least the changes wrought by the oil boom. The gardawa were seen as ignorant and traditional by both the ilimi and the Islamiyya scholars, but the latter conspicuously enjoyed the prestige and patronage of the state and characteristically were appointed as *alkalis* (local judges). The 'Yan Izala and the gardawa were, conversely, united in their antidarikat beliefs.[39] The ilimi and the gardawa were both marginalized by the fact that the proliferation of Islamiyya schools (in conjunction with the growth of UPE during the oil years) systematically eroded their traditional networks.

Finally, there is the legacy of the millenarian and Mahdist tradition of social protest in northern Nigeria. Mahdist discourse and practice have provided a critical ingredient for major reform movements in Nigeria—including the jihad of dan Fodio—and have been responsible for large-scale migrations eastward (Clarke 1987). During the 1840s one Sufi sect fled Kano to establish a state in the Ningi Mountains (Patton 1987), and during the last two decades of the nineteenth century, three Mahdist communities were established in northern Nigeria, but the arrival of the colonial forces (symbolically seen as the anti-Christ) represented the sure sign of impending collapse. The Satiru rising in 1906 was in some respects the most politically central millenarian revolt, since it sealed the alliance between the British and the sarauta class, but Mahdist sentiment flourished, especially between 1915 and 1925, generating an extraordinary paranoia among colonial officers. In the postwar years, Mahdism entered the melting pot of reformed Tijaniyya and Wahabi radicalism in northern Nigeria and has been associated with some of the most influential marabouts, including Ibrahim Niass. In all of these movements, of course, the call for a new world has often assumed a strong antiaristocratic, antimodernist, and antibusiness luster.[40] Indeed, in 1983 one such Mahdist sect (the Mintalla Ibrahima Hanifa Antakuma Lillahi) was discovered in Kaduna State, in the town of Dutsin-Ma preaching against all social amenities and modern artifacts, including watches and hospitals. The antimaterialism of Maitatsine was, in other words, not unusual or historically unprecedented, nor, indeed, was the millenarian vision of redemption and proclaimed prophethood. Indeed, in some respects it was a short step from some of the "legitimate" reformism of the 'Yan Izalas to the "fanatical" and "heretical" antimodernism of Maitatsine and his followers.[41] Not least, 1979 marked the onset of the new century in the Muslim calendar, a passing that is widely held to promise the coming of a Mahdi and the clearest sign of the imminent end of the world.

To recapitulate a rather complex argument, the advent of petrodollars and fast capitalism was directly experienced and reworked through the symbolic matrix of Islam. But Islam is not a monolithic lens through which the lived world is unproblematically filtered. The radical populist or jacobin interpretation of social change—the Muslim moral economy—is central here, but I have attempted to reveal the complexity of these struggles over Muslim "tradition" within the northern Nigerian community. Debate over Islam and modernity long predated the oil boom and was part of a serious and deep reformist debate within an ideologically fragmented Muslim population. The brotherhoods were hegemonic in the sense that they provided the necessary language that any opposition is obliged to employ to make its objections known (Terdiman 1987:62). But the popularity and following of Sheikh Gumi in relation to the powerful brotherhoods is a measure of the fact that a counterdiscourse of revivalism—and in some cases an "antimodernist" revivalism—was debated, discussed, and widely supported. As with all counterdiscourses, however, revivalism inhabits and struggles with the dominant that inhabits it.

Maitatsine was, in this regard, legitimately part of a wide-ranging struggle among Muslims (one aspect of which was the role of sharī'a law in the writing of the Nigerian constitution, which surfaced with particular acrimony in 1978[42]), and that debate provided a social space, and in a sense tacit support and legitimacy, for Marwa's admittedly unconventional preaching. While the language of Muslim reformism resonated with some sections of northern Nigerian society—Marwa was not, in other words, simply an "isolated fanatic"—the struggles over the meanings of central Muslim symbols (the centrality of the Qu'ran, the role of the sunna and the hadith) conducted by sects, brotherhood, mallams, alkalis, and state officials increasingly marginalized the gardawa and the Maitatsine movement. There was, as Christelow (1985:384) observes, a breakdown in the traditional mechanisms of assimilation. But this dissolution is more complex and recondite than he infers. It was the fragmentation of the social world of Islam, the marginalization of the almajirai/gardawa system, and the exploitation of the Maitatsine followers by political forces that at once enabled and constrained the movement, and that ultimately propelled Marwa to establish an independent religious community, to provide the grist for a particularly radical interpretation of the moral economy (a literal interpretation of the Qu'ran), and finally to defend his beliefs militantly against a state presence (the police) explicitly seen as the embodiment of the devil.

Idioms of Accumulation: Money, Commodification, and Muslim Identity

There's a peculiar thing about money. . . . In large quantities it tends to have a life of its own. . . . The power of money becomes very difficult to control.

Philip Marlowe, *The Long Goodbye*

Kudi cinye gaskiya [Money corrupts truth].

Popular Hausa adage

The Maitatsine insurrection sprang up in the interstices of Nigeria's oil-based modernization, within what I have referred to in shorthand as fast capitalism. More precisely, the appeal of Marwa must be located in a series of complex articulations: between Islam and capitalism, between precapitalist and capitalist institutions, and between class and culture. It would be much too facile to see the millenarian qualities of the movement as a lumpen insurrection plain and simple. The 'Yan Tatsine were, according to Maruf (1986), uniformly poor; 80 percent had income well below the minimum wage. But the "fanatical" qualities of the social explosions that occurred between 1980 and 1985 can be fully comprehended only in terms of the material and status deprivation of 'Yan Tatsine recruits scrambling to survive in an increasingly chaotic and Hobbesian urban environment and the unprecedented ill-gotten wealth and corruption of the dominant classes in urban Kano. In theoretical terms, this requires an analysis of "class relations . . . as they are experienced in terms of both everyday and canonical texts by producers and reproducers of the hegemonized transactions of the ruling bloc's socially extended and pervasive alliance systems with all the latter's split loyalities . . . feuds and betrayals . . . and their ambivalent awards of social success or failure" (Rebel 1989:130).

Marwa was, first of all, a long-time resident of Kano and was witness to the extraordinary transformation in the political and cultural economy of urban Kano during the oil years. As a charismatic preacher with a compelling, if idiosyncratic, reading of the Qu'ran, Marwa recruited followers from the influx of migrants and students into the city and from the marginal underclass of Kano. His disciples recruited at the truck stops and railway stations in Kano, where they typically sustained themselves by selling tea and bread (Nigerian Federal Government 1981a). The 'Yan cin-rani and gardawa more generally were products of the same Qu'ranic system as was Marwa (the makarantar allo); a survey by Maruf (1986) established that 80 percent of the Kano followers were educated in this system. Furthermore, Marwa's use of syncretist and pre-Islamic powers resonated strongly with migrants from the rural areas, where the *bori* cult and other vestiges of ancient Hausa metaphysical belief remained quite influential. Slowly Marwa was able to build up an enclave in 'Yan Awaki (see Figure 2.7) fashioned around a disciplined and self-consciously austere, egalitarian community of Muslim brothers (*'yan'uwa*), who supported themselves largely through alms. A survey conducted by Saad (1988:118) among the arrested 'Yan Tatsine revealed that 95 percent believed themselves to be unequivocably Muslim. As Marwa's following grew, land and urban gardens were appropriated to support the devotees.[43] Marwa's unorthodox and literalist interpretation of the Qu'ran focused specifically on the icons of modernity: bicycles, watches, cars, money, and so on. By the same token, Marwa addressed not only commodities per se but, of course, the means by which they were acquired. Indeed, the two were inseparable. Consequently, many Kano merchants, bureaucrats, and elites were implicated. The state emerged in Marwa's analysis as the most illegitimate and morally bankrupt part of the Muslim ummah, and the police as its quintessential embodiment. By the same token, any Muslim affiliation with the state naturally contaminated Islamic practice.

The 'Yan Tatsine did not necessarily stand in opposition to the popular classes among whom they lived.[44] In the 1980 conflicts for example, 'Yan Tatsine who had ocupied a cinema on the Kofar Mata Road told local residents that their fight was strictly with the police, while young immigrant workers living in Fagge (see Figure 2.2) "appeared to be just as fearful of the police and of the vigilantes as they were of 'Yan Tatsine" (Christelow 1985:377). Marwa himself scrupulously returned property to its rightful owner if it was unlawfully appropriated by his followers.

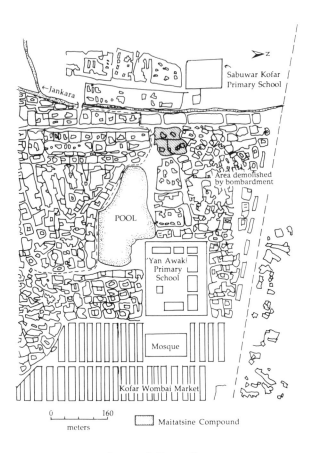

Fig. 2.7 'Yan Awaki Ward, Kano City

And it is to be recalled that Marwa was held in high esteem by certain extremely influential sections of Kano society. Among large sections of the talakawa there is reason to presume that Marwa's own discourse was anything but marginal or irrelevant. The geography of the violent conflict that broke out in December 1980 in the wards around 'Yan Awaki is especially interesting: specifically, it was the mercantile and petty bourgeois quarters (the purveyors of modernity) that felt the brunt of the attack. In Koki and Yan Awaki wards, the heart of the struggle, five times as many kiosks, shops, and market stalls as residences were destroyed (Nigerian Federal Government 1981a:154). Similarly, Marwa appropriated land as he needed it, and stole food as his followers grew in number, but this popular appropriation was directed at the state and the market.

We have already alluded to the fact that any social protest must contain "molecular processes of contrasting speed" (Stinchcombe 1978; Burawoy 1989) that explain the conjunctural forces and processes generating the insurrectional momentum. The Kano disturbances occurred during the dry season as many young male migrants poured into the city, drawn by the second oil boom. Further, the wider Muslim environment was animated by both the onset of the new century and the debates surrounding the role of sharī'a in the constitution. But it was the return to civilian rule and its attendant corruption, combined with the rise of the PRP in Kano, that explain the significance of 1980 and the timing of the final insurrection. The PRP was, on ideological grounds, certainly loath to intercede in the 'Yan Awaki Ward among a large constituency of "commoners," while the tensions between the left-leaning Kano State administration and the conservative federal oligarchy created a critical two-week hiatus between the ultimatum sent to Marwa on November 26, 1980, and the first efforts to arrest his followers.[45] During this critical time, Marwa drew in new recruits, armed his followers, and developed a siege mentality. The appearance of the police on December 18 elicited cries of "infidels!" from the well-organized 'Yan Tatsine and promptly initiated ten days of bloodshed and slaughter.

While there are structural conditions that account for the experience of modernity among the Kano popular classes, commodification and money are clearly central to understanding the ideology of Maitatsine. Harvey (1989) has suggested that capitalist restructuring in the core countries produces a type of time-space compression in which money is central. The same argument may be made, I think, for those periods of transformation of peripheral capitalism. There is a long line of thinking, of course, on the erosive, glacial qualities of money and on money as a form of domination (Simmel 1978; Harvey 1985; Shipton 1989). Suffice it to say, however, that the social relations of money strike to the core of Maitatsine and his ideological appeal. The gardawa mallams were conspicuously nonsalaried, and the 'Yan Tatsine carried little or no money on their persons. Further, there was a strong sentiment among the gardawa that wealth, especially in the 1970s, was ill-gotten (*haram*); in the popular imagination, behind every instance of wealth there is a crime. Indeed, this builds upon an important cultural distinction embedded in Hausa society between fruitful and barren capital. Money capital (literally "mother of money," *uwa*) may be fertile (*uwa mai amfani*) or ominous (*jarin tsiya*), a distinction rooted in cultural notions of work and proper conduct. Certain money is bitter and illegitimate (for example, interest for Muslims), and this is powerfully expressed in popular reactions to the petronaira in Nigeria.[46] Karen Barber (1982, 1986) has documented, for example, the recurrent theme of good and bad money in Nigerian popular plays and literature, and it is clear that the notion of the "benevolent rich man" was culturally transgressed in the robbery and venality that flourished around a corrupt state during the oil boom.[47]

There is a cultural economy of money in Islam, which requires serious intellectual exploration, and this is necessarily the case in northern

Nigeria, where the consequence of the oil boom was to produce wealth on a hitherto unimaginable scale; in oil economies money seems to literally appear out of thin air and without the expenditure of effort. Money was, however, experienced as a form of domination and social power, and this was expressed in symbolic and metaphorical terms.[48] There is good reason to presume that the sentiments of the Venezuelan diplomat who in lamenting his own country's predicament referred to petroleum as "the devil's excrement" may have found much support among Maitatsine and his followers (Watts 1992).

Insofar as money constitutes one aspect of the oil-based transformation in Nigeria, commodification—and specifically the profusion of Western "things"—provides another. Commodities, in fact, loom large in Marwa's preaching. The basis of his provocative reading of the Qu'ran as the *only* valid guide to human conduct (thereby excluding the sunna and the hadith) rested on the revelation of hidden meanings within the sacred text, and in his rooting of verse in local conditions. Marwa's vehement denunciation of cigarettes, motor vehicles, buttons, apparel, and so on, was revealed within the text through his careful textual analysis. Marwa deconstructed Qu'ranic texts in part by playing on the meanings and phonetic associations of certain Hausa and Arabic words. Furthermore, he played creatively with the relations between signs and their referents. In his public preaching, he pointed to the physical similarity between the Arabic character for Allah and a simple graphical depiction of a bicycle. This homology not only validated his accusation that all persons who rode bicycles were by definition pagan but also confirmed his far-reaching attack on the corruption of Islam at the highest levels by virtue of its association with Western modernity. Perhaps more than anything else, Marwa's preaching vividly illustrates how a "sign becomes an arena of class struggle" (Volosinov [1929] 1979:23), how symbolic struggles over the definition of "legitimate culture" strike to the heart of political economy.

Making Sense of Maitatsine

To theorize hegemonized social experience we need to theorize not only "experience" as such but, in addition, the textual limits of determined social relations.

> Hermann Rebel, *Cultural Hegemony and Class Experience*

The history of subaltern groups is necessarily fragmented and episodic.

> Antonio Gramsci, *Prison Notebooks*

The Maitatsine insurrection represented a powerful, counterhegemonic reading and critique of the Nigerian oil boom and of the Nigerian ruling classes. To this extent one should not be diverted by the syncretist character of Marwa, by the use of juju and other magic, by the possible Mahdist overtones, and by accusations of cannibalism. Marwa's self-identity, including his prophethood, are perhaps of less relevance than the antimaterialist, class-based reading of the moral superiority of the Qu'ran that led him to attack decadence, profligacy, and corruption. His antimaterialism was in one sense an effort to fashion a sort of Muslim modernity, yet it also contained an explicit class antagonism: specifically against corrupt ulema, the wealthy merchants, an illegitimate state, evil police, and private property more generally. Maitatsine's recruits typically were young men—unskilled migrants, Qu'ranic scholars and rural destitutes—products of shifting relations between town and countryside during the 1970s. Like the Kano insurrection, the subsequent Maitatsine conflicts in the north were led by low-status workers and craftsmen schooled in the Qu'ranic networks. It was the presence of the police that invariably triggered outright conflict.

The Maitatsine insurrection speaks directly to the question of hegemony and counterhegemony. Like any Marxist concept, hegemony is susceptible to what Raymond Williams (1977:112) calls "epochal" as opposed to "historical" definition, and "categorical" as opposed to "substantive" description. I have tried to situate the symbolic and interpretive struggles within Islam in northern Nigeria in terms of such historical and substantive specificities—in terms of the details of oil-based capitalism, the changing social organization of Islam, and the historical legacy of certain local class identifications. In this way one can come to appreciate the necessary preconditions for counterdiscursive assertions to be made, the space and modalities for discursive contestation, and the place of discursive engagement (Terdiman 1987:65). Hegemony can accordingly be seen less as a bundle of techniques to orchestrate consent than as a moment when "socially engaged selves, already split and de-centered . . . , in addition have to act in order to hold together *within themselves* a society that has split and turned against itself in irreconcilable and mutually inconstruable social relations" (Rebel 1989:129). At a certain point, these hegemonic processes could no longer occur, and one has, from within the belly of the beast, counterhegemonic movements as a response to these irreconcilable social relations. The Maitatsine movement as a form of resistance was finally choked off, of course, through, in Gramsci's language, repressive rule rather than hegemonic consent.

Two final matters are striking in the case of Maitatsine. First, struggles of a class nature are also fundamentally cultural; in this sense Islam and the other cultural traditions fought over provide an *active* part of social change. As Paul Willis (1981:124) put it, the cultural does not simply mark or in some simple sense live out wider social contradictions; "it works upon them with its own resources to achieve partial resolutions, recombinations, limited transformations to be sure but concrete . . . and the basis for actions and decisions that are vitally important to that wider social order." My second point, however, is precisely the limited nature of the transformations and of the cultural vision of this specific form of Muslim populism. Maitatsine represented a serious challenge to the Nigerian ruling class and to its fragile hegemony. Indeed, one can only understand the ferocity of state coercion, and the bloodbath that ensued, in relation to the fact that Maitatsine had exploded the myth of what Rebel (1989:129) calls "hegemonized social experience." The movement revealed the serious fractures *within* the dominant northern regional ruling bloc and jeopardized the fragile political unity *among* the regions in what was interpreted in the southern regions as a drift toward Islamic fundamentalism. It was also, of course, a self-consciously Muslim movement, speaking directly to the then–Muslim President of Nigeria, employing a revolutionary rhetoric of Islam. Unlike the Shi'ite revolution in Iran, however, it was not transformative. And I would suggest that the contrast resides in the fact that Maitatsine had a limited social base outside the gardawa and 'Yan cin-rani, especially among the middle classes. To this extent Muslim populism was hampered by its incapacity to generate an alternate social vision, and in particular an alternative economic vision, to mobilize segments of Nigerian society.

The question of the social basis of recruitment resonates strongly with the present nevertheless, because the period since the Maitatsine insurrections has seen a further deterioration in living conditions for the Nigerian industrial working and middle classes (see Table 2.3). The oil bust, a gargantuan debt service, and a Draconian structural adjustment program (SAP) have collectively imposed a terrifying burden on labor and state functionaries in particular (see Bangura and Beckman 1989; Bierstecker et al. 1987; IBRD 1988; Main 1989; Usman 1986). Several industries slashed their workforces by 60 percent between 1982 and 1988; industrial capacity utilization fell to 27 percent; and real wages fell by at least 25 percent. Staple food prices grew by close to 300 percent between 1981 and 1987, and public sector layoffs were widespread. Negotiating the bust in the immediate wake of the halcyon years of the boom deepened the legitimation crisis of the Nigerian military and the ruling coalition more generally. The conflation of legitimation and accumulation crises produced a quite ferocious sort of authoritarianism. Three laws— the Constitution Decree #1 (1984), the State Security Decree #2 (1984), and the Robbery and Firearms Decree #5 (1984)—deny the most basic civil liberties. One might venture to say that organized labor, students, and many professional associations have felt the state violence that Maitatsine so vividly captured in his condemnation of the police as "devils." In May and June of 1989 the police and state security forces surfaced as central actors in a wave of massive detentions, arrests, and murders.[49] In

TABLE 2.3. *Economic Structure of the "Bust" in Nigeria, 1981–1988*

Macroeconomic indicator	1981	1982	1983	1984	1985	1986	1987	1988
GDP at market prices (billions of N)	52.2	54.5	54.0	70.1	80.3	82.9	107.6	135.0[a]
Real GDP growth (%)[b]	−2.9	−1.9	−6.4	−5.5	1.2	−2.1	1.8	4.1[c]
Consumer price inflation (%)	22.3	6.4	23.2	39.6	5.5	5.4	10.2	25.0[c]
Population (millions)[d]	83.3	86.1	89.0	92.0	95.2	98.5	101.9	n.a.
Exports (billions of $ f.o.b.)	17.94	13.66	10.70	11.90	12.57	6.80	7.60	6.90[a]
Imports (billions of $ c.i.f.)	20.53	15.00	9.06	9.40	8.89	4.44	4.46	4.60[a]
Current account (billions of $)	−6.2	−7.2	−4.1	0.1	2.6	0.4	1.6	−0.5
Reserves, excl. gold (millions of $)	3,895	1,613	990	1,462	1,667	1,081	1,165	686[e]
Total external debt disbursed (billions of $)[f]	5.90	8.49	11.76	18.66	19.52	24.47	28.71	29.50[a]
Debt service ratio (%)	4.6	10.3	18.6	25.5	30.7	17.9	10.0	n.a.
Crude oil production (millions of barrels per day)	1.44	1.29	1.24	1.37	1.48	1.46	1.28	1.38[a]
Exchange rate (average N per $)[g]	0.614	0.673	0.724	0.764	0.892	1.347	4.006	4.429[b]

SOURCE: Economist Intelligence Unit 1981–1989.

[a]EIU estimate.
[b]At 1984 factor cost.
[c]Provisional official figures.
[d]IMF estimates; no reliable census data.
[e]September 1988.
[f]Including private and short-term debt.
[g]The two tier rates were unified as of July 2, 1987.
[h]January–November 1988. As of January 30, 1989, N6.77 per $.

1990 President Babangida decreed that the anticipated return to civilian rule in 1992 (including the process of party formation) must accept structural adjustment as a precondition for political debate.[50]

Oil and Islam no more determine revolutionary, or, indeed, insurrectional, outcomes than does a mixture of copper and Christianity. But Muslim populism, which possesses a great capacity to resist cooptation and to provide a culturally convincing critique of "oil prosperity," constitutes a powerful ideology in weak Islamic states experiencing the petroleum boom (Burke and Lubeck 1987). Maitatsine revealed in a fantastic way that the efforts by the Nigerian state to form a stable class coalition by redistributing oil rents were morally bankrupt. The fantastic intermingling of the old and new that Maitatsine wove from certain Muslim texts and the experience of oil-based capitalism also shaped, I would argue, new personal and collective identities, and in so doing fashioned a curious and ambiguous sort of Muslim modernity.

My reading of the Maitatsine movement and the preachings of Marwa himself suggest that it is less about "fanatics and heretics" than about the compelling need for a radically new class coalition and social compact. But manufacturing political consent and consensus in an era of petroleum bust and structural adjustment is a different story altogether. At the very least, as Nobel Laureate Wole Soyinka observed, this demands a national debate and dialogue. At this historic juncture in Nigeria, it is precisely this debate and dialogue that, as the Nigerian Civil Liberties Organization has made perfectly clear, is wholly absent in the face of state repression.[51] In these circumstances, to return to the motif of the Maitatsine movement, a charismatic leader with a coherent ideology and capable of speaking to the uprooted, excluded, and oppressed, could generate oppositional energies capable of a quite different outcome than the brutal oppression that transpired in a dusty, impoverished quarter of Kano in December 1980.

Appendix 2A
Maitatsine Disturbances, 1981–1985

In the aftermath of the Kano insurrection, large numbers of 'Yan Tatsine were imprisoned in spite of the fact that the precise nature of the charges leveled against them was ambiguous. On October 1, 1982, President Shagari, in a hotly debated and heavily criticized decision, pardoned 923 of those incarcerated in two Kano prisons. The 'Yan Tatsine followers—223 of whom were designated as foreigners and were immediately deported—dispersed to communities across the northern states. In the three years following this act of clemency, at least four major Maitatsine insurrections occurred (and there were rumors of several more in Lagos in 1984, in Yola in 1985, and in Benin City in 1986 and 1987). Judicial Commissions of Inquiry were established under Justice Muhammedu Jimeta in 1983, Justice Uwai in 1984, and Justice Okoye in 1985. None of the reports of or testimony before these tribunals has ever been officially released, in part because of the political character of the testimony and the threats of communal violence. According to NIPSS (1986:27), for example, four volumes of the report on the Jimeta Ward, Yola, insurrection were formally submitted, but the principal preoccupation of the committee (consisting entirely of Muslims) was to establish conclusively that "Maitatsine was not a Muslim group." The four major Maitatsine protests in the wake of the Kano insurrection are described below and represent my own summary of the events drawn from the sources listed at the end of this appendix.

Bulumkutu, near Maiduguri, October 26–29, 1982

The influx of Maitatsine disciples released from Kano prisons caused apprehension among law-enforcement authorities, who arrested sixteen of them on October 25 for illegal preaching outside the Shehu of Borno's palace in Maiduguri, in northeastern Nigeria. Following a police search and arrest at a village 15 km from Maiduguri (see Figure 2.8), Maitatsine followers (some of whom had fled to Bornu from Kano in 1980 and others following the state pardon in 1982) launched an attack armed with "guns, cutlasses, daggers and clubs" (*West Africa*, November 8, 1982, 2873). Two principal activists, Bukar Tella (a gasoline tanker driver) and Haruna Mainama (a butcher), had established a sect (referred to locally as *kalo-kato*) in Maiduguri town, but its spiritual leadership was provided by Mohammedu Rufai, who was killed in the subsequent riots. In the four days of armed struggle that ensued, an estimated 3,350 persons were killed. Of the 411 arrested, 79 were foreigners, principally from Chad.

According to a Radio Kaduna broadcast of January 11, 1982, there

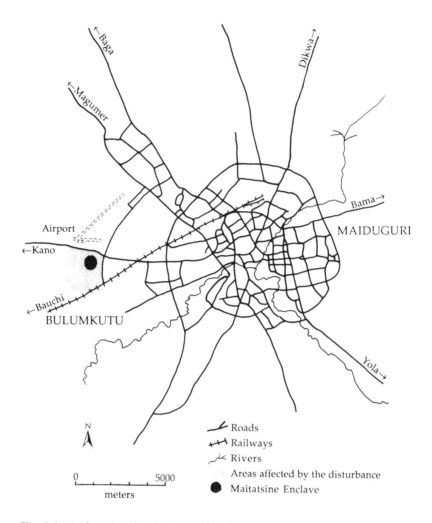

Fig. 2.8 Maiduguri and Bulumkutu Suburbs

had been previous religious conflict in the Ingbandje Ward of Maiduguri when "fundamentalists" attacked various hotels in the town. Apparently a "rampage" was triggered by a partial eclipse of the moon, which, according to the "fanatics," was "due to evil being committed in the town."

Rigasa, near Kaduna, October 29, 1982

An assistant commissioner of police, following a report that "fanatics" fleeing from Bulumkutu had regrouped in Rigasa, appears to be have been the catalyst for communal violence. Reportage was scant and often contradictory. In a somewhat hysterical atmosphere, accusations were made in Rigasa, and a group of migrants fled for their lives. Conflict spread to Kaduna city, where at least forty presumed 'Yan Tatsine were killed by the civilian population.

Jimeta Ward, Yola, February 27–March 5, 1984

Many 'Yan Tatsine had fled to Yola in the wake of the Maiduguri massacre and had apparently lived peacefully in the community (see Figure 2.9) until rumors of a possible attack on the Yola mosque prompted a police investigation. According to NIPSS (1986:23), Makaniki (who was almost certainly an assistant to Maitatsine in Kano) and his lieutenant, Shaibu Maitatasai, had been questioned by the national security forces and the police following accusations by another Muslim sect, the Yan Izalas, that their own preaching had been restricted while that of the 'Yan Tatsine continued unabated. With a change of state government in 1984, the state security committee directed the police to arrest the Maitatsine followers. The 'Yan Tatsine, organized around three defense groups (led by Musa Makaniki from Gombe, Danbarno, a cobbler from Borno, and Bagobiri, a barber from Yauri, Sokoto), preempted police assault by attacking and destroying the Yola market. Fifty-nine police officers were dispatched to confront the Jimeta-Dubeli enclave, but they were successfully repulsed, and their arms and ammunition seized. Seven days of violence followed, in which one thousand police were called into Yola and troops of the Fifth Battalion (aided by the air force) launched a major assault on the Maitatsine *tsangaya* on March 3. Estimates of the dead were put at 718 (*Guardian*, March 11, 1984, 9); hundreds more were injured, and 914 detained (of whom 47 were non-Nigerian).

Gombe, April 26–29, 1985

Musa Makanaki, who had esaped from Yola, resided in the Pantami Ward of Gombe until complaints led police to attempt an arrest. Fighting broke out, and the 'Yan Tatsine withdrew to central Gombe, fighting with considerable skill and substantial military hardware (amidst rumors of involvement of ex-Biafran mercenaries). Again the police forces proved to be easily intimidated and extremely disorganized; the chaotic performance of the law enforcement agencies was compounded by the fact that the Bauchi governor's orders were not promptly acted upon. One hundred one people were killed and hundreds (there are no official estimates) injured. One hundred forty-six individuals were imprisoned, but the Maitatsine leader, Yusufu Adamu, and many of the followers

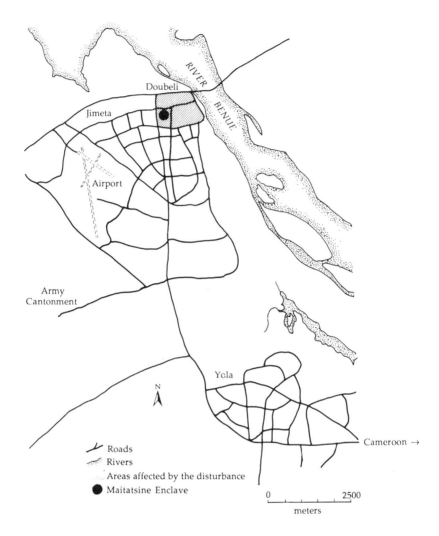

Fig. 2.9 Greater Yola, Including Doubeli Ward

escaped. According to the NIPSS (1986:36) study, there was "strong evidence" of external influence from Iran, Libya, and Syria.

Sources

Isichei 1987; Kasfelt 1989; Omoniwa and Abu 1986; *Guardian*, March 11, 1984; *New Nigerian*, March 22, 1984; *Africa News*, May 6, 1985; NIPSS 1986.

Appendix 2B
Excerpts from Report of Tribunal of Inquiry on Kano Disturbances [Anagiolu Report]

Maitatsine's band of fanatics were estimated to number between 6000 and 10,000.

Evidence before the Tribunal revealed that the person or group of persons involved in acts of negligence which caused the breaking out of the disturbances may be traceable to:

(i)   principally the Nigeria Police Force and the Nigeria Security Organisation . . .
(ii)   the Kano State Government and its organs and functionaries . . .
(iii) the Governor of Kano State, the Alhaji Mohammed Abubakar Rimi . . .

("Findings and Conclusions," p. 6)

The Tribunal found that the actual causes of the disturbances were as follows:

(i)   the objectionable preaching of Maitatsine . . .
(ii)   Maitatsine's deep-rooted hatred of the Authorities . . .
(iii) Maitatsine's hostile attitude to his neighbours . . .
(iv)   the build-up of a contingent of armed students . . .
(v)   the leakage of official secrets to Maitatsine
(vi)   the death of Maitatsine's first son: and
(vii) the Governor's ultimatum issued in a letter dated November 26th, 1980. . . .

(From "Findings and Conclusion," p. 7)

Living under Contract: Work, Production Politics, and the Manufacture of Discontent in a Peasant Society

Work may seem to be a simple category. . . . [H]owever when seen from an economic point of view even this simple category is as historical a concept as the social relations which have given birth to it.

Karl Marx, *Capital*, Volume 1

The plainness and the iterativeness of work must be one of the things which make it so extraordinarily difficult to write of. . . . [H]ow is it possible to be made clear enough that the same set of leverages has been undertaken by this woman in nearly everyday of the eleven or twenty five years since her marriage, and will be persisted in nearly every day to come in the rest of her life. . . . how is it to be calculated, the number of times she has done these things, the number of times she is still to do them; how conceivably in words is it to be given as in actuality, the accumulated weight of these actions upon her . . . and what has it made of her mind and of her heart and of her being?

James Agee, *Let Us Now Praise Famous Men*

The issue is rather one of the ongoing struggle for meaning. The struggle is formed in the context of the social relations of individuals, groups, classes and cultures which at the same time are constituted by the struggle.

Hans Medick, *Missionaries in a Row Boat*

Introduction

"FARMERS TURN TO HOG RAISING FOR A FEE" proclaimed the *New York Times* (May 29, 1988, 12) in a recent account of the changing fortunes of the American family farm. Propelled by high interest rates, falling land values, and the sluggish hog markets of the early 1980s, pig farmers in Arkansas, Missouri, North Carolina, and much of the Mid west, have made a dramatic shift to contract production for corporate processors (Wilson 1986).[1] Household or family-based pig growers working directly under company supervision, fatten corporate hogs owned by the likes of Cargill Inc. (the largest privately held corporation in the United States) and National Farms (owned by the Bass brothers of Texas) in grower-financed production facilities built to company specifications. Contracting now accounts for at least 10 percent of national hog production, a quintupling in less than five years.

The restructuring of U. S. hog farming is simply one reflection of the complex and divergent logics of reproduction within North American agriculture in general and within the family farm sector in particular (Gilbert and Akor 1988). Contract production is, of course, a well-trodden path on the U.S. and, indeed, on Western European agrarian landscapes, bearing the footprints of previous restructuring in the poultry, dairy, and specialty crop sectors. But it also represents a fast-growing, and, in fact, a much touted, mode of agro-industrial integration for a debt-laden Third World engaged in a desperate search for foreign exchange (Sanderson 1986a, 1986b; Glover 1983, 1984, 1987; Williams and Karen 1985). The genesis of these agricultural enclaves, still clinging to the classic export commodities, such as sugar, tea, and rubber, but distinguished by standardization, nonequity forms of control over production, and a relative homogenization of production technologies, suggests both a new social character to the "old" international division of labor and a new wave of aggressive industrialization of peasant agriculture (cf. Lipietz 1986).

The dispersion of contracting marks an important phase in the social transformation of the rural sector in agrarian societies. Less a terrain of independent peasantries and commodity circulation through trade (or, for that matter, a world of large plantation systems under foreign-transnational, or state control), Third World agriculture has become a crucible in which new forms of social integration and subordination link peasant growers to state and private capital. Kostas Vergopolous puts it succinctly: "Integration is no longer anonymous as it was previously but personalized through the emergence of "companies.' It uses as its means *contracts integrating direct producers* . . . conform[ing] to the microeconomic pattern of the company" (1985:291, emphasis added).

The well-known case of fruit and vegetable processors, freezers, and canners in the Mexican Bajío illustrates how contract production—in this case between U.S. agribusinesses, such as Campbells Soup, Birdseye, and Green Giant, and heavily capitalized Mexican growers of strawberries, carrots, asparagus, corn, and green beans—has blossomed since the late 1950s (Runstan and Archibald 1986; Young 1987; Rama 1985). Kindled by the postwar industrialization of the U.S. food system, contracting reflected an emergent, distinctively new agricultural regime, what Kenney et al. (1987) call an emergent Fordist agriculture. Gerber, Campbells, Del Monte, and Heinz all established canneries in the Bajío between 1959 and 1963, geared almost wholly to the internal market but provisioned by large-scale and heavily capitalized Mexican contract growers. However, the collapse of local purchasing power in the wake of the 1982 devaluation of the peso drove many of these enterprises to the U.S. export market, a flight actively promoted since 1967 by Birdseye with its establishment of a freezing plant for broccoli, cauliflower, okra, and zucchini. Frozen and fresh vegetables produced under contract tripled between 1950 and 1980 (Young 1987). Throughout the 1980s Mexican horticultural crops proved to be even more attractive to U.S. investors, attracting new capital and substantial agro-industrial investment (for example, Green Giant in 1983). In short, the last decade has witnessed a second boom in contract production. The average rate of growth of contracted frozen broccoli exports from the Bajío was an astonishing 28.6 percent per annum in the 1980s (Young 1987:68).

Contracting is a form of industrial agriculture[2] whose genesis and dispersion can be explained in part by commodity characteristics that create variable incentives and disincentives to scale in the crop industry, processes that are shaped, however, by specific historical and class relations (Friedland 1984; Wells 1987; Friedmann 1987). That is to say, the contracting crop system must be embedded in the local and regional constellations of state, political, and social forces. In this sense, the proliferation of contracting suggests certain parallels between certain transformations in industrial organization—for example, subcontracting, outsourcing, and flexible specialization in certain sectors of underadvanced capitalism—and restructuring of agriculture in the Third World (FitzSimmons 1984; Watts 1989). To employ language that harks back to the classic debates of Marx, Kautsky, and Lenin over the "agrarian question," contracting represents one means by which agriculture and industry seem to achieve a higher synthesis.

In this chapter, I shall explore what one might call configurations of production, power and culture, the "cultural economy" of peasants drawn into the circuits of the world economy as contract growers. In general I seek to situate this process on a larger terrain of capitalist restructuring, and of the current phase of agro-industrialization in particular. Broadly speaking, there are three narratives. The first is a general and theoretical discussion of contract farming, its particular form and character, based on an examination of the U.S. poultry industry, and its dispersion from the heartland of agrarian capitalism in the United States to Third World peasant societies. The second addresses one case of contract farming in Africa, specifically of contract rice production on irrigation schemes in The Gambia, West Africa. The intention is to trace out at the local level—the level of the farming household and the minutiae of farm work—the intersection of new labor processes, the struggles over meaning, associated with contracting and deeply sedimented property rights, cultural structures, and gender roles in one particular African setting. In the third, we return to some general matters on the character of contracting as a production regime, and the way in which peasant contracting during a period of globalization and emerging Fordist agriculture sheds light on the relationship among the development of capitalism, culture, and unfree labor; in short, to illuminate a particular reworking of modernity via a refashioning of work.

Contracts, Contracting, and Contract Farming

The notion of contract is central to any understanding of the social integration of peasants into corporate relations of production.[3] For Maine and Durkheim and classical sociological theory more generally, the contract represented a historically unique form of sociopolitical linkage, standing as a counterpoint to the notion of status. In Maine's lexicon, the contract enables social unequals to negotiate and enter binding agreements as legal and political equals (Goodell 1988). The contract extracts political life from the interpersonal and private into the public domain, and in so doing promotes the creation of a legal personality, individual and inalienable rights, public accountability, and collective bargaining. This legal but nonetheless essentially Eurocentric definition—in essence, a general legal form of agreement between abstract individuals proscribed by civil authority—provides the foundation for a large part of economic theory (Hart and Holmstrom 1987; Williamson 1985; Mead 1984). For example, as a quid pro quo, any trade must be mediated by some form of explicit or implicit contract; in fact the analysis of contracts covering a small number of actors lies at the heart of the new institutional approaches to the economy, what Elson refers to as the "third hand of networks and relationships" (1988:22).[4]

The legal and so-called "complete" expression of contracts must be expanded, however, to include the variety of forms in which contracts appear in agrarian contexts throughout the Third World. To the extent that complete contracts (that is, those in which each party's obligation are specified for *every* eventuality) are quite rare, contingent or incomplete contracts conversely allow for the introduction of social relations, culture, and custom (Akerlof 1984). Market relations are frequently undeveloped in Third World agriculture, and transactions often take the form of complex contractual relations, such as sharecropping, interlinked contracts, so-called forced commerce, patronage, and labor-recruitment, deeply embedded in local social relations (see Binswanger and Rosenzweig 1984).[5] These indigenous contractual arrangements can refer to any oral or written agreement between individuals that specifies fixed terms in advance and is subject to customary proprieties (Robertson 1987).

Contracts, in the expanded and incomplete sense, are found in agriculture everywhere and are extremely heterogeneous in form ("World Agriculture" 1976). Simple market specification contracts or future-purchase agreements (typically determining price, quantity, and time of delivery) are commonplace between growers and buyer-shippers in U.S. agriculture (Sporleder 1983; Marion 1986). Labor contracting, in which certain on-farm operations are performed by contractors, characteristically supplying labor and machinery, is also endemic in Western European agricultural systems. Ball (1987) found, for example, that contract work is ubiquitous in Britain's arable and dairy industries, and in California, growers' use of farm labor contractors has exploded in the 1980s as a flexible means to capture cheap, nonunion field labor.[6] The switching of labor from the *internal* (that is, household) or local labor markets to *external* sources through dense networks of contract relations is also extremely widespread in the farm economy of Japan. One-third of all Japanese farming households habitually contract in for certain on-farm operations, while at least 25 percent contract out their own labor.[7]

Contract farming or contract production must, however, be distinguished from the multiplicity of simple marketing or labor contracts.[8] Specifically, contract farming entails relations between growers and private or state enterprises that substitute for open-market exchanges by linking nominally "independent" family farmers of widely varying asset holdings with a central processing, export, or purchasing unit that regulates prices, production practices, product quality, and credit arranged in advance under contract (Davis 1979). The classic, all-encompassing definition provided by Roy refers to "[t]hose contractual arrangements between farmers and other firms, whether oral or written, specifying one or more conditions of production and marketing of an agricultural product" (1927:3). Contracting, or vertical coordination in U.S. agriculture stands, in other words, between the spot market and the vertically integrated agribusinesses (that is, integrated corporate production, input supply, processing and distribution), which it now exceeds in terms of gross output.[9] By 1980 one-quarter of U.S. farm output by volume (one-third by value) was produced under some form of contract.[10] Not only in the United States but also across much of Western Europe and Japan, in fact, contract production is the centerpiece of contemporary food and fiber complexes.[11]

Insofar as contract farming minimally demands a crop agreement made in advance, the processor-buyer-exporter (the nonfarm firm) has title to a portion of on-farm resources and shares, in varying degrees, the decisionmaking power with the grower. The grower lends to the production process his/her labor power and the effective property within his/her possession. Conversely, the contractor provides some of the production inputs, participates in production decisions and supervision, and holds title to the product. The contract circumscribes what one might call the social space of autonomy and subordination that the grower occupies in relation to the labor process. It maps, in other words, the topography of direct and indirect control at the point of production (Davis 1980). In a descriptive sense, contract farming is defined by three broad attributes:

(1)   *A futures, or forward market, contract* for a specific product is entered into by a grower (who typically controls the means of production and labor power in some way) and a buyer/processor or contractor. There is no presumption that the contractor must be an agent of international agribusiness; contractors may be local merchants, the state, or joint enterprises. Both parties commit to buy and sell at specified volumes and/or acreages though the completeness, duration, and specificity of the contract varies considerably.

(2)   *Production contracting links product and factor markets.* Purchase commitments rests in some determinate way on the provision of inputs, services, and supervision to growers, who may or may not be organized. Contractually linked markets generate a marked division of labor in the realm of farm management and hence a complex field of autonomy and subordination (that is, the labor process contains a clear separation of execution and conception (cf. Braverman 1974). There is no presumption of market destination (that is, the crop may be destined for local or foreign markets with or without processing).

(3)   *Production contracts differentially allocate production, price, and market risks.* Crop-share contracts without price determination share production risk between contractor and grower. Conversely, in price-specified contracts, the grower is bound in a sort of piece-rate system in which he/she bears production risk but none of the price risk.

For our purposes, contract production presupposes some form of regulation and control, a sort of direct fashioning, of the labor process by the contractor, and a web of social relations, which are practically and ideologically central to the production system. To this degree Asano-Tamanoi (1988:450) is quite mistaken when he states that *contract farming* is "nothing but a technical term"; rather it represents quite specific social relations of production, in which independent commodity producers are subordinated to "management" through a distinctive labor process.

Contract Farming in North America: The Case of the "Perfect Broiler"

In 1986, U.S. consumers ate more chicken than beef for the first time in history. The average American consumed 61.5 pounds of chicken in 1988, an increase of over 450 percent in thirty years.[12] Growing sensitivities to a healthy diet combined with the proliferation of the fast food industry has converted the poultry sector into a giant sixteen-billion-dollar a year industry.[13] Concentrated principally in the southern states, where it employs 20,000 contract farmers and 150,000 workers in processing plants, the poultry industry is larger than peanuts in Georgia, tobacco in North Carolina, and cotton in Mississippi (*Southern Exposure* 1989).

The picture of a huge integrated poultry industry resting on contract production must be painted on the larger historical canvas of the U.S. political economy. The Great Depression, and the New Deal in particular, proved to be a watershed, which "transformed an agriculture dependent upon extensive growth using relatively low levels of manufactured inputs into a commercial agriculture prepared to adopt any innovations [to] improve productivity" (Kenny et al. 1987:9). The farm production system was routinized, subsidized, and mechanized at the same moment that the rural U.S. constituency was brought into line with national consumption norms. In the postwar era of high Fordism—the social contract linking mass production and mass consumption—a rehabilitated agriculture was inexorably drawn into a buoyant consumer market. Fordism made possible a revolution in the food delivery system, and simultaneously converted the agricultural sector into a market for Fordist inputs, such as tractors, fertilizers, and manufactured wage goods. Not only was the poultry sector caught up in this vortex of postwar growth as workers demanded meat as part of a social contract— Roosevelt had, after all, promised to put "a chicken in every pot"—but in many respects it became the model of "development" within an increasingly industrial agriculture.

Over three decades, the U.S. poultry industry has been converted from "hundreds of competing mom-and-pop farms, feedmills and processors" (Hall 1989:12) into vertically integrated agribusinesses, usually called "integrators." Prior to World War II, chicken breeders were in effect open range grazers until they were driven out of business by the likes of Swift and Ralston Purina in the 1950s. Massive investment in the sector between 1945 and 1955 simultaneously transformed both the market and the geographic structure of the industry. The spatial core of the industry shifted from Maryland, Virginia, and Delaware to the southeastern states, where surplus labor and "chronically depressed conditions" (Reimund et al. 1981:5) were widespread as a result of the westward shift of cotton. In addition, production materials (especially for chicken-house construction) were cheap, and feed prices substantially lower. Over the same period, the market was also restructured; concentration and integration proceeded apace. In 1960 there were 286 firms selling commercial fryers. By 1989 there were only 48, close to 40 percent of production being accounted for by only five companies (Tyson Food, ConAgra, Good Kist, Holly Farms, and Perdue Farms) (Hall 1989:12). One of these integrators, Tyson Foods, a massive Arkansas-based agribusiness, has been in the vanguard of U.S. poultry contracting for several decades. Currently it realizes an annual output of 8.3 billion chickens, drawn from its 8,500 family-farm contractors, scattered around thirty-two company processing units, almost all located in the southeastern states (*The Economist* 1989:84).

Each integrator typically controls at least two levels within the six stages of the commodity system, namely, broiler breeders, hatchery, growout, feedmill, processing, and distribution. The complex divisions of labor within the commodity system are a product of the harnessing of an advanced poultry science in the search of the "perfect broiler."[14] Standardized growing and processing systems have systematically upgraded maturation rates, killing and bleeding procedures, and chicken "stress management" in order to enhance productivity.[15] By the late 1980s, 40 percent of all poultry was destined for the fast food market, a trend that propelled the integration of processing units and slaughterhouses geared, to use the words of the CEO of Tyson Foods, "to products [that is, processed chicken commodities] we didn't produce seven years ago."

The spine of the poultry system is the contract grower attached to the broiler breeding, hatchery, and, especially, growout systems. Growers receive day-old chicks in flocks, which can, under tightly controlled conditions, be matured to four–five pounds live weight in less than two months. In North Carolina, to take one illustration, 4,200 growers provide the houses ($385,678 for a two-story, 64,000-bird house), feeding equipment (specified by the company), and labor. The company supplies the flock of birds, as well as the feed, and imposes quality standards. Grower schedules determine the number of birds supplied, and the frequency of delivery and collection. Almost all growers have "bunch to bunch" contracts, in which there is no guarantee that the family farm will receive more than one flock of chickens (Aho 1983). The conspicuous absence of any form of price negotiation, coupled with the fear that all growers experience of being cut off with a high debt overhang, acts to subordinate family labor and limit grower militancy. And not least, the maturation process and the growing regime is extremely labor-intensive in relation to economic returns. Wellford's study in the early 1970s determined, in fact, that labor returns were minus thirty-six cents per hour with depreciation taken into account (1972:101).[16] A grower in Alabama lamented to a researcher in 1971 that "us folk in the chicken business are the only slaves left in this country." Almost two decades later, the Rural Advancement Fund in Pittsboro, North Carolina, referred to contract farmers as little more than "serfs on their own land" (cited in Yeoman 1989:22).

The poultry industry reveals that contract farming is a singularly distinctive mode of the social organization of agriculture in which plants and animals are produced on land in relation to the complex and changing profit conditions under global capitalism. More generally, its genesis and proliferation reflect important links between specific commodities, and equally specific manufacturing processes, which are characterized by particular social relations among, and within, farm enterprises (Friedmann 1987).[17] Rhetorically, contract farming is characteristically touted in populist and Jeffersonian terms, as the savior of small farms on the verge of collapse in the American Midwest. Family farmers under contract have, as the manager of the country's largest swine enterprise put it, "given up the privilege of going broke" (*New York Times*, May 29, 1988, 12). In the same fashion, French farm policy has actively promoted contract production of seed corn, tobacco, and pigs, all of which theoretically require little or no land, and hence would be particularly suited to family production (Groger 1986).

As the savior of the family farm, and the voice of twentieth-century agrarian populism, contract farming turns out to be deeply ambiguous. It is clearly a means to introduce distinctive work routines, introduce new on-farm technologies and labor processes, and promote a further concentration and centralization of capital in agro-food systems. And not least, it deepens the process of appropriation by which rural production processes (farm inputs and services) are converted into industrial products by agro-industries and subsequently reincorporated into agriculture (Goodman et al. 1987).

Contract Farming and Global Restructuring

While contract farming was hatched, in its contemporary guise, in the United States in the 1930s (Pfeffer 1985), it is no longer confined to advanced Euro-American agro-food complexes but now operates through international circuits of capital as part of globalized agricultural commodity markets (Glover 1984; Watts 1990b; de Treville 1987). In the Third World, however, contract farming appears to have a dual origin. First, contract farming is competing with, and partially replacing, traditional plantation and estate forms of production employing free wage labor because foreign agribusiness is subject to nationalist pressures, threats of expropriation, and local regulation and to new conditions of profitability within a changing international division of labor (Graham and Floering 1982). Plantation and estate capital may, in spite of these pressures, retain a foothold in agricultural production by contracting for export—for example, United Fruit shifted its banana operations in Honduras from plantation production to contracting with local large-scale growers. Another illustration is provided from Fiji. Estate production of sugar in Fiji employing indentured Indian labor collapsed in the early twentieth century because of a labor shortage created by freed laborers' taking up peasant production on leased land. Companies accordingly shifted to contracting with smallholders, creating a huge outgrower system, which was nationalized in 1973 (Ellis 1988). Confronted by some

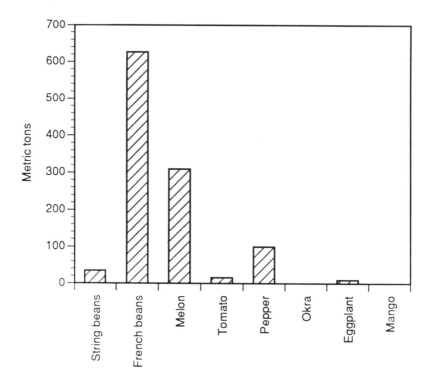

Fig. 3.1 SENPRIM Exports by Commodity: 1985–1986

Source: Watts and Little, forthcoming.

combination of worker militancy, nationalist agitation, and international competition, foreign agribusiness may, indeed, terminate plantation production altogether. California-based Bud Antle liquidated its horticultural operations in Senegal in 1976, which were promptly acquired by a state-owned firm (SENPRIM), which contracted for fresh vegetables (French beans, tomatoes, melons), primarily with women growers, for European Economic Community (EEC) markets (see Figure 3.1) (Mackintosh 1989; Horton 1987). Whatever the local dynamics, contracting emerges with the full or partial *decomposition of plantation/estate production*. The classic export commodities (sugar, tea, and palm oil) persist, but cultivation now occurs under contract by a variety of local growers (cf. Sajhau and von Muralt 1987; Vlaverde 1980).

In the second form, independent peasants, households, and sometimes newly settled pioneer families in frontier regions are drawn into contracting under state and/or private auspices, producing a variety of commodities for domestic consumption and export. In Mexico, for example, Pillsbury, Campbells, General Foods, and other U.S. transnationals engage in contracting farming for strawberries, tobacco, tomatoes, and cocoa, while state corporations contract for sorghum and soy. Many of the African and Malaysian settlement schemes funded by the World Bank and host country governments are quite radical efforts to create, or at the very least relocate, peasants through land redistribution and heavy fixed investment in centralized processing facilities for the production of contracted perennial tree crops, such as palm oil, rubber, and cocoa. In this case, contracting represents a *recomposition of peasant producers;* nominally independent growers are institutionally captured by, and socially integrated into, new production complexes (Bernstein 1986).[18] Whatever its origins, contract farming is a particular form of petty commodity production, generated by a restructuring of capital-labor relations, in which peasants are increasingly subsumed in real and formal terms to capital (see Mblinyi 1988:578).[19]

The dispersion of contracting is not unrelated to the growing hegemony of IMF/International Bank for Rural Development (IBRD) reform and economic adjustment in a debt-ridden Third World and the chaotic search, by donors and local functionaries alike, for private sector mechanisms to revive flagging export sectors, to alleviate foreign exchange shortages, and to occupy the spaces previously accounted for by government parastatals. Since the early 1980s, U.S. agribusiness and the L.S. Agency for International Development (USAID) have actively promoted contract farming as a "dynamic partnership" between small farmers and private capital, a union that promises rapid market integration, economic growth, and technical innovation while protecting the rights and autonomy of the grower via the contract.[20] The World Bank (IBRD 1980) in its influential assessment of the agricultural crisis in sub-Saharan Africa— the infamous Berg Report—specifically identified contracting as an exemplary means to revive what it deemed to be a moribund private sector. The International Finance Corporation (a division of the IMF), the IBRD, and the Commonwealth Development Corporation (CDC)[21] have all pioneered so-called smallholder palm oil, cocoa, and rubber contracting—in their nomenclature, core-satellite, nucleus-estate, or outgrower schemes—across Asia, Africa, and Latin America for at least three decades. Self-consciously advertised as models for technology transfer, the outgrower schemes purportedly encourage small-farmer settlement and integrated rural development, which in practice means nurturing a conservative, middle peasantry. Contracting also confers a certain ideological legitimacy on Third World ruling classes and state managers, politically imperiled by liquidity crises, who gravitate to the populist rhetoric of "targeting the rural poor," and "putting peasants first." Some of the largest contracting schemes—tea production in Kenya, tobacco and livestock in Thailand, rubber in Malaysia, palm oil in the Philippines—are public sector enterprises in which the state is typically the dominant partner in joint ventures with transnational agro-industry and foreign banks.[22]

Contract farming signals something of a watershed in the process of peasant subordination to the world market. In particular, the export-oriented horticultural industry in Central America, southern Europe, and parts of North and East Africa has been a pioneer in this process (Mac-Kintosh 1977).[23] To withstand the rigors of storage and transportation, the physical properties of horticultural crops have been revolutionized over the last three or four decades, a trend related to the clamor for standardization and quality control in the international fresh fruit and vegetable trade. Mexico was already accounting for almost one-third of U.S. strawberry consumption by 1960, but horticultural contracting throughout Central America was a veritable growth sector throughout the 1960s. There were already forty-one North American processing plants in Mexico, nineteen in Costa Rica, and several each in Honduras, El Salvador, and Guatemala by 1970. Eighty-five percent of these enterprises employed contracts in which prices, delivery dates, and at least half of the

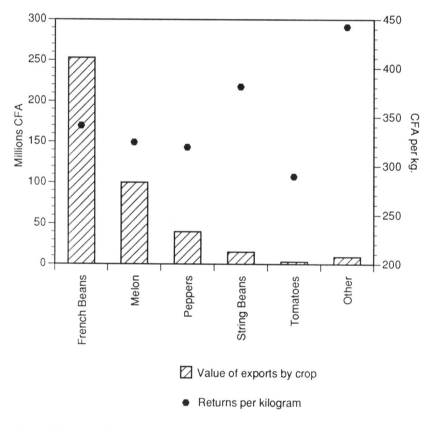

☑ Value of exports by crop

● Returns per kilogram

Fig. 3.2 Fresh Produce Exports and Returns, Senegal, 1985–1986

Source: Watts and Little, forthcoming.

inputs were specified (Morrissy 1974). By 1978, the U.S. alone imported $1.23 billion worth of fresh fruits and vegetables, its primary trading partners being Mexico and Central America. According to Ray Goldberg of the Harvard Business School, about fifty U.S. distributors in Nogales, Arizona, handle almost all of the Mexican fresh vegetables exported to the United States, contracting with large, well-organized growers, who must meet the stringent quality standards of the U.S. market and the substantial investment requirements of transnational agribusiness (Glover 1984; Morrissy 1974). In a quite different part of the world, Senegal in West Africa, the growth of horticultural contracting for EEC markets was equally rapid in the 1970s. By the 1980s, thirteen companies accounted for five thousand tons of produce, especially green beans and melons, valued at 0.5 billion CFA [see Figure 3.2 and Table 3.1). The irony associated with the proliferation of contracting, however, is that while peasant growers do produce for a market, at the level of production, contract farming actually subverts the market. Contract farming advances the *erosion* of market relations between growers and their immediate bosses, the exporters, freezers, canners, and brokers.

The Peasant Labor Process and the Logic of the Contract

Contracting is frequently assumed to be commodity-specific. Minot (1986) notes, for example that 75 percent of all contract farming schemes in Africa involve horticulture and "classical export commodities." This view, articulated most explicitly by Binswanger and Rosenzweig (1986) in their discussion of the material determinants of productive relations in agriculture, sees contract farming as arising from the intersection of technological conditions and crop characteristics—specifically, crops in which there are important economies of scale associated with processing and coordination requirements and long-term crops (for example, palm oil) requiring high maintenance, labor intensity, and extended maturity periods. Contracting is, in this view, associated with classic world commodities, such as sugar, tea, and rubber, and its modal organizational form is the large, centralized outgrower system. Hence its spokespersons conclude, quite incorrectly, that "contract farming has never been able to survive in food grains" (Binswanger and Rosenzweig 1986:529).

Binswanger and Rosenzweig's narrow technological explanation privileges a view of contract farming that radically underestimates the crop heterogeneity of contracting and produces a distorted theory of its origins and determinants. Many commodities grown under contract *are* destined for some form of processing—and, indeed, *are* highly perishable. Oil palm and sugar cane must be crushed within a matter of hours; tobacco and tea leaves deteriorate immediately if uncured; and fresh fruit, flowers, and vegetables must, of necessity, reach foreign markets in prime

TABLE 3.1. *Distribution of Fresh Produce Commodities Exported from Senegal, 1985–1986 (metric tons)*

Exporters	Beans (filet)	Beans (bobby)	Melons	Tomatoes	Peppers	Okra	Eggplant	Mangos	Total tonnage	Average total tonnage	
										1973–1978	1978–1983
SENPRIM	31.65	626.30	306.47	15.79	95.85	0.00	3.12	0.00	1,079.18	n.a.	n.a.
SIDCA	100.36	40.05	0.00	0.00	4.30	0.00	0.00	0.00	144.71	n.a.	n.a.
Toll Selection	610.51	236.46	0.00	0.00	105.44	0.00	0.00	0.00	952.40	n.a.	n.a.
SEPAM	390.45	161.04	433.83	5.02	85.67	1.87	0.00	12.73	1,090.60	n.a.	n.a.
SAFINA(AGROCAP)	239.26	92.51	254.71	148.88	39.98	4.28	0.00	0.00	779.61	n.a.	n.a.
SOEX	186.01	35.64	0.00	0.00	21.09	0.00	0.00	0.00	242.74	n.a.	n.a.
Ets. T. Drame	107.78	222.14	11.48	0.00	17.00	0.00	0.00	0.00	358.41	n.a.	n.a.
SAAF	0.00	0.00	79.99	0.00	0.00	0.00	0.00	0.00	79.99	n.a.	n.a.
GIPES	n.a.	n.a.	n.a.	n.a.	n.a.	n.a.	n.a.	n.a.	n.a.	n.a.	n.a.
Jardima	580.98	265.42	1.64	4.70	134.46	0.44	0.00	0.00	987.64	n.a.	n.a.
SCOMI	106.05	97.52	16.17	0.00	56.27	0.00	0.00	0.00	276.01	n.a.	n.a.
SAO	3.26	34.02	0.00	0.00	2.26	0.00	0.00	0.00	39.54	n.a.	n.a.
SENIMEX	4.46	7.72	0.00	0.00	0.00	0.00	0.00	0.00	12.18	n.a.	n.a.
Total tonnage by commodity	2,360.78	1,818.81	1,104.29	174.38	562.33	6.59	3.12	12.73	6,043.02	7,750.00	4,900.00
Commodity as % of total tonnage	39.07%	30.10%	18.27%	2.89%	9.31%	0.11%	0.05%	0.21%			

SOURCES: Senegalese Plant Health Inspection Service, Yoff International Airport, Dakar, 1986; Mackintosh 1989: 200.

condition. Contracts, unlike spot markets, *are* a means to ensure a regular throughput of commodities for contractors engaged in processing. But Binswanger and Rosenzweig tend to neglect those crops neither processed nor subject to long-cycle growth and significantly underestimate the array of other crops grown under contract, including cotton, oilseeds, rice, bananas, cassava, spices, and livestock. Table 3.2 provides some sense of these crops and the organizational diversity in sub-Saharan Africa.

What is clear is that contract crops are especially linked to demanding grade and quality standards—freshness, fragrance, appearance, color, weight, moisture content, shape, odor, absence of blemish, and so on—which allow the commodity to be classified, screened, and priced in the contract. Partly as a response to these standards, contracted crops are labor-intensive and may be relatively resistant to mechanization for agronomic reasons (it is, for example, difficult to mechanize strawberry harvesting). Tea in Kenya, for example, demands a very high standard of husbandry and maintenance. Only two or three of the top young leaves on every bush are plucked ("two and a bud"), a pattern that demands almost year-round attention (at least 250 days annually), physically arduous and painstaking field labor, and detailed attention in the plucking process. French beans demand even more labor, absorbing more than 500 days per hectare (see Figure 3.3). To take a quite different crop, snowpea cultivation in Central America is also extremely labor-intensive. The peas are sown in rows and the maturing plants tied to simple trellises, and during the first eight weeks they must be regularly weeded and sprayed. Over the subsequent ten to twelve weeks, the peas are continually picked. In view of the year-round, twenty-week growing cycle and the rigorous international standards pertaining to color, texture, and shape, snowpea cultivation is almost six times more labor-absorptive than cultivation of the local staple, maize (613 days per hectare as opposed to 119 days per hectare for maize).[24] In a study of snowpea contracting in Guatemala, all the net increase in labor among the smallest grower class originated from the family, doubling total labor input (von Braun, et al. 1989:52).

In neoclassical economics, the contract not only reflects commodity characteristics but is the embodiment of a sort of laissez-faire mutualism (Binswanger and Rosenzweig 1986). Freely entered into, the contract allows growers to make better use of their specific endowments in imperfect markets and to arrive at combinations of income, effort, and risk reflecting their resources and tastes. Contracts are enormously diverse in content and legal character, however, and some so directly shape, regulate, and discipline the production and labor processes of the grower that the neoclassical perspective is seriously compromised. To take the example of smallholder tea production in East Africa, Mblinyi (1988:566) vividly captures this aspect of the labor process:

TABLE 3.2. *Typology and Classification of Contract Farming Schemes in Africa**

Commodity	Class[a]	No countries with contract farming schemes	No. contract farming schemes in sample	Schemes with nucleus estate as % of all schemes	Ownership as % of all schemes			Average no. outgrowers	Average contracted acreage per outgrower (ha)	Average size of nucleus estate (ha)	Export or domestic market	Services[b]	Organizational form[c]
					Private	State	Joint venture						
Tobacco	Q	6	6	0	10	45	45	5,500	0.6	0	D	C, E, I, T	3
Spices	Q	1	1	0	n.a.	n.a.	n.a.	100	Small	0	E	E, I, T	3/4
Coffee	Q	4	4	50	50	50	0	500	1.5	n.a.	D/E	C, E, I	1/3
Seed millet	Q	2	2	n.a.	50	50	0	100	n.a.	n.a.	D	E, T, I	3
Tea	P/Pr	5	7	60	33	67	0	26,000	0.5	8,600	D/E	C, E, I, T	1/2
Horticulture	P/Q	9	10	10	80	0	20	1,160	0.2	n.a.	E	C, E, I, T	2/4
Dairy	P/T	3	3	25	0	100	0	4,000	n.a.	n.a.	D	n.a.	1/4
Cotton	Pr	4	4	50	33	67	0	9,500	n.a.	n.a.	D/E	C, E, I, T	3
Palm oil	Pr	5	8	100	0	80	20	2,000	4.0	10,500	D/E	C, E, I, T	1/2
Sugar	P/Pr	6	12	90	33	33	33	5,000	2.3	5,000	D/E	C, E, I, T	1/2
Pineapples	Pr	2	2	50	50	0	50	25	n.a.	n.a.	E	E, I, T	1/2
Rubber	Pr	2	2	100	0	50	50	1,200	5.0	12,600	E	C, E, T	1/2
Oilseeds	Pr	1	1	0	100	0	0	1,500	1.5	0	D	E, T	3
Poultry	T	1	1	100	0	0	100	20	400[d]	120,000[e]	D	C, E, I, T	1/2
Rice	F	2	2	0	0	0	100	2,000	0.2	0	D	C, E, I, T	2
Gari (cassava)	F/PR	1	1	0	100	0	0	141	1	0	D	E, I, T	2

SOURCES: Watts 1986. This table is based on published sources available as of 1987.

[a] Q—Quality control; P—Perishability; Pr—Large-scale processing; T—Throughput; F—Food contract.

[b] C—Credit; E—Extension; I—Inputs; T—Technical.

[c] 1—Nucleus estate + processing; 2—Centralized outgrowers + processing; 3—Decentralized outgrowers + processing; 4—Outgrowers + marketing company.

[d] Number of birds.

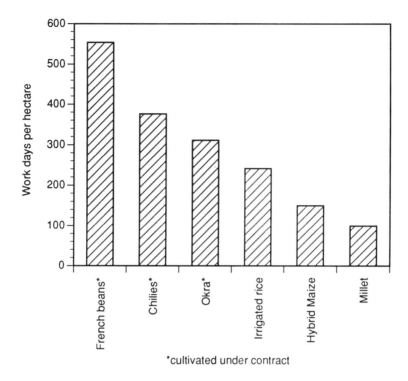

Fig. 3.3 Labor Intensity of Kenyan Crops

Source: Little 1991

[T]ea is plucked from two to four days a week, from eight to nine months a year. When the bushes are mature, the task of plucking may take up to eight hours a day. . . . The pace and rhythm of work is set by TTA [Tanzania Tea Authority] timetables. The organization of the working week is fixed by the number of pick-ups per week, and its timing and regularity. On the pick-up days, tea plucking takes precedence over all other household activities. . . . The frantic urgency with which the growers rush to take their leaves to the buying station . . . illustrates the effective loss of control over the labor process itself.

The tea outgrower schemes certainly are not unusual. On the Mphetseni pineapple project in Swaziland owned by Libby's (Levin 1986), and on the state-run Kibirigwe horticultural project in Kenya (Makanda 1984), the production management contract determines crop choices, rotations, and *all* on-farm operations in highly regimented work routines.[25] Field operations are compulsorily performed by the company's own field labor force in the event of grower default, and the company retains the right of eviction if the provisions of the lease are contravened. In all forms of contracting in which the household is contracted (that is, in which the family enterprise is the unit of production), the contractor in effect exploits a peasant "labor market" rather than a class of rural proletarians. The grower lends to the production process labor power and property, while the contractor supplies inputs, makes the critical production decisions, and holds title to the product. The contract frames the degree to which the grower retains any measure of autonomy over work conditions and expresses the juridical control by the buyer over many aspects of production and exchange.

Contract production is a form of petty commodity production with a distinctive labor process. To this extent, the neoclassical view obscures both the degree of economic compulsion and hence the entire field of power exercised by and contained within the contract. These aspects are quite pivotal if contract farming is posed *as a form of the labor process,* as a structured relationship between labor and the means of production, to employ Marx's language. Contract farming is, in short, a "particular technical organization of production combining certain kinds of means of production and labor-power and . . . achieving a certain level of productivity" (Callincos 1988:45). Whether this abstract combination occurs empirically depends on specific social relations determining both the distribution of the means of production and the control of labor power itself. The contract precisely maps the topography of the labor process linking grower and buyer/processor, and speaks directly to these social relations shaping what Marx called the "effective control" of the means of production and of labor power. While the grower may retain procession of land and nominally of domestic labor, the contractor provides other critical means of production and directs the application of labor, and by extension the pace and rhythm of work. Authoritarian and despotic forms of contracting establish and regulate work conditions in a manner that renders household labor in effect *unfree.* In other words, grower labor is unfree in the sense that it is directly distributed, exploited and retained by politico-legal mechanisms (Miles 1987). Nominally independent growers retain the illusion of autonomy but have become in practice what Lenin labeled "propertied proletarians," de facto workers cultivating company crops on private allotments.

The particular unity of the household labor-property complex with some form of management, a relationship that Davis (1979) aptly terms "property without power," highlights the three distinctive aspects of the contracting labor process. First, as Braverman (1974) notes in his discussion of the capitalist labor process, there is a distinct separation of *conception* and *execution* even though capital does not directly control the point of production. This raises the question of the degradation of work and the ways in which contracting may involve a sort of deskilling, and by extension the alienation of the grower from his/her product as one aspect of the commodification of social life. "We do not know how our canes go in or how the sugar comes out," remarked a Kenyan sugar grower. "We only get money." Growers take on the character of a self-employed proletariat (Chevalier 1983).

Second, because the grower is paid in relation to quantity and quality, there are fewer incentives to shirk, since the family members share in the profits. Under contract in centralized satellite systems, peasants work as de facto piece workers, typically laboring more intensively (that is, longer hours) and extensively (that is, using children and other nonpaid household labor) to increase output or quality.[26] The basis of peasant contracting is, in Kautskyian fashion, self-exploitation, which, in the context of the peculiarly labor-intensive attributes of such crops as tea and tobacco, implies a sort of parallel to Marx's discussion of the enslavement, impoverishment, and exploitation associated with the industrial labor process under capitalism. A woman Tanzania tea grower puts it more succinctly: contract work, she said, is like "the big slavery! Work has no boundaries, it is endless" (Mblinyi 1988:574). And third, while Bernstein (1986) is right to suggest that petty commodity production does not *necessarily* presuppose either the provision of "cheap" labor power (and hence a subsidy to capital) or the exploitation of peasants as disguised wage-labor equivalents, the particular labor process of contract production would seem to provide compelling evidence for both.

Insofar as there are interesting parallels between Marx's discussion of the industrial labor process and the social relations of contract production as a form of agro-industry, it is only right that we turn to the question of production politics (Burawoy 1985)—that is, work as a terrain of compromise, consent, and struggle. If contract production among peasants aims to exploit nonwage household labor through dense networks of dependence and subordination, in what sense is a disciplined labor force—a quiescent "peasant workforce"—actually produced? As Marx and Weber asked of capitalism, can contractors manufacture consent among peasants under hierarchical and coercive conditions in which, in contrast to capitalism, surplus appropriation is not obscured at the point of production? Is the system self-reproducing and self-disciplining? What forms of resistance and discontent are engendered?

Property, Power, and Politics: A Case Study of Irrigated Rice Contracting in West Africa

Has the work force been sufficiently prepared by famine, impoverishment and proletarianization to constitute a reliable, hardworking, paddy-field peasantry? My assessment is that it has not. Agricultural intensification means getting people to work harder and that undertaking usually requires coercion. . . .
Keith Hart, *The Political Economy of West African Agriculture*

Returning to The Gambia from home leave in late 1952, the director of Wallikunda Irrigation Project[27] discovered that a substantial slice of the project rice harvest, some four hundred bags of paddy, had mysteriously disappeared during his absence. Petty theft and pilferage by Mandinka

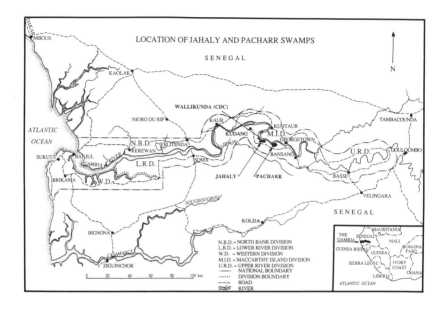

Fig. 3.4 Location of Jahaly and Pacharr Swamps

tenants had been commonplace since the scheme was hatched in 1949 by the Colonial Development Corporation (CDC), but the scale of the latest popular appropriation implied, at the very least, some sort of collective organization and collusion by local chiefs.[28] Given birth by a postwar West Africa Rice Mission sent by the colonial government, the Wallikunda project represented a heady mix of ambition and risk: to introduce and foster mechanized double-cropping of rice throughout the largely Mandinka middle-river districts of The Gambia, a region in which swamp and tidal rice production was of some antiquity (see Figure 3.4).[29] Wallikunda actually linked to adjacent rice-growing swamps—Jahaly and Pacharr—and the original blueprint proposed extensive bund and canal construction designed to bring 10,880 acres under irrigation. The project proved, in fact, to be an expensive and embarrassing failure. The CDC alone was implicated to the tune of over five million U.S. dollars, and the entire development was plagued by a Chaplinesque succession of basic design flaws. Massive rice theft, following close on the heels of extensive flooding, inadequate surveying and leveling, canal collapse, and rumors of the exploitation of child labor and wild debauchery by the British construction crew, brought the project to its knees. "If these Gothic predations are to continue," observed the exasperated director, referring to the rice theft, "we may as well pack the whole thing up."[30] Indeed, they did.

The gothic predations were incubated in the fertile soil of colonial folly, notably in the large-scale appropriation of rice lands by the CDC—

initially on a thirty-year lease from the local Native Authority—which imperial administrators quite wrongly assumed to be "uncultivated." The land seizure initiated a flood of property claims and disputes; indeed, it was the belief of the peasants themselves that they were taking the rice "because the *tubabos* [whites] had taken their land." The collapse of the CDC scheme in 1953 ushered in direct government control and the creation, on a much more modest scale, of The Gambia Rice Farm. This was, in essence, a state farm with limited water control employing largely female wage labor for most farm operations, particularly rice weeding and harvesting. Local resistance once again proved intractable. Wage workers were almost impossible to recruit and discipline because rice labor bottlenecks conflicted directly with the primary demands of the work routines of other rainfed upland crops (notably, groundnuts, millet, and sorghum). In addition, the productivity of hired labor was low, and rice pilferage was endemic. In desperation in 1954, the farm management introduced women sharecroppers onto the farm, many of whom had lost, and were then contesting, their claims on swamplands in the wake of signing of the thirty-year lease. But extensive underreporting and the retention of too much paddy by ornery sharecroppers lead to the dissolution of share contracting after only two years. A return to direct cash rental persisted until 1958, by which time the explosion of farm debt, primarily by the women tenants who had borrowed from the Department of Agriculture for tractor ploughing and other services, marked the final humiliating demise of The Gambia Rice Farm.

Some twenty years after the almost farcical collapse of the Wallikunda project marked the abrupt closure of the first in a succession of efforts to harness the water resources of the Gambia River, the Gambian government has returned to irrigation and has offered, amidst much pomp and fanfare, the latest incarnation of mechanized rice irrigation. Seen as a prototype for what is envisaged as a massive expansion of irrigation and double-cropping permitted by the construction of an antisalinity barrage across the lower reaches of the Gambia River, the new Jahaly-Pacharr project[31] bears an uncomfortable resemblance to its much-maligned colonial predecessor. Not only is the new high-tech perimeter located on the selfsame site of the failed CDC scheme but it also operates on a leased-land-tenancy basis. A large pump-irrigated system under centralized management employing labor-intensive on-farm operations, Jahaly-Pacharr rests on the bedrock of household production. Unlike the earlier colonial scheme, however, project management subordinates producers under contract in a rigid work routine, appropriating a share of paddy as payment for production credit advanced during the growing season to cover water and land preparation costs. By 1985, the double-cropping regime appeared to be in place, yields for both seasons averaged in excess of five tons per hectare, and the loan repayment was 98 percent. But the first blush of technical success has been partially eclipsed by social problems strikingly reminiscent of the earlier CDC project. Contract farming at the Jahaly-Pacharr scheme has, from its very inception, generated militancy among many women rice cultivators, a spectacular escalation in conflicts over land claims and crop rights, and signs of domestic violence centered on the withdrawal of female labor power from domestic production. As Marx once noted, paraphrasing Hegel, events in history may occur twice, the first time as tragedy, the second as farce.

The Historical Origins of Rice Contracting in The Gambia

Well before the first European presence, rice was a widely cultivated staple foodstuff in Senegambia. As a rainfed cultivar, it was grown on the well-drained sandy uplands, and as a lowland paddy crop, it was sown in saline and freshwater tidal swamp and on the heavy, alluvial soils typically associated with riparian depressions.[32] An elaborate indigenous rice-growing technology included complex drainage and water control, which drew praise from early British and French explorers. The production system also proved flexible enough to incorporate several highly productive Asian rices introduced by Portuguese traders in the sixteenth century.[33] As a consequence, in the period of informal empire prior to the nineteenth-century groundnut boom, Mandinka rice cultivation flourished. By the 1760s, the French were purchasing large quantities of paddy rice near the mouth of the river, and there was some speculation by British and French administrators alike that the territories of the Senegambia might be converted into a veritable rice bowl, a large-scale exporter of paddy, comparable to the Carolinas and Georgia (see Watts, forthcoming; Carney 1986, 1988, 1991).

Alas, this early enthusiasm proved to be short-lived. As British territorial acquisition inched forward, the meteoric rise of commercial groundnut production during the 1830s, a revolution actively promoted by British and French merchant houses, sounded the death knell for the nascent rice trade. Groundnut exports took off after 1843—output quadrupled in the following fifteen years—drawing male labor into the export sector and leaving rice as a residual "women's crop."[34] The groundnut boom, in other words, presaged an important transformation in the social relations of production, propelling a shift from a task- to a crop-specific sexual division of labor. This culturally distinctive, and seemingly rigid, association of crop and gender, which is often seen as a permanent hallmark of rural Mandinka society, was in fact a product of nineteenth-century mercantilism. Furthermore, the growth of export production placed new and onerous demands on women to cover domestic subsistence needs as male labor was gradually diverted from upland cereals (millet and sorghum) to the relatively lucrative groundnut. Women shouldered these expanded foodstuff, and specifically rice-growing, responsibilities from the 1850s onward,[35] but the spiraling demand for staples rapidly outstripped local supply. By the end of the century the new colony of The Gambia had a major food deficit, and beginning in 1894, but most particularly over the period of 1908 to 1933, the colonial state was forced to advance large quantities of imported rice to Gambian farmers to preserve the flow of migrant labor (so-called "strange farmers") that was so central to the export structure of the colonial political economy.[36]

Spiraling rice imports and the escalation of rural debt—held by peasants who refused to repay food credits advanced by the government—prompted efforts by the colonial state to expand domestic rice output. After some half-hearted efforts at seed improvement and local water control in the 1920s, the rice import-substitution program began in earnest with the 1940s mangrove campaign. Stimulated by the outbreak of World War II, the mangrove campaign provided for the improvement and expansion of the seasonally saline swamps. The area devoted to swamp rice production grew from twenty-three thousand acres in 1946 to sixty-five thousand acres in 1965, but the expansion rested almost wholly on an intensification of women's labor, a process subject to obvious limits.[37] For largely cultural reasons, men steadfastly refused to work in the swamps in spite of the fact that mangrove clearance potentially enhanced women's land holdings, and hence threatened male hegemony within the household property complex. In the final analysis, however, the first phase of Gambian rice expansion foundered on the reefs of labor shortage; men could not be cajoled to work in the swamps, and labor productivity had yet to be radically enhanced by mechanization. In short, the prospects for national food self-sufficiency were distinctly bleak.

An early attempt at Wallikunda to introduce mechanized irrigation for rice cultivation in the 1950s proved to be, as we have seen, an embarrassing and expensive failure, but the search for an effective irrigated double-cropping regime was renewed with vigor following Independence. From 1966, the Gambian state, in conjunction with foreign assistance provided by Taiwan, the People's Republic of China, and the World Bank, developed 2,900 hectares of irrigation perimeters in the central (MID) and eastern (URD) salt-free zones of the Gambia River. The schemes were community-focused perimeters (typically twenty to thirty hectares) in which small eight-inch diesel pumps, rototillers, seeds, and inputs, were provided both on credit and at subsidized rates to peasant growers (see Figure 3.5). In essence, these irrigatation schemes provided Green Revolution inputs and laid the foundations for a second dry season rice crop in a region in which rice swamps had hitherto been cultivated solely during the rains. In spite of the enthusiasm for the development of irrigation provided by the Sahelian drought in the early 1970s, these initiatives to raise labor productivity and enlarge the marketed surplus of rice proved

Fig. 3.5 Aerial Photograph of a Taiwanese-Funded Irrigation Perimeter, MacCarthy Island

to be an expensive failure. Cropping intensities were low (in 1980, only 18 percent of the total wet and dry season acreage was cultivated), debt recovery was almost nonexistent (ca. less than 20 percent), and by the late 1970s many of the perimeters had been abandoned (see Kargbo 1983; Brautigam 1987; Dey 1980; Carney 1986, 1988, 1989; and Watts forthcoming).

What the irrigation schemes lacked in efficiency they more than compensated for in social impact. For the first time men did indeed get their feet wet. In a historic transition to rice growing, men gradually entered the paddy fields, particularly during the dry season cropping cycle, although they typically returned to upland groundnut cultivation during the rains.[38] Women meanwhile were compelled to divide their time; they labored with their husbands on nominally household irrigated plots during the dry season but retreated to their rainfed swamps during the wet season. More critically, the introduction of a dry season, *noncustomary* cropping cycle raised the question of who within the Mandinka household production unit was to provide the labor, under what conditions, and for what return. In the same way that the mangrove clearance of the 1940s had animated struggles between men and women over access to and control over newly cleared mangrove swamps, the irrigation schemes—whatever their technical and economic limitations—triggered a new round of intrahousehold struggles over domestic land, labor and resources.

The Emergence of Contract Farming in the 1980s

In the context of growing rice imports,[39] the collapse of the small-scale perimeter, and the significant deterioration in rainfall since the late 1960s, the Gambian state, in conjunction with its primary donor, the International Fund for Agricultural Development (IFAD),[40] has pioneered a new strategy to expand rice output in the 1980s. The Jahaly-Pacharr project, which began operations in 1984, is a large-scale irrigation project embracing two thousand peasant households drawn from seventy villages in the MacCarthy Island Division in central Gambia (see Figures 3.4 and 3.6).[41] Designed to support the double-cropping of rice, it employs a centralized pump system in which water delivery is organized through ten-hectare blocks divided into half-hectare field units. Each rice cycle covers approximately 120 days: from January to May for the dry season, and from June to December for the wet season. In order to ensure

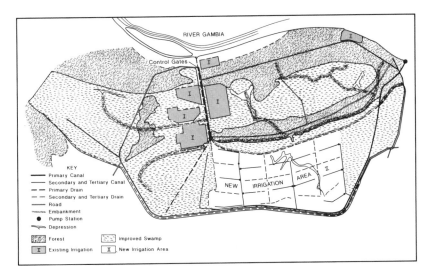

Fig. 3.6 Smallholder Irrigation Project, Jahaly Swamp

both high cropping intensities and full repayment of production credit (the basic flow of previous rice schemes), the Jahaly-Pacharr management integrates peasant households under contract. Project management advances inputs and determines the cultivation routines (water distribution, planting times, weeding, fertilizer application) through extension agents. Management appropriates a share (roughly one-third) of the rice harvest to cover input costs, while grower households provide all on-farm labor (see Watts and Carney 1990, 1991; Carney 1988; von Braun and Webb 1989).

Land for irrigation development was appropriated and centralized by the Gambian state on a thirty-year lease, and usufructary rights were redistributed to participating growers, registered in the first instance with male heads of household. In some cases, land sequestered by the project was "collective" household property, but in many others it included swamp rice fields owned individually by Mandinka women, who naturally stood to lose an important and highly valued source of personal income. In any event, the question of intrahousehold access to, and control over, the new plots and their product is the nucleus of the new relations of production imposed by the schemes. Retention of plot usufruct is, according to the contract, subject to the growers' compliance with cropping schedules, production targets, and loan repayment.

In sum, the Jahaly-Pacharr project inaugurated a new work regime and social relations of production designed to rapidly commercialize a staple food crop, rice, which had historically been the domain of Mandinka women. In order to capture the potential income benefits of enhanced on-farm productivity, growers confronted radically new labor demands not only in a quantitative sense (rice production under full irrigation required 60 percent more labor per unit of land than did traditional swamp systems)[42] but also qualitatively insofar as peasants had to conform to regimented work schedules and routines imposed by project management. Furthermore, the Jahaly-Pacharr project promoted dry season production for which there were no customary labor arrangements and crop disposition rights as such. Mandinka women specifically stood to lose control of their own rice fields as a consequence of the process of land centralization and redistribution. Under conditions in which peasants are contracted as household units of production (in contradistinction to a wage contract) in which familial labor is recruited and employed, the central question is *Who will work, under what conditions, with what rewards?* The Jahaly-Pacharr scheme reveals that these questions are, in practice, deeply political and contested. Contract production animated intense intrahousehold struggles over the nature of domestic obligations and customary forms of labor recruitment. These adjustments, which took the form of intrahousehold struggles, were articulated in terms of gender, conjugality, and property.[43]

Life under Contract: Struggling over Land and Labor

The Jahaly-Pacharr swamps in MacCarthy Island Division have long been a crucible for serious land disputes. Occupying the very same site, the controversial CDC Wallikunda rice scheme of the 1950s had leased 10,800 acres from local authorities. But, unbeknownst to the CDC and the colonial state, large swaths of the swamps were already owned by women rice growers. With the collapse of Wallikunda and the scramble to regain use rights, considerable juridical confusion existed in local land tenure; some of the leased land was not returned to the original cultivators[44] and male heads of household, who were, in any case, ambivalent about their wives' control of individual property, interceded to exacerbate an already Byzantine and conflictual process of reclamation. The subsequent development of community perimeters by the Taiwanese and Chinese in the 1960s and 1970s only compounded the local complexities of land tenure. The leveling and draining of the irrigated plots was undertaken by the foreign donors with the assistance of male heads of household, who invoked local custom, backed by local district authorities, that land clearance conferred ownership, a principle that overrode prior claims by women who held individual rights in the swamps. Many women felt, quite rightly, that the era of irrigation heralded dispossession and poverty as much as enhanced food security.

Not surprisingly, land rights were controversial in the Jahaly-Pacharr swamps from the outset. Local opposition to long-term leasing was assuaged by the establishment of Land Committees constituted by local political elites and notables, typically men drawn from the influential founder lineages (Figure 3.7). The gender bias was legitimated on the grounds that Mandinka marriage is customarily virilocal and that women, in any case, lacked the ability to mobilize sufficient labor for irrigated cultivation.[45] During the first land allocation in 1984, 87 percent of the 220 hectares was registered in the names of men, and hence centralized land rights within the household under the jurisdiction of the patriarch. Women expressed opposition to the loss of their individual rights and, indeed, with the hindsight of the earlier irrigation experiences grew increasingly militant. One Mandinka women observed that "this project is just like the Chinese one when we suffered before . . . [but] we aren't going to put up with that again." Quite by chance, a British feminist filmmaker was resident on the scheme, shooting footage for a film on agrarian change in Africa, and women enlisted her support in sending a deputation to the capital city to protest the system of land allocation.[46] The national Women's Bureau yielded to the pressure and lobbied the project management. As a consequence, the major donor, IFAD, intervened directly in land distribution and adjudication in the following year. Of the 340 hectares distributed in 1985, 99 percent of the plots were

Fig. 3.7 Household Head
from a Founding Lineage

registered in women's names, although some 110 original tillers remained without access to irrigated plots. The restructuring of the land
allocation process was roundly praised as an equitable solution in which
"the rights of women to possess their own plots, against the pressure
from male farmers, was protected . . . [which] was a notable achievement
in male-dominated Gambian society" (*African Business*, January 1986,
22).

The reregistration, however laudable, was obviously imposed on
households from without and could not be monitored nor policed *within*
the domestic unit. Hence an unintended consequence of the project management's desire to enforce a contract in which women's legitimate
claims were respected was to convert, or more properly to deepen, the
latest tensions within the domestic realm over property rights and labor
obligations. In order to fully grasp these tensions and understand why
land rights are as much about social relations as material things, one
must be sensitive to the nuances of Mandinka social structure and the
household property complex. Specifically, Mandinka society distinguishes between two types of land use on family property, namely, individual fields (*kamanyango*) and collective or familial property (*maruo*).
Each land use category confers specific crop rights to *which specific labor
claims are attached* (Carney 1988). Quite specifically maruo fields contribute directly to "collective" subsistence needs, and hence all household
members are obliged to contribute. Characteristically, men cultivate upland millet, and women labor in the lowland rice swamps; but the control and disposition of the collective product is under the jurisdiction of

the senior male. In return for their contributions to domestic consumption needs, the male head typically allocates land rights to junior members (sons, wives), the product of which is appropriated individually. Kamanyango usufructary rights are, then, central to the terms on which family members exchange services and labor. As previously noted, however, women may also possess kamanyango rights in rice lands, not as a function of the marriage but as a result of clearance. In other words, the land is their own in perpetuity because they cleared the field—or, alternatively, inherited it through the agnatic line from kin who themselves cleared the swamp. This tension between individual and collective responsibilities is structurally part of the Mandinka domestic sphere and is played out annually in the pattern of labor allocation in wet season farming activities.

The direct consequence of Jahaly-Pacharr land registration was to call this property complex into question. First, dry season production introduced productive activities for which there were no customary reciprocities and obligations. Second, in spite of the formal registration of plots by women, men endeavored to claim that the irrigation plots were maruo and hence under their control. Insofar as these maruo fields now produced substantial marketable surpluses, men gained control over a very substantial cash disposition. Third, many women had contributed their own individual rice fields (typically inherited from their mothers) to the project and hence contested the classification of the new irrigated fields as household property. Minimally, they questioned the classification and demanded compensation for the new claims over their labor exercised by men in the name of familial responsibilities. And fourth, even in cases in which women had not experienced the loss of their own kamanyango rice fields, the unprecedented labor demands associated with irrigated rice production necessitated a renegotiation of work conditions and compensation. For senior males and project staff alike, the resolution of these domestic matters was fundamental since the new production regime created major labor bottlenecks (especially in November/December and May/June), which presupposed that men could mobilize and recruit domestic labor promptly and efficiently.[47]

Land registration was in some respects a gloss, a papering over, of deep-rooted domestic contradictions among property, patriarchy, and labor. A technological change coupled with the imposition of new cropping patterns and new relations of production placed heavy strains on the internal social architecture of the peasant production unit. The naming and classification of land and the nature of domestic labor obligations, especially between senior men and their wives, who possessed critical knowledge and skills related to rice production, were among the issues that were subject to a complex process of domestic bargaining and negotiation. The Jahaly-Pacharr project demonstrates how efforts to raise peasant productivity can trigger a variety of cultural and social struggles over meaning: the meaning of customary land rights, the meaning of traditional labor obligations, and the meanings to be attached to new agricultural practices.[48] Contracting generated its own production politics, which took the form of symbolic contests and negotiations employing the domestic lexicon of rights, obligations, gender, and conjugality.

Adjusting to the Contract:
Reworking Conjugality, Autonomy, and Wages

From the first harvest in 1984, the production targets and the cropping intensities projected by IFAD in the early planning documents were achieved with little difficulty. Rice yields from the fully water-controlled plots in the 1984 dry season were in excess of 5 tons per hectare and one year later rose to close to 7.5 tons per hectare (three times greater than traditional swamp rice productivities). Furthermore, in sharp contrast to the community irrigation schemes of the 1970s, double-cropping and high-yielding varieties accounted for a marked increase in marketed surpluses; in seven villages surveyed by the International Food Policy Institute (IFPRI),[49] for example, 35 percent of the total irrigated rice output was sold. The income effect was quite dramatic; one half-hectare plot was capable of generating between two and three times the preproject per capita income. The question of the disposition of what is, in local terms, a very substantial cash inflow naturally places a premium on domestic labor in terms of who works on the irrigated plots and for what remuneration.

The confluence within the domestic arena of systematic efforts by men to centralize property rights under their control and the accompanying loss of traditional individual rice plots by many women enhanced the likelihood of interpersonal struggles over the distribution of rice income. Specifically, the erosion of women's autonomy in cases of outright dispossession coupled with new and heavy demands for their dry season labor for which there were no customary labor obligations generated unstable and contradictory relations within the domestic unit and hence complex bargaining and negotiations between male heads of households and their wives. In this regard, the struggles over work obligations and the disposition of rice surpluses—in short, production politics—were typically conducted in the idiom of conjugality, that is to say, the customary reciprocities and exchanges between husbands and wives.[50] In this sense, the domestic arena experienced a form of what James Scott (1985), in referring to the everyday resistance of peasants, calls the "war of words." Women naturally wished to preserve the measure of economic autonomy conferred by their prior (that is, preproject) control of traditional rice swamps, but the negotiations over what form (if any) compensation might take were invariably expressed through cultural notions of

Fig. 3.8 Woman Rice Grower Working on Lowland Nonirrigated Swamp Field

marital and domestic harmony, cooperation, and balance (*badingya*), long-standing social traditions (*tarakuo*), and Muslim ethical responsibilities (*adoo*).

What, then, were the sorts of adjustments and resolutions that emerged from the bargaining process between husbands and wives over working on, and the returns from, irrigated rice production? According to Carney (1988), three broad adjustments were in evidence by 1987. First, women provided labor on the irrigated plots and received compensation through other usufructary rights in tidal-irrigated and rainfed plots on the project (Figure 3.8). While this reflects a maintenance of *some* property rights—and a source of personal income—by Mandinka women, these ricelands are less productive than the irrigated fields, are often shared among several women, and confer crop rights only while the wife is resident in the compound of her husband. Resolutions of this sort typically occurred in well-to-do households blessed with adequate project land for both subsistence and commercial needs. Second, women were compensated for work on irrigated plots by receiving a fixed share of the rice yield. In the community studied by Carney, for instance, the share amounted on average to roughly 10 percent of total paddy output.[51] In practice, this adjustment entailed the *internalization of the external (that is, grower-management) sharecropping relationship within the conjugal contract.*

The third, and most commonplace, adjustment was the absence of any compensation and the withdrawal of female labor from irrigation activities. Women had lost their individual rice fields, and were in effect proletarianized by project development. The lack of compensation, in other words, the failure to establish a conjugal resolution, compelled women to both withdraw from domestic farming responsibilities on irrigated plots and simultaneously sell their labor power or engage in other income earning enterprises. In the main, the project contributed *to the creation of a local labor market;* roughly 25 percent of all irrigated farm labor is hired, typically by propertyless women endeavoring to compensate for their loss of rice income. Many of these women sold their labor power, however, not as individuals but as participants in traditional female age-grade, that is, nonwage, reciprocal labor networks (*kafo*), which employed customary social relations as the basis for recruitment but in practice functioned as proletarian gang labor.[52] In these households, the adjustments are especially radical because when women appear as de facto wage workers, men increasingly have to resort to the hiring-in of paid labor, and domestic tensions are deepened by the withdrawal of female labor, which constitutes, in the eyes of the patriarch, abrogation of domestic responsibilities. It is precisely in such circumstances that domestic violence and even divorce attend the withdrawal of female labor.

Household adjustments, then, assumed a variety of forms, in which women sometimes maintained land rights, sometimes secured a share of the rice income, and sometimes neither. However, these adjustments were the products of often long and intense negotiation and struggle, a bargaining process whose consequences occasionally extended beyond the rather porous boundaries of the Mandinka household itself. The genesis of gang labor is one dramatic case in point, insofar as it engages new and politicized social forms in the name of the "traditional" collective work party. But there are other examples. Some women contested the loss of project land rights upon divorce by taking their cases to the local courts, and women more generally have become active voices in the project Land Allocation Committees, which provide the forum for property disputes.[53] Further, the dissent manufactured by the project, building upon a history of domestic struggles over swamp clearance and women's property, has in a profound sense put the prevailing cultural notions of patriarchy and gender to the test of social practice. Reflecting on the impact of irrigation, a women from the Jahaly area referred to this changing consciousness when she observed that woman "were asleep in the past [but] now we are awake."

New Spatial Divisions of Labor and the Question of Gender

The new conditions of profitability wrought by rice mechanization on the Jahaly-Pacharr scheme and the deterioration of groundnut prices in the 1980s throughout The Gambia, have laid the foundations for a new social, and hence *spatial*, division of labor. Mandinka agroecology is typified by a sharp division between the lowland swamps and riparian flats, characterized by heavy clay soils, and the sandy plains of the upland guinea savanna soils. Small benches and terraces situated between the two are often the sites for marketing gardens and rice nurseries. The map of land use also corresponds to a symbolic and cultural polarity between upland and lowland, expressed most vividly in the sexual division of labor by crop (cf. Moore 1986). The lowland rice-growing swamps are very much the domain of women, (men typically refer to rice growing as "women's work" and women see rice as "women's sweat"), and much of the ritual and ideological activity associated with female work groups and age-grade socialization takes place in and around the alluvial flats. Women rarely have land rights in the heavily tilled, sandy loams on the higher elevations. Upland production, conversely, is dominated by groundnuts, which in Mandinka society are the male crop par excellence. Men customarily assist in the transportation of rice seedlings to the swamps or take part in the arduous work of bringing paddy back to the village from peripheral fields; in the same way, women help in the cultivation of millet for collective consumption on the upland fields or, in the care of maize, in gardens adjacent to the compounds. But in general the geography of upland-lowland cultivation is deeply embedded in culturally sanctioned notions of sexuality and crop production.

Notwithstanding its brief history, the Jahaly-Pacharr project has already opened up fissures within the traditional Mandinka nexus of spatial and sexual divisions of labor. First, rice production is clearly no longer solely or even predominantly a female activity. Unlike the Taiwanese and Chinese schemes of the 1970s, in which men participated as part-time, and somewhat laconic, dry season growers only, Mandinka men are now deeply committed to irrigated rice in the improved swamp areas (Figure 3.9). Men provide close to half of the farm labor on the irrigated plots during the dry season, and according to von Braun and Webb's data for the 1985 wet season, almost half of the labor during the *rainfed* cropping cycle (von Braun and Webb 1989; see also Carney 1986, 1988). As a consequence men are not only physically rooted in the lowlands in "women's work" but are significantly diverted from upland production. An IFPRI study estimates that groundnut production has fallen by 30 percent since 1984; in practice men are now spending at least two-thirds of their on-farm labor time in lowland rice production and derive the majority of their cash income from irrigated production.

Second, evidence suggests that women are exercising, or perhaps more accurately, are winning, claims over upland farms for individual use, and hence breaking through the barrier of sex-specific crop production. This is especially the case for women who have lost control over their kamanyango swamps. In some cases women have been granted improved rainfed

Fig. 3.9 Male Rice Grower Preparing Plots for Rice Germination prior to Transplanting

land as compensation for the loss of their tidal rice fields. In other cases there is some evidence that women have access to upland groundnuts fields, which they now cultivate for their personal disposition. While this is certainly the case for Wolof and Serrahuli women on the Jahaly-Pacharr scheme, the evidence for new incursions by Mandinka women into the groundnut sector, a bastion of male control, remains quite limited. Nonetheless, in general the deepening of male labor allocation in the lowland rice sector has a counterpoint in the growing involvement by Mandinka women in upland production.

And third, some women who have lost swampland and who received little or no project compensation have been spatially marginalized in the sense that they are compelled to search for traditional tidal swamps outside the project area or take up dry season gardening, either of which can account for a substantial increase in travel time. It is not unusual, for example, for women to commute more than five miles each way to reach the alternative unimproved swamp sites.

Almost a century and a half ago, the cultural economy of Mandinka peasants was fundamentally shaped by their rapid incorporation into a growing world capitalism under the auspices of European merchant capital. One of the consequences of this incorporation was a deepening of gender-specific crop production, a sexual division of labor firmly rooted in cultural, social, and property relations. In spite of growing commercialization and market involvement throughout rural Gambian society since the early nineteenth century, it is only in the last decade that a relatively rigid Mandinka space-crop-gender complex is, in an uneven and complex way, once again being refashioned by a conjuncture of world systemic forces. In this regard, the changing geography of labor allocation—where men and women work in agriculture—points to a more profound realignment of cultural and social practices, adjustments by and within the household, which call into question the very essence of local notions of what it is to be Mandinka, for men and women alike.

Struggles over Meaning and Reconfigurations of Power

The cultural does not simply mark, or in some simple sense "live out" wider social contradictions. It *works* upon them with its own resources to achieve partial resolutions, recombinations, limited transformations which are uncertain to be sure, but concrete, specific to its own level and the basis for actions and decisions which are vitally important to that wider social order.

Paul Willis, *Learning to Labor*

The Jahaly-Pacharr project manufactured a sort of symbolic discontent. This is not surprising because every social field is a site of struggles over the definition of legitimate principles of the division of the field: "In the symbolic struggle over the production of common sense, or more precisely, *legitimate naming*, . . . agents engage the symbolic capital they have acquired in previous struggles . . . [that is] all the power they possess over instituted taxonomies" (Bourdieu 1985:731–732, emphasis added). It is largely through language that local practices are instituted, but meanings are never fixed and outside forces can often determine what is to be endowed with meaning. The introduction of contract production in Jahaly-Pacharr throws into relief the symbolic aspect of political economic transformation, and one can readily appreciate why the debate over the naming of irrigated plots is, in Mandinka society, so charged and so political. While it is within the language of everyday life that meaning is mobilized in the defense of domination, the outcome of struggles, such as those initiated within Mandinka farming households, is far from predetermined. This is not simply to suggest that the wage relation may have "liberating" consequences for women, but more generally that culture is a field of struggle contributing toward the creative, tense, and uncertain social reproduction of diverse kinds of relationship; "cultural reproduction always carries with it the possibility of producing . . . alternative outcomes" (Willis 1981:172). Mariama Koita, an active rice grower in Wellingara, put the matter succinctly: "I am prepared to change tradition if I have the power and money."

The discontent manufactured by the Jahaly-Pacharr project suggests the beginnings of a resistance to domestic discipline and to the culturally dominant representations of gender and property (Moore 1986). The politicization of women's communal labor groups, the presence of women on Land Allocation Committees, the rumblings of juridical change, female deputations to government ministers, and the like all suggest important changes. The change in consciousness that this statement implies, arising out of the ashes of previous conflicts over women's land, is suggestive of how important internal resistance has been. Quite by chance, this resistance was captured in a dramatic fashion in 1985 when a BBC film crew visited the project in the course of making a film on agrarian change in Africa. Jahaly women sought out the film producer—as it happened, a British feminist—and enlisted her support in organizing a deputation of senior women from the area to the Ministry of Agriculture in Banjul in relation to land claims. As a result, a hitherto-lethargic Women's Bureau latched onto the Jahaly-Pacharr affair, and some pressure was brought to bear on project management. The release of what became a critical and explicitly prowomen film in The Gambia, generated anger and resentment among male village heads, project personnel, and government officials alike. But international exposure of the land conflicts—not least to the donors—has without question been seen by local women as a political triumph. The fact that the Land Committees of both swamps have a female representation of almost 50 percent pays testimony to the efficacy of women cultivators seizing the political moment created by the fortuitous presence of an unsuspecting film crew. These events, needless to say, have further politicized the Jahaly-Pacharr scheme, and management sensitivities are such that it is shrouded in secrecy.

Production Politics: The Reworking of Work

[U]nfree labor can be explained as both anomalous and necessary to the reproduction and spread of the capitalist mode of production within and to an increasing number of social formations. [They are] anomalous when viewed in relation to the tendency for the emergence for increasing dominance of free wage labor, and yet [they are] necessarily introduced and reproduced because historical conditions obstruct the universalization of wage relations of production.

Robert Miles, *Capitalism and Unfree Labor*

Contract farming necessitates some sort of control over household labor. Growers are contracted as household units of production and the domestic sphere becomes a terrain of production politics (Burawoy 1985), the terrain on which the details of work conditions and surplus appropriation are fought out. In some cases, these struggles may be collectively resolved through grower organizations or cooperatives, as the historically militant smallholders' sugar association in Fiji reveals (Ellis 1988).[54] But the efforts to create a disciplined class of growers by the companies may also generate production politics of another sort, specifically tensions and contradictions *within* grower households themselves. This is especially true when contracting introduces new technologies and labor-intensive work routines.[55] Put differently, the external contractual relation between grower and company demands that labor allocation and new work obligations be effected, and resolved, *within* the family.

These resolutions are seen vividly in the previous Mandinka case study, but they seem endemic to contract production among peasant growers.[56] Labor intensification and intrahousehold conflicts associated with contracting were widespread for example in the SEMRY irrigated rice scheme in Cameroon. Jones (1983) describes how contracted rice conflicted with women's production of upland sorghum and Vela wives refashioned the contract through renegotiating the terms and conditions of conjugality. In a similar development, Bassett's (1986) study documents the efforts of northern Ivory Coast women to redefine the traditional "working week" in relation to new labor claims associated with the introduction of cotton. Sorensen and von Bulow (1988:93–94) working in a tea-growing location in Kericho District, Kenya, among Kipsigis contract growers, paint a picture of sharp conflicts between male heads of household and both wives and adult sons. Conflicts arose if dependents felt exploited by the male head, who directly controls tea income for personal disposition. Sons and wives may, in such cases, simply refuse to work. In 7 percent of cases in which the Kenya Development Tea Authority (KDTA) complained of negligence (that is, inadequate weeding and pruning), the tea-growing family was wracked, indeed, incapacitated, by domestic conflicts. While adult men physically abused women when they withdrew their labor, the household head typically employed his power to defer land allocation to his sons as a means to sanction ornery dependents and impose domestic discipline.[57]

Suzette Heald's (1991, 1988, 1985) research among new tobacco growers in western Kenya is an intriguing illustration of this class of domestic production politics because it throws into relief the mediating role of two quite different social structures. In 1975 a tobacco conglomerate launched an intensive program to develop leaf growing in several provinces in Kenya, following the disruption of high-quality supplies from Uganda in 1972 and from Tanzania in 1976. Among the Teso in Western Province, the farming unit is the conjugal family, marked by a relatively small size and a division of labor by gender. Teso women had considerable autonomy vis-à-vis one another and their husbands but this was associated with "a radical separateness of goods and services [that] are not exchangeable" (Heald 1988:24). The introduction of tobacco conflicted directly with the millet crop (a major food staple) for female labor, and hence animated tensions between husbands and wives over subsistence, labor scarcity, and the control of tobacco income.

Conversely, among the Kuria in Nyanza Province, the modal homestead is a two-generation, large extended family, in which there is a more flexible division of tasks by gender and age and a strong ideology of joint interest. In addition to the large size of the homestead, the Kuria (unlike the Teso) were able to mobilize a wide variety of work groups for the labor-intensive tobacco operations. According to Heald, a strong Kuria authority pattern mandates the head of household to organize activities as a solitary family enterprise. Tobacco introduction thus posed a limited threat to subsistence among the Kuria and diminished tensions between household members over labor and income claims. In this sense, for the Kuria, contracting was mediated by social structure to produce what Burawoy (1985) in describing industrial systems (what he calls "production regimes") refers to as a *hegemonic regime*, distinguished by relations of consent. Conversely, among the Teso, contracting generated conflict and intense intrahousehold struggles—in Burawoy's lexicon, a *despotic regime*—in this case, centralized and authoritarian domestic rule by the patriarch.

Peasant contracting thus raises the possibility of what Ellen Wood (1986) describes as the head of household's acting as the agent of his own exploiter. The extrahousehold effort to enforce the labor process generates struggles over who, within the domestic unit, will work and under what conditions. Insofar as peasant enterprises are social structures in which patriarchy and property are at stake, the contract may provoke gender and generational conflicts (that is, patriarchal and domestic politics). How, and in what ways, this conflation of production and domestic politics is played out, negotiated, and resolved (if at all) is always, of course, an open question capable of generating a variety of new political configurations within the farming household. Contracting reveals how, to use Medick and Sabean's felicitous phrase, "emotions and material interests are socially constituted and . . . arise from the same matrix" (1984:3–4), embedded in property relations, working processes, and the structure of domination.

Unfree Labor in the Fields?

Contract production in agriculture generally bears striking resemblances to so-called post-Fordism or flexible accumulation in sectors of advanced capitalism that rely on multiple outsourcing through industrial subcontracts (Scott and Storper 1985; Lipietz 1986; Storper and Walker 1989). The genesis of non-Fordist production strategies in some productive sectors signals a wider industrial restructuring (see Chapter 1)—a new geography of production, switches from inert mechanical to programmable electronic technologies, the recomposition of capital and labor, and industrial reorganization, such as vertical disintegration by firms—which takes different forms depending on the institutional characteristic of labor and capital. Large manufacturing firms may vertically disintegrate by deploying dense networks of subcontractors or just-in-time delivery systems as a way of sustaining accumulation in the face of heightened competition. The contract relation generally determines product features, technical specifications, price, and technical or financial support.

The contract represents, in other words, a deepening of the division of labor external to the firm, yet reintegrates control under dispersed conditions. Industrial contracting is, as geographer Allan Scott (1983:243) observes, a "self-regulating mechanism ensuring wage discipline and a method of balkanizing the labor force;" it transfers labor demand from high-wage, organized labor to outworking labor forces in secondary labor markets. The flexibility conferred by the contract in the most extreme cases of industrial disintegration can eliminate centralized factory production altogether by the putting-out of industrial work to independent households. What appears as industrial deconcentration of production is in reality, however, the technical and social integration of dispersed producers and workers formally subordinated and controlled via credit and patterns of tied contracting (Harvey 1982; Massey 1984).

The emergence of the world car and the diffuse factory have their agrarian counterparts in the so-called world steer, in the corporate strawberries grown by Mexican sharecroppers in California, and in the highly standardized "designer vegetables," such as the Kenyan green beans embellishing Parisian dinner tables. These parallels reside in the integration of Third World peasantries into industrial enterprises through contracting, standardized technologies, and production conditions and nonequity forms of private and state control over production. In these new forms of integration and flexible organization, peasants are controlled and subordinated through a sort of agrarian "corporatism." Like their industrial counterparts, farm contractors are able to reduce fixed costs (that is, land) and to disperse much of the price and/or production risks to the direct producers. The dispersal of growing "helps us protect use from the vagaries of weathers," as the chairman of the British American Tobacco Company (BAT) put it (cited in Currie and Ray 1986:473). Like the putting-out system in textiles, the farm contractor exercises direct and indirect control over the household labor process.

Unlike other industrial sectors, however, agricultural commodity production contains its own biological and geographical peculiarities. Labor demand is shaped by biological growth processes, production time exceeds labor time, land is relatively fixed, and land markets are often quite sticky. Yet it is precisely these attributes, combined with the self-exploitative logic of household-based forms of contracting, that establish conditions in which the interest of capital is better served by disciplining and controlling a peasant labor market than by engaging directly in production. Under contract, the technical division of labor and the overall production process is regulated, directly and indirectly, by the contractor, who controls a dispersed and typically unorganized class of growers.[58] The so-called flexibility of household commodity production, and the apparent barriers to accumulation presented by agriculture (cf. Mann and Dickinson 1978) are thus converted into the building blocks for capitalist development. In the process, the free peasant is converted into a unfree grower, a sentiment vividly expressed by a Kenyan sugar grower: "Since you agree to plant sugar there is a rope around your neck that connects you to the company."

Contract farming entails new configurations of state, capital, and small-scale commodity production within a changing international division of labor. In this sense, it challenges the essentialist views of agrarian capitalism and labor-capital relations more generally. First, capital can dominate agriculture not so much by an advancing frontier of capitalist enterprises—the establishment of factories in the fields through the expropriation of the means of production from the direct producer—but rather through dense institutional networks of social control and domination. The nature of capitalism, as Suzanne Berger puts it, is "not to create a homogeneous social and economic system but rather to dominate and to draw profit from the diversity and inequality that remain in permanence" (1980:136). And second, contract production suggests that unfree labor is both an anomaly and a necessity in capitalist development (Miles 1987). In those cases in which peasants are subordinated under contract, capitalism exploits household labor, which is in a fundamental sense "unfree." The state is naturally pivotal in the enforcement, arbitration, recruitment, and, indeed, direct exploitation of this unfree labor. It is the political and ideological requirements of contracting that explain why the state is imperative in the reproduction of this particular production regime and why contracting is often conducted directly under state auspices. Peasant producers under contract are located in varying positions of unfreedom and constitute a distinct class or a fraction of an emerging global proletariat.

Contract farming and the exploitation of household labor reveal that capitalism may contribute to the reproduction of nonwage labor not simply because free labor presents an obstacle for capital (that is, labor markets do not arise "naturally") but because in some sectors it is not required. In agriculture the use of unfree nonwage labor can fulfill the same function as technology in industrial capitalism, namely, as a means to cheapen and subordinate labor or to substitute for free wage labor (Brass 1986). It is entirely possible that contracting is a preferable strategy where class configurations threaten capital's control over the point of production. Whether the conditions—political, legal, and ideological—required to maintain this contractual form of unfreedom and its dominant relations of production can be maintained is, of course, a question of class capacity and class action in actual social situations. What is clear is that the contradictions within contract farming of all forms generate oppositional energies, popular struggles, and symbolic conflicts capable of challenging the relations of dominance on which the "free" contract rests. It is the refashioning of "modern" work routines—in the Mandinka case a reworking of marriage, property relations, and rules of domestic conduct—which provides a crucial link to the case studies, from quite different times and places, that follow.

Capitalisms, Crises, and Cultures II: Notes on Local Transformation and Everyday Cultural Struggles

Society is a battlefield of representations, on which the limits and coherence of any given set are constantly fought for and regularly spoilt.

T. J. Clark, *The Painting of Modern Life*

For the victims as well as the beneficiaries of the large abstraction we choose to call capitalism . . . the *experience* itself arrives in quite personal, concrete, localized, mediated forms.

James C. Scott, *Weapons of the Weak* (emphasis added)

[Raymond Williams gave Gramsci's notion of hegemony] a characteristic twist by emphasizing the continual processes of adjustment needed to secure any political or cultural hegemony above, and *its perpetual failure*—as an inherently selective definition of reality—*to exhaust the meanings of popular experience below.*

Perry Anderson, "A Culture in Contraflow" (emphasis added)

Not only is the cultural construction of meaning and symbols inherently a matter of political and economic interests, but the reverse also holds—the concerns of political economy are inherently about conflicts over meanings and symbols.

George E. Marcus and Michael J. Fischer,
Anthropology as Cultural Critique

Prelude

ONCE AGAIN THE QUESTION: From what vantage points are we to understand the various guises, metamorphoses, and reconfigurations of historical and contemporary capitalisms? The partial answers to be offered here build upon a recognition that the reconfiguration of historical or contemporary capitalisms always encompasses processes of local transformation, processes that cannot be divorced from the concrete experiences of act-ual women and men, processes that involve a "trialectical" tension between meanings, situated practices, and power relations.

As the agents of different forms of early and modern industrial capitalism
have constantly attempted to reach into new markets,
to develop new products,
to restructure existing economic activities,
to move their resources from activities with falling rates of return,
   to activities which promise higher rates of return,
as the agents of capitalism have exercised their creative energies,
   while restlessly divesting and investing,
while repeatedly coping with crises of overinvestment,
as they time and again have abandoned existing technologies,
                        labor processes,
   and their associated working conditions,
as they thereby have engaged in "creative destruction,"
they constantly have constructed new geographies
   and eradicated old geographies,
they constantly have affected some locations, some places and regions
but not others.
Thereby,
as the ever more globally extensive processes of capitalism have unfolded
   during various phases of mutation dating back to the nineteenth
   century,[1]
they have yielded particular local transformations,
they have become integrated
   into locally sedimented forms of everyday life
   in singular ways,
they have led to the place-specific introduction
of new production- (and consumption-) related practices
                     and power relations,
they have resulted in place-specific experiences of modernity,
   in place-specific experiences of disjuncture,
   in place-specific cultural (re)form(ation)s,
   in localized meaning-centered everyday struggles
   that are at once political and cultural.

Put more tersely, the intersection of economic restructurings—of historically and geographically specific forms of capitalism—with already existing local-ized patterns of everyday life almost inevitably elicits some form of cultural response or negotiation, some overt or covert form of symbolic contestation.[2] The repeated but varied cultural responses that emerge as a part of local transformation, as a part of the local introduction (or removal) of specific forms of capital, as a part of the articulation of the local and the global, are central to all four of the empirical stories of everyday struggle recounted in this book. The research underlying the two (geographical-hi)stories that I will narrate has been self-consciously informed by a particular conceptualization of culture, by a particular view of the cultural content of concrete everyday practices and their associated power relations, by a particular perspective regarding the meaning-filled qualities of culture, language, and everyday life. This fundamental conceptualization is here spelled out in a somewhat unconventional manner—in a montage of aphorisms and propositions—so as to influence your author-ized reading of these tales, so as to add a final word to the intertextual screen through which your reading is filtered.[3]

Culture, Language, and Everyday Struggles

Culture does not stand   isolated
    on its own, immutable and uncontested.
It is neither fixed, nor confined to the traditional,
    neither completely stable, nor a unified monolith of coherence.
It is not an autonomous entity,
    existing in a territory of its own,
    beyond the realms of materiality and social reality.
Culture is embodied and lived,
    actively produced and expressed,
through all social practices,
through all that is concrete and everyday,
through all that is enmeshed in power relations
    and their associated discourses,[4]
    their associated representations and rhetorics.
Culture is one with "the *meanings* and values which arise amongst distinctive social groups and classes on the basis of their given historical [and geographically specific] conditions and relations,"
one with the meanings through which women and men "handle and respond to the conditions of [everyday practical] existence,"[5]
one with the mean(ing)s through which "a social order is communicated, reproduced, experienced, and explored"[6] in the flow of everyday life.
Culture is one with the meanings both through which distinctive social groups and classes are constructed by others and through which those groups and classes (re)make themselves.
Hence,
cultural dynamics,
the birthing and rebirthing of meanings,
are embedded in social process and the unfolding of human biographies,
    in the corpo-real execution of act-ivity,
    in the exercise of agency,
    in the sit(e)-uated reproduction of the ordinary and the extra-ordinary,
    in the intricate dialectic between conditions and consciousness,
    in the simultaneous making of histories
        and construction of human geographies.[7]
Or,
in the actual course of localized everyday life,
the cultural,
the intertwining of meaning and practice,

of meaning and event,
of meaning and object,
the production of local and more widely spread meanings and values,
cannot be   uncoupled
  from the social,
  from the historical,
  from the human geographical,
just as the social, the historical, and the human geographical
cannot be   severed
  either from each other
    or from the cultural.[8]

As people move through their lives,
as thinking, feeling subjects
  bodily engage
    in an unbroken succession of time-space specific activities,
the meaning-filled dynamics of culture are played out
at the intersection of that which is locally sedimented,
      that which is locally ongoing, and
      or that which locally penetrates from a distance,
at the junction either where different elements
    of local interest and discourse collide in new ways,
  or where the locally distinctive and the global,
      the locally originating and the nonlocally originating,
      the microprocessual and the macroprocessual,
  meet head on.
Or,
the meaning-filled dynamics of culture are played out
at those various crossroads of practical and relational tension,
      of practical and relational con-front-ation,
where responses of active resistance or covert opposition are called for
            almost unavoidably.[9]

" . . . cultural situations [are] *always* in flux, in a perpetual historically
sensitive state of resistance and accommodation to broader processes of
influence that are as much inside as outside the local context."[10]

"Language is . . . primarily a practical tool that gains in *meaning* from
doing as doing gains its *meaning* from language. Language is therefore
always in a state of becoming. . . . It is a semantic field that shifts as the
practices and projects of the material world alter, setting new limits as
old ones are overtaken, inventing new [local or wider] *meanings* for old
words, or bringing new words and *meanings* into existence."[11]

Languages are not things in themselves.
Languages are lived and situated.
Languages do not exist outside of people and places.
They cannot be   detached
  from the human practices of the areas in which they occur,
  from the human activities in which they are learned
            and employed,
  from the human activities out of which they emerge
            and to which they give rise.
They cannot be rent   asunder
  from the social conditions in which they are produced,
      reproduced, and utilized.

Especially in the form of the *meaning*-filled spoken word,
situated languages are inextricably bound up
with the practices of everyday life,
with quotidian activities of production or employment,
          of consumption and social interaction,
with the execution of recurrent routines and rituals
     in private and public spaces.
This being practic(e)ally the case, the words and meanings associated
with language usage are not only geographically and historically specific,
not only always in a state of becoming, but always entangled—at some
level—
with power relations
     that ultimately are a matter of who may or may not do what,
          where and when,
          under what conditions of control (if any),
with power relations
     that en-gender and class-ify,
     that otherwise simultaneously open up and restrict
          the times and spaces of human action,
               of human engagement in the world.
It is within the realm of everyday practices,
     within the flow of thought, conduct, and experience
          passing through them,
     within the field of power relations bearing upon them,
     within their attendant meanings,
     within the arena of meaning(s) in action,
that cultures and languages   lcaunlgtuarges
     overlap and disappear into one another,
     become inseparable from one another,
          except by academic legerdemain.
Or,
no matter what the scholarly sleight of hand,
in the act-ual world,
on the ground,
in place,
locally or more widely shared elements of culture and language—
     shared symbolic knowledge and meanings—
arise out of
and merge into
the experience of shared practices,
          shared asymmetrical power relations,
          shared situations.
In any historical-geographical setting,
the experiencing of shared practices and unequal power relations
     by those who are subordinate,
     by those who are subject to the practical rule(s) of others,
          to rules that are not of their own making,
     by those subject to "the social experience of
       indignities, control, submission, humiliation,
       forced deference, and punishment,"[12]
     by those whose use of time and space
       is in some measure subject to the command of others,

is apt to be given some cultural or linguistic expression,
is apt to result in some form of everyday cultural struggle,
    some form of open or clandestine word warfare,
    some form of symbolic discontent.

The content of locally occurring language usages and symbolic forms is
not fixed,[13]
for among other reasons,
because they are so often an outlet for discontent
    with the content of everyday practices and power relations,
because they are so often a means of contention,
    a medium for sign-aling dissatisfaction,
        for staking out the shifting grounds of practical struggle,
because they are so frequently the scene of ideological contestation,
because they are not only the means by which local struggles
    are described and communicated,
but also themselves frequently a site of struggle and resistance,
        an arena of conflict.

The circumstances are legion where
the spoken word, body language, or any other symbolic mode,
may serve the weak as a weapon
    for opposition, protest, or struggle,
    for rejecting reigning discourses,
    for rejecting the class-ification and categories
        of those above,
        of those who exercise power
            over the conduct of everyday practices.

The weak may deepen their opposition or resistance
    to the conditions of everyday practice and power relations,
by using the uttered word,
    the meaning-filled symbol,
    the cultural weapon,
as an instrument of social distinction,
an indicator of difference,
an underliner of division from others,
a boundary marker of exclusion and inclusion,
a cementer of collective identity,
a reinforcer of solidarity,[14]
a commitment to community.

The weak may express symbolic discontent
through opposing visions of the same social wor(l)d,
through opposing categorical divisions of the same social
                    (and material) world,
through opposing representations of group identity
    and characterizations of collective self,
through opposing taxonomies and images of social position,
through opposing classificatory systems of class,
through opposing verbal constructions of reality.[15]
Or,
symbolic discontent may be expressed through struggles
over what is to be construed as common sense,
over which categories are allowed to make sense,

over which words are to make a difference,
    are to construct a difference,
over which names and meanings are to be taken as legitimate,[16]
over the symbolic import of past "facts" and present everyday realities
    and thereby over the future making of local (or wider) histories.
The circumstances are legion where language and other symbolic forms
may serve the subordinate as a vehicle
    for spurning the "appropriate" meanings
      of those who appropriate,
    for scorning the "propriety" of meanings
      proclaimed by those who control property,
    for casting aside the governing meanings
      pronounced by those who politically govern,
    for giving shape to grievances,
    for turning the social world upside down.[17]
But, it is especially in conjunction with the local introduction of new
practices and their associated power relations that the spoken word (or
some other representational form) is apt to become an instrument of opposition and struggle—even if only uttered at offstage sites where one
may speak freely, where one may fearlessly offer rejoinders to those who
practically control and ideologically dominate.

New practices frequently involve a juxtapositioning of unconventional,
unprecedented contexts of action with conventional, established contexts
of action.
It is also so that "new meanings [generally] emerge from the interface
between one context and another."[18]
Therefore,
participation in new local everyday practices,
    in new social interactions and social relations,
may bring about an experience of opposed meanings or symbols,
may create a threat to existing accepted-as-natural meanings or symbols,
may evoke a defense of existing meanings
    and their unexamined idea-logics,
may trigger a struggle over meanings or symbols
    that is at once political and cultural.[19]

If the locally spoken word and other symbolic forms are embedded in
local practices and their associated power relations, and if conflict over
locally occurring practices and power relations almost always involves
some linguistic or symbolic expression, then there will be some (repeated)
impact on local representation, some active cultural response, some
(re)making or (re)invention of culture, wherever the workings of modern
industrial capitalism extend, wherever the actions of entrepreneurs, corporations, investors, and other profit-seeking, accumulation-oriented
agents are implemented.
In each of its successive periods of mutation,
    of accumulation crisis and self-reinvention,
    of modernization anew and accelerated,
industrial capitalism has been characterized
    by a furthering of "time-space compression,"[20]
    by a temporal and spatial shrinking of the world,

by advances in transportation and communications technology
   that have increased the mobility of goods and capital,
      the spatial reach of investments,
      the ease with which everyday practices and
         power relations are transformed at a distance,
and thereby by a tendency
   for the articulations between nonlocal capital
      and local cultural contestation
    to be more geographically extensive,
by a tendency
   for the truth of experience to no longer coincide with the place
      in which it takes place.[21]

As globally extensive processes of capitalism make their distinctive local
        appearances,
        exits, and
        reappearances,
as they generate particular local transformations of practice,
those processes inevitably contribute
to some transformation of locally encountered symbols,
    of the locally spoken word,
    of locally shared meanings,
to the introduction of new terms, expressions and meanings
   regarding newly erected built facilities
    and newly modified local landscapes,
   regarding new types of machinery, equipment, and production inputs,
   regarding the organization, details and moments
    of new labor processes,
   regarding the new social relations of those processes,
   regarding who is to interact with whom under what circumstances,
   regarding who is to supervise whom under what conditions of control,
   regarding new relations between employers and wage earners.

The local appearance of new forms of capitalism is not only about the
physical deployment of new technologies or about the implementation of
new labor-process moments and their associated social relations.
The local appearance of new forms of capitalism
is also about the *experience*
of its new everyday practices and power relations,
about newly experienced oppositions,
about political and cultural opposition
   to the new material circumstances and rules of the game
    those forms force into everyday life,
about the (re)shaping of subordinate cultures
   in the face of new conditions of domination,
   in the face of newly shaped hegemonic discourses.
It is about the mediation of new experiences by past experiences,
about the previous and the ongoing forming new experiential
        and perceptual constellations,
about the conflicts and struggles that thereby emerge.
It is about the experience of,
and open or covert resistance to, that which was not before.

It is about experiencing
disjuncture and discontinuity,
incongruity and rupture,
the shocking newness of the new.
It is about experiencing
what appears extraordinary in light of the established ordinary,
what does not make sense in light of preexisting sensibilities,
what appears illogical in light of a long-acted-upon idea-logic,
what seems immoral in light of a long-practiced moral economy,
what seems unethical in the light of a long-held ideal-ogic.
It is also, thereby, about the experience of modernity,
about everyday opposition to initial modernization,
        to further instances of (re)modernization,
        to episodes of "post"-modernization,
about efforts—
   sometimes isolated and subterranean, sometimes organized and above
     ground—
on the part of women and men to cope with, or even change,
    the world that is changing them,
about the local simultaneity of modernization, modernity,
                and modernisms.
Or, it is also about the experiences and off-stage or on-stage resistances
that result when locally sedimented ways of doing things and forms of
consciousness, or locally sedimented patterns of action and thought, are
confronted by practices and power relations that have been locally
(super)imposed.

Whether occurring in connection with early appearances of industrial
capitalism,[22] or in connection with its late-twentieth-century manifestations, such localized confrontations between some form of "tradition"
and some form of "modernity" are not likely to involve an automatic,
unproblematic capitulation of the former to the latter, an effortless ab-
sorption of the former by the latter—
even if, sooner or later, those who are subordinate
"consent" in practice to their new conditions,
accommodate themselves to new power relations.
Instead, such confrontations between the traditional and the modern are
almost certain to generate cultural tension between classes, groups, institutions, or gendered
women and men with different interests,
almost certain to bring the cultural modalities of different classes,
groups, institutions, or
gendered women and men into new forms of opposition.
Instead, such localized confrontations are
almost certain to call into question the appropriateness of some names
and classifications that until then had been pivotal to navigating the
    everyday world,
almost certain to require some re-cognition of difference,
        and the representations thereof,
almost certain to open to contestation the fact-uality of the present moment and its antecedents,
and,
by striking at the heart of collective memory
    and taken-for-granted differences,

thereby threaten personal or collective identity.[23]
Instead, such localized confrontations are
almost certain to demand some translation,
              some rewording,
              some reworking of the new into the old
                    or the old into the new,
almost certain to animate cultural struggles and representational contests
that are given voice in the private- or public-space languages and symbolic tactics of everyday life,
almost certain to redefine the everyday interplay of the hegemonic and
the counterhegemonic.[24]

It is not only through terms that label new tactics of everyday resistance
or in some way refer to the execution of those tactics that the local appearance of new forms of capitalism further impacts
upon local linguistic and symbolic expression,
upon the representational register,
    linguistic repertoire and
    multiple daily discourses of specific women and men.

In the wake of new forms of capitalism,
in the wake of new polarizations between capital and labor,
the locally spoken word and other symbolic forms
are also very likely to be altered in central ways
by cultural struggles,
by ideological battles,
by everyday power contests,
over the appropriateness of meanings,
over the legitimacy of namings,
over the preservation of identity.

Yet again,
where new forms of capitalism make their entrance,
where the custom-ary is consequently suspended,
where experiences of modernity
    are consequently in-corpo-rated into everyday life,
some precipitation of symbolic discontent is almost certain to occur.

However, the symbolic discontent following in the train of new forms of
capitalism is far from always synonymous with politically effective, protracted, and organized forms of local resistance.

Especially when it is confined to off-stage or subterranean expression,
symbolic discontent may serve much more as an adaptive safety-valve
than as an effective form of resistance.

Admittedly, symbolic discontent may merely serve as a haven of critical
acquiescence,
as a resort to safe subversion,
for those who seek to survive,
for those who are somewhat resigned to accommodation,
for those who consciously or subconsciously recognize the futility, danger, or impracticality
    of direct confrontation,
    of more active forms of struggle or open rebellion.

And yet,
through the recognition and penetration of power relations
    that is necessarily a part of it,
through the unveiling or underlining of everyday injustices
    that comes with it,
symbolic discontent may serve as a latent foundation for more organized
forms of resistance or pressured negotiation—
if it is not actually a prerequisite tinderbox for such collective agency.
For,
in symbolically challenging their domination and control,
in (re)constructing or (re)inventing their culture,
in (re)forming elements of their collective consciousness,
in making common sense of their situation,
locally subordinate groups
may revive their sense of community or their sense of place,
may (re)awake some sense of collective dignity, of solidarity,
and, in so doing,
may sow the seeds of future political action.

(Dis)contents to Come

Both of the remaining chapters tell a (geographical-hi)story of economic restructuring and symbolic discontent, of capital-based local transformation and experiences of modernity. But these stories of economic restructuring involve quite different forms of capital intersecting with quite different "First"-World settings, with quite different situations of the past and present, with quite different locally sedimented forms of practice, power relations, and consciousness. Both accounts of capital-centered articulations of the local and the global involve a highly pivotal—but geographically singular—historical juncture, a highly important mutational period of modern capitalism: on the one hand, the spread of large-scale factory production during the era of competitive industrial capitalism; on the other hand, the internationalization of production systems during the current era of "flexible accumulation" and crisis. Each narrative unveils shocks of modernity that are rather different, unveils experiences of modernity that are synonymous with rather different foci of symbolic discontent. Here, I will not be dealing with issues of gender, property, and labor relations (as in Watts's account of contemporary Gambia), or of fundamentalist religious discourse (as in his account of contemporary urban Nigeria). Instead, I will turn to one instance where symbolic discontent centers around the issue of urban space (late-nineteenth-century Stockholm) and to another instance where issues of nationalism, morality, and identity are conflated with those of labor/capital relations (the contemporary San Francisco Bay Area).

The story of the "popular geography" employed among Stockholm's working and periodically employed classes at the end of the nineteenth century (Chapter 5) is a story of the embeddedness of cultural/linguistic struggles in the practices and power relations of everyday life. It is a story of everyday cultural struggle that cannot be separated from the economic restructuring of the Swedish capital during that period, from the increasing concentration of manufacturing output in large-scale factories rather than artisanal workshops, from the city's changing position in the European world economy and the international division of labor.

The tale of multiple forms of symbolic discontent among construction laborers and steelworkers in Pittsburg, California (Chapter 6) is from the outset a tale of how South Korean government capital came to articulate with U.S. corporate capital, of how a global crisis in the steel industry impinged upon the everyday life of men and women who worked, or wished to work, in an industrial suburb situated at the northeastern periphery of the metropolitan complex surrounding San Francisco Bay.

While the particulars are distinctive, while the circumstances involved are extremely different, each tale resembles the other three insofar as it reveals a set of cultural contestations that accompanies the local insertion of new forms of capital and the consequent transformation of everyday life, insofar as it attempts to reveal the links between political economy and cultural forms through an in-depth examination of what Geertz (1983) terms "local knowledge."

Languages of Everyday Practice and Resistance: Stockholm at the End of the Nineteenth Century

Gramsci is, I believe, misled when he claims that the radicalism of subordinate classes is to be found more in their acts than in their beliefs. It is more nearly the reverse. The realm of behavior—particularly in power-laden situations—is precisely where dominated classes are most constrained. And it is at the level of beliefs and interpretations—where they can be safely ventured—that subordinate classes are least trammeled.

James C. Scott, *Weapons of the Weak*

Preamble

STOCKHOLM BETWEEN 1880 AND 1900. A becoming city. A city becoming. A city being swept into a new phase of capitalist mutation. A city thereby undergoing perhaps its most dramatic era of social and spatial transformation. A city becoming transformed largely through the appearance of new forms of industrial capitalism, through the appearance of forms of *competitive* industrial capitalism already characteristic of many urban centers elsewhere in Western Europe and North America. A two-decade period during which the local economy was restructured in fits and starts, during which manufacturing output became increasingly concentrated in large-scale factories, thereby undercutting the relative role of artisan and small workshop production. (By 1900 over one-half of the city's manufacturing jobs were to be found in 53 of 2,765 establishments [Gustafson 1976:263].) A two-decade period during which the city's youthful industrial capitalism—borne along by the uncontrolled, unfettered actions of investing agents—arose from the depression of the late 1870s, surging and lurching forward from 1880 onward, stumbling temporarily first in the mid-1880s, again between 1889 and 1891, and yet again in the final year of the century. A two-decade period during which the city's industrial capitalists repeatedly responded to transformations in the international division of labor and the European world economy, all the while contributing to those same transformations, either by opening markets for specialized machinery, tools, and equipment in Russia and Finland, or through other strategies. A two-decade period in which the metalworking and machinery industries flourished and grew technologically more advanced as their growth became intertwined with increasing agricultural mechanization, the local construction boom of the eighties, and the mounting domestic demand for modern railroad and shipping equipment generated by export activities. A twenty-year span during which modernity made its many-guised entrance. A twenty-year span during which consumption became marked by a whirl of quickly passing fashions and fads, during which commodity fetishism took hold, during which the circulation of money accelerated, during which the iron cage of bureaucratic regulation and surveillance was dropped down over previously ungoverned details of daily existence, during which everyday life on the streets was ever more characterized by restless and anonymous movement, by fleeting, fragmented impressions. A score of years of demographic ferment, of high population turnover, of people flocking into the city, of people returning to the countryside and lesser towns, of people departing for destinations across the Atlantic, of people making repeated residential shifts within the city. A score of years during which the population of Sweden's largest urban center expanded at an unprecedented rate, growing from well under one hundred seventy thousand to more than three hundred thousand. A tumultuous time during which the city's urban geography was radically modified by successive waves of speculative investment and "creative destruction." A tumultuous time during which remnants of the rural and pastoral were obliterated, during which hills of moraine and bedrock were leveled and sheer cliffs blasted away, during which the construction and reconstruction of housing led to a more pronounced spatial segregation of the classes, during which areal expansion, the appearance of broad esplanades, and other forms of infrastructure development were generally inseparable, during which new monumental buildings and signifiers of technology triumphant were erected.[1]

Stockholm's end-of-the-century engulfment by industrial capitalism and modernity, its simultaneous economic, demographic, and spatial transformation, its conversion from an overgrown small city into a modern European capital, its constant becoming, were synonymous with the appearance of new production, distribution, and consumption practices, with the modification or elimination of previously existing practices. The transformation of practices characterizing daily life in Stockholm was, in turn, one with new or modified power relations, with altered languages of practice among the city's working and periodically employed classes, with new practices of linguistic resistance and symbolic discontent among those same classes.

Languages of Production and Consumption, of Social Reference and Address

Within the realm of manufacturing, production workers developed different occupation-specific languages as the handicraft division of labor was replaced, as larger-scaled production units and mechanized, new-technology factories appeared. (Parallel new languages also developed with the modernization of construction and distribution activities.) These languages emerged as manufacturing became characterized by centralized planning within the firm, by a more finely divided and specialized division of labor, by a more closely controlled integration of production moments, by wages paid per unit of time worked rather than per unit of output produced, by machine-dictated labor tempos, by foremen who were overseers rather than consulting experts, by, in short, strict time discipline and a greater emphasis on rule compliance and subordination, or by a reduction of mental and reflective labor and a disappearance of most semblances of worker self-determination on the job.

The new spoken languages did not merely refer to new tool types, equipment, and machinery, or the parts thereof. And those same languages did not merely further refer to the distinctive tasks, separate labor-task moments, and specialized spaces to be found within the newly created production units.

As the division of labor grew more specialized and production became more large-scale and mechanized (especially in the metalworking and machinery, printing and publishing, and textile and apparel industries), the new deskilling and time discipline that emerged in Stockholm's manufacturing establishments did not go unopposed. Neither was there mere passive acceptance of the stricter labor discipline—the tighter coordination and surveillance—that began to develop at the city's docks and construction sites in connection with the increased scale and pace of activities conducted at those locations.[2] Nor, in particular, were the variously originating commands, demands, and pleas for the cessation of alcohol consumption at workplaces of all types met with the universal obedience of docile bodies and inactive minds. Instead, on all of these scores, bodies and minds proved to be frequently unruly and far from totally governable. Instead, there were innumerable daily skirmishes and contests, daily on-the-job struggles against those who commanded the use of time and space as a consequence of commanding money.[3] Instead, there were instances of resistance which were not confined to the trade union activities, occasionally occurring strikes, and political mobilization conventionally focused upon by many labor historians.[4] Instead, there were episodes which unfolded in the surveillance-free nooks and crevices of everyday production, construction, and distribution projects; episodes which brought immediate gains rather than the satisfaction of long-term objectives. Each newly emerging language of production, construction, and distribution practices therefore subsumed a new language of discipline avoidance and retaliatory tactics. Many occupation- and workplace-specific words and expressions served, for example, to label and describe tactics which involved stealing goods, other items, or potential income or profits from one's employer. Others referred to the wide range of tactics devised to consume alcohol on the job. Yet others pertained to the tactics relied upon for individual footdragging, to collective workpace slowdowns and rule violations, or to the prank tactics chosen to deliver resistance messages (such as arranging to sound the end-of-the-day signal at 6 P.M. rather than 7 P.M.).[5]

Whether these languages were employed to refer to the actual conduct of work or the execution of discipline avoidance and retaliatory tactics, they were always cross-cut and peppered by folk humor, by the mustering of malicious metaphors, by a vocabulary of comic irony and irreverence, by expressions of mocking and ridiculing social inversion, by verbal projectiles of laughing lewdness and licentiousness, by high levels of symbolic discontent. This was equally true of the consumption-practice languages utilized by Stockholm's working classes, of the spoken languages that not only labeled items of food and clothing, forms of housing, and periodically purchased novelty and fad goods, but also encompassed the survival tactics to which many were forced to resort in order to keep their stomachs and throats satisfied, their bodies warm, their heads beneath a roof. It was likewise true of the working-class language of social reference and address, the language used for tagging groups and individuals with nicknames, the mode of speaking that subsumed a language of social boundary drawing, social orientation, and social boundary transgressions.[6]

In order to demonstrate the richness of these spoken languages and the nature of their symbolic discontent, I will detail and interpret yet another working-class language of this era of new forms of industrial capitalism, a language of popular geography, or spatial orientation.

The Language of Spatial Orientation and Footing about the City

The production, distribution, and consumption practices through which late-nineteenth-century Stockholm was constituted, reproduced, and transformed were interwoven by human movement along the ground and through seconds, minutes, hours. Amidst the extended entrance parade of modernity, amidst the frequently frantic rhythms and dizzily paced march of newly emerging industrial capitalism, at the level of everyday life, was an endless stream of convergences and divergences, of people bringing their daily paths together to form joint presences, of people moving off in different directions leaving absences behind them.[7] To conduct one's daily routines, to be caught in the constraining and enabling web of local power relations, to be swept down in the maelstrom of the social, was repeatedly to get from one here and now to another, to go from location to location, to trace out one's daily path, to construct one's own geography, to negotiate and navigate the streets, usually anonymously, often among a restless and hustling crowd. The practices of production, distribution, and consumption, in short, demanded another set of practices: those of footing it about the city and of spatial orientation. (While walking was by far the most important form of movement, it did not monopolize urban circulation. For those who had the means and chose to do so, walking the streets as well as the connecting bridges of Stockholm could be avoided by hiring a horse-drawn cab, taking a stream-driven launch, or, during the early 1880s, paying for the services of a rower-woman (*roddarmadam*). Horse-drawn trolleys, which first operated in the Swedish capital in 1877, and one line of steam-driven trolleys, which first appeared about ten years later, were together carrying an average of 29,065 passengers per day by 1895. However, as this figure is equivalent to approximately fifty-four daily round trips per thousand people for the city as a whole, and as the corresponding figure for predominantly working-class Södermalm was equivalent to about twenty-seven daily round trips per thousand people, it would appear that fare costs discouraged the use of trolleys as an alternative to walking among the city's low-income population.[8])

Footing about Stockholm a hundred years ago, like walking about the streets of any modern city, involved a "spatial acting out of the place" (de Certeau 1984:8), just as it re-presented one's place in the local world. In act-ualizing only a few of the possibilities permitted by the constructed street network, in following the steering rules generated by the particular alignment of physical barriers, in trudging a well-trodden route, in creating shortcuts and detours to interrupt the humdrum of the accustomed, in self-imposing obstacles and intentionally avoiding accessible pathways, in making (ground-)marks that were immediately erased, the Stockholm pedestrian, like his or her present-day counterpart, made a statement. But, if pedestrian acts were statements made within rules, and were thereby analogous to speech acts, if pedestrian acts involved the use of languagelike "stylistic" devices,[9] then the very use of that language frequently required an actually spoken language.

To describe to another how to reach a particular destination required a language of spatial orientation. To convey to another where one had been and how one had gotten about required a language of spatial orientation. To arrange convergence at a meeting place required a language of spatial orientation. To make inquiries and comprehend responses regarding where activities or things were situated required a language of spatial orientation. To convey elements of one's own cognitive map, one's own "situational representation . . . [of] that vaster and properly unrepresentable totality which [was] the ensemble of the city's structure as a whole," required a language of spatial orientation, a set of locational formulations that was recognizable to others.[10] And, indeed, such a language existed among the working classes of Stockholm, as it would have among their counterparts dwelling in other urban settings, living at other times and places.

This language, however, was characterized not only by a vast shifting vocabulary of generalities and nuances, of broad areal designations and pinpoint precise details. As reflected in available sources, it was an assemblage of terms and phrases that was remarkable for its relatively infrequent reliance on official street names and other "proper" locational signifiers, for its frequently unrestrained, uninhibited expressions.[11] Among the city's lower social strata, at least, to speak the language of spatial orientation, to express the language of getting around the streets, was in large measure to utter a "folk geography," or "popular geography," that was intermingled with relatively standard and official locational designations. The lower end of Stockholm's social hierarchy did not fully monopolize this popular geography; certain terms occasionally managed to transcend class boundaries as a result of workplace contacts between employers and employees, the on-the-job talk of servant girls, more or less prolonged liaisons, a certain amount of social mobility, and the circulation of humor magazines, variety-show couplets, and popular songs. However, it is quite likely that in order to ensure recognizability, members of the "underclass"[12] generally resorted to more conventional, restrained, and official locational designations when addressing those higher up in the social hierarchy.

The Vocabulary of Working-Class Popular Geography: Words of Mouth for Negotiating the City Streets

Stockholm as a Whole and Its Areal Components   Stockholm itself went by other names among those commanding more than a few words of the city's popular language of spatial orientation. To some it was simply *byn*, or "the village" (Thesleff 1912:30), a term perhaps more employed by in-migrants who had resided locally long enough to grow comfortable with their new setting. Such individuals, presumably, were therefore able to draw a parallel between the familiar atmosphere of their customary sphere of daily activity and that of the rural settlements from which they came. More commonly, working-class residents referred to Stockholm as Stockhäcken, Stockeken, or, in abbreviated form, Eken, all of which were traceable to Månsing, the long-standing secret language of traders from the province of Västergötland, which served as a rich word source for the city's lower-class slangs (Thesleff 1912:30, 95; Bergman

1951:28–29; Stahre et al. 1984:30–31). Other Swedish urban centers were similarly renamed through substitution of the location-designating suffix *häcken* for the city's final syllable. Thus, for example, Göteborg became Götehäcken, Borås became Borhäcken, and Falköping became Falhäcken (Bannbers 1944:358; Gjerdman 1937:182).

While the folk-geographic verbal repertoire of individuals varied with the length of time they had been living in Stockholm and with the character of their past and present daily paths, and while some elements of that vocabulary were discarded or newly adopted in accord with the city's ongoing physical transformation, a small number of words indicating large areas appear to have been used almost universally. If biographic and quotidian circumstances prevented any one person from fully mastering the language of street negotiation, footing about Stockholm, bodily navigating its world of industrial capitalism, usually required an ability to distinguish among the city's geographically separate or distinct components. Thus, Södermalm, Norrmalm, and Staden mellan broarna (the City between the Bridges, or what is currently known as the Old City) (see Figure 5.1), the three parts of Stockholm in which the majority of the working classes were most apt to circulate, were respectively known by virtually all as Söder (the South),[13] Nor (the North), and *stan* (the city), just as Djurgården (Animal, or Deer, Park), the most popular destination for Sunday and holiday outings, was widely spoken of in its corrupted form, Djurgårn, and as the name Ladugårdsgärdet (The Cattle-Herd Field), the vast undeveloped area at the city's eastern margins, was generally uttered in a much abbreviated manner, *gärde* (field). The island of Kungsholmen [The Royal Islet], whose eastern half became increasingly populated between 1880 and 1900 by industrial laborers and other working-class groups, was eventually known to its poorer occupants and some of their elsewhere residing counterparts as Svältholmen, or The Starvation Islet. A portion of northeastern Norrmalm, or Vasastaden, an area relatively distant from the city's active core, where wooden buildings and shacks had long dominated the landscape, was likewise labeled with bitter irony as Sibirien (Siberia), in much the same way as the northern edges of some medieval Swedish urban settlements had been called Helvete, or Hell (Rehnberg 1967:117).

In a city of uneven topography and waterways that both fragmented and unified, the attachment of names to prominent physical features served to differentiate areas and subareas, and thereby greatly facilitated learning or explaining how to get from any one location to another. The city's variously scaled hills and heights—the consequence of the block faulting of primary rock and of glacial residue in the form of densely packed end moraines and eskers—proved a particularly important source of areal and subareal designations: Fyllbacken (Booze Hill), Galgbacken (The Gallows Hill), Himmelsbacken (The Hill of the Heavens),

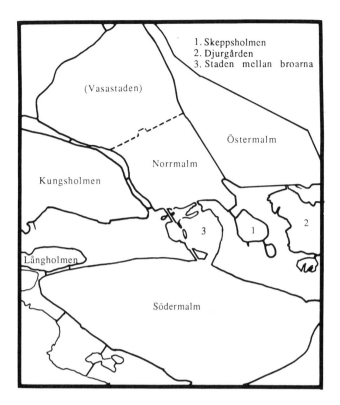

Fig. 5.1 District and Island Designations within Stockholm

Note: Northern Norrmalm was not officially designated as Vasastaden until 1926.

Lusberget (The Louse Mountain, or Hill), Postmästarebacken (The Post-master Hill), Rörstrandsbergen (Rörstrand's Mountain, or Hill), Tioöresbacken (The Ten Öre, or Penny, Hill), Stjärnkikarbacken (Tele-scope Hill), etc. Properly named smaller islands and peninsulas, such as Skeppsholmen, Långholmen, and Blasieholmen, when popularly rebap-tized (Holmen [The Islet], Långis [Long-*is*], and Blasan), filled the same purpose, as did the terms used for the markets, parks, and meeting grounds situated on flat, open land surfaces (Bondtorget [The Small Farmers', or Peasants', Marketplace], Lill Jans [Little Jans], Torget [The Marketplace], Träsktorget [The Marsh Marketplace], etc.) and the terms used for inlets and portions thereof (Brunsis [Well's-*is*], Pankis [The Broke-, or Penniless-*is*], etc.). And, in at least one instance, even an iso-lated oak tree functioned as an areal signifier (Luseken [Louse Oak]) for part of Djurgården.

In addition to its folk-humoristic characteristics, this areal terminology shared a number of attributes with much of the more finely detailed folk-geographic lexicon. Certain words, like those in other categories, represented the preservation of older usages; for example, Träsktorget had been the publicly acknowledged name for Roslagstorg until 1865, Träsket (The Marsh) had been the mid-seventeenth-century designation for a shallow lake then covering the area of Östermalm in question, and Lill Jans had, since 1731 or earlier, been a popular expression derived from the name of an inn operator (Stahre et al. 1984:150, 301). In many terms, the nonsense ending -*is* or -*an* was combined with either an abbreviated or a corrupted version of some official place name (Blasan, Brunsis, Långis, etc.) or with a noun or adjective from standard or dialectal Swedish (Pankis, Rackis [The Straight-*is*, a rock outcrop hill on Södermalm], etc.).[14] Some appellations were ambiguous, capable of causing confusion because they were applied to two different locations and descriptive of shared activities or attributes of the same type (Bondtorget, Fyllbacken, etc.). Others were substitutable for one another, since the singular characteristics or reputation of the specified area lent themselves to a number of alternative representations. Långholmen, an island that was synonymous with the prison situated upon it, was known by no fewer than six names—Framtidsön (The Island of the Future), Gråbo (Gray Nest, or Home), Långis, På den andra sidan (On the Other Side), Tavet (The *Tav*), and Vita Tavet (The White *Tav*).[15]

Especially during the late 1880s and 1890s, the areal distinctions included within the language of street navigation were supplemented or reinforced among some groups by a separate set of terms referring to young male gangs, who, unlike their counterparts in British cities, rarely engaged in major criminal transgressions (Sperlings 1973:47–48). The names of these gangs invariably indicated the territories within which their members hung about in the evenings, socializing with one another, playing cards, pulling pranks, committing mischief, intimidating strangers, now and then jumping somebody, and occasionally organizing forays against their rivals.[16] Thus, those having knowledge spoke of the gang from around the Atlas Locomotive Works in northwestern Norrmalm, or Vasastaden, as Atlasligan, the gang from Katarina Parish, on the eastern half of Södermalm, as Katarinaligan, the gang from the Träsket area of Östermalm as Träskligan, the gang from around Roslagstull, or Roslag's Toll, near the northern extremity of the city, as Roslagstullsligen or Tulligen, the gang from Kungsholmen as Kungsholmsligan, the gang from Norrtull, or North Toll, in the vicinity of the city's northern-central border, as Norrtullsligan, the gang from the neighborhood of Hornstull, or Horn's Toll, at the western end of Södermalm, as Horntullsligan, the gang from around Nytorget, or the New Marketplace, in Södermalm, as Nytorgsligan, the gang from a section of northern Norrmalm, or Vastaden, centering on Surbrunnsgatan (Acidic Well Street) as Surbrunnsligan or Surbrunnsgrabbarna (the Acidic Well Boys), and so on. Not surprisingly, the gangs also used derogatory names for one another. The gangs of Södermalm, for instance, termed members of the Kungsholmen gang as *kumminostar*, or "caraway cheeses," and referred to the members of any gang from Norrmalm as *norrbaggar*, or "northern beetles."[17]

Drinking and Eating Establishments as Points of Reference and Heteroglotic Reinforcement   The syntax of any Western language of urban spatial orientation builds in large measure upon a juxtapositioning of variously scaled general areal designations, precise reference points, and streets or other linear route indicators. As the folk geography of late-nineteenth-century Stockholm revealed in available sources was an overwhelmingly male language, and as public bars and cafés, where drinking and eating could be combined, were the primary loci of male working-class sociability, such establishments were the most frequently occurring points of locational reference. (The preponderance of public bars and cafés among the total array of folk-geographic references may not be ascribable only to the fact that the ethnographers responsible for key sources interviewed more men than women. It may also mean that women tended to have less need of locational referents, that because of their household chores and responsibilities, working-class adult females on the average had more spatially confined daily paths than did working-class adult males, especially if they had no wage-providing job.)

Since a great many drinking and eating establishments did not hang out signs or otherwise post identification, it usually fell to their frequenters to devise a name. The designations that stuck often directly invoked the current or former operator's name (Forsbergs, Karlbergskan [Karlberg's Wife], Solen [the Sun, from Solberg], Zetterholmskan [Zetterholm's Wife], etc.) or played upon that person's geographic origins, previous place of residence, or nonlocal ancestry (Ryskan [the Russian Woman], Skånskan [the Woman from Skåne], Småländskan [the Woman from Småland], etc.). Others alluded, in an often unflattering manner, to some real or rumored attribute, previous occupation, or past circumstance of the operator(s) (Vackra frun [the Beautiful Wife], Tre fittor [Three Cunts], Mor i arslet [Mother up the Ass], Halta Lottas [Lame Lotta's], Mälardrottningen [the Queen of Lake Mälar—"queen" being based on the caretaker's copious bust], Stämmar-Kalles kafé [Tuner-Karlsson's Café], Godhjärtamor [Good-Hearted Mother], Glaskalles [Glass Karlsson's—in reference to Karlsson's supposed dependence upon a glass tube for urinating], etc.). Some labels were similarly based on the characteristics of the establishment's personnel (Yngsjömörderskan [the Yngsjö Murderess], Barnkammaren [the Nursery Room—after the young relatives of the operator who made up most of the staff], etc.). The physical configuration, details, and general atmosphere of public bars and cafés, as well as the type and perceived quality of food they served, also inspired lasting names (Futten [the Shabby Place], Oredan [the Disorder],

Mässingsstången [the Brass Handrail], Stentrappen [the Stone Stairs], Dockskåpet [the Doll's House], Konstgödningen [the Artificial Fertilizer], Himmelriket [the Kingdom of Heaven—signifying two ascensions, from a basement location in the building next door, and from café to public bar], Pannkakan [the Pancake], Fläskoset [the Pork Fumes], Soplådan [the Garbage Box], Döden i grytan [Death in the Pot], Lilla helvetet [the Small Hell], Sprutmojet [the Squirting Thing—reflecting a large squirt gun from which soup was served into hollows carved into the establishment's tabletops], etc.). The past or present clientele most characteristic of an outlet also could occasion the appearance of a name that caught on (Socialistkafét [the Socialist Café], Sotaren [the Chimney Sweep], Målarfördarvet [the Painters' Ruin], Tullfördarvet [the Custom's Officers' Ruin], Skräddaren [the Tailor], etc.).[18]

In numerous instances fabricated names functioned as more direct locational referents, indicating where establishments were actually situated by the use of house numbers, street and alley designations, which were usually abbreviated, or some other device (Systa Styvern [the Last Penny—near steps of the same name], Hisskaféet [the Elevator Café—in view of the imposing outdoor elevator, Katarinahissen, in Södermalm, completed in 1884], Trebackarlång [Three Hills Long—on what until 1885 had been a street of the same name in Norrmalm], Hötorgskrogen [the Hay Marketplace Tavern—near Hay Marketplace, in Norrmalm], Kilen [the Wedge—on a triangular wedge between Kammakargatan, or Comb-Maker Street, and Wallingatan, or Wallin Street, in Norrmalm], Brunnsan [the Well-*an*—on Brunnsgränd, or Well Alley, in the Old City], Mittens krog [the Middle's Tavern—in the middle of Österlånggatan, or East Long Street, in the Old City], Timmermansorden [the Carpenters' Order—on Timmermansgatan, or Carpenter Street, in Södermalm], Fyran [Number Four—at number 4 Nytorget, or New Marketplace, in Södermalm), Saltmätarkrogen [the Salt Weighters' Tavern—on Saltmätargatan, or Salt Weighters' Street, in northern Norrmalm, or Vasastaden], Skepparkrogen [the Skippers' Tavern—on Skeppargatan, or Skippers' Street, in Östermalm], Femman [Number Five—at number 5 Kornhamnstorg, or Grain Harbor Marketplace, in the Old City], Mor på höjden [the Mother on the Heights—atop Kronoberget, or Crown Heights, in Kungsholmen], Funkens [on Funckens Gränd, or Funck's Alley, in the Old City], Majorskan [the Major's Wife—on Majorsgatan, or Major's Street, in Östermalm], etc.).

For a variety of anecdotal and singular reasons beyond the pale of this chapter, the nomenclature of many, if not most, other drinking establishments that were part of the popular geography more closely resembled the names conventionally associated with English public bars (Ankaret [the Anchor], Stjärnan [the Star], Tärningen [the Die], Flaggan [the Flag], Klotet [the Ball, or Globe], Lokomotivet [the Locomotive], etc.).

As the most significant loci of male working-class sociability, eating and drinking establishments, and public bars in particular, provided an environment in which the city's folk geography was constituted and re-produced, casually invented and passed on. This occurred through idle chatter and gossip, through the discussion of personal experience—of one's own being in the world—and events in the world at large, and through the telling of quick-witted jokes. It also occurred via the recount-ing of stories and the spinning of yarns, a good number of which appear to have been more or less straightforward narratives of workplace epi-sodes that either highlighted recently successful discipline avoidance and retaliatory tactics—the triumph of simulation and dissimulation, the mo-mentary reversal of power relationships—or celebrated, often via exag-geration, the cleverness and irrepressibility of fellow workers, the foibles of foremen, the evilness of employers, and the stupidity of seemingly om-nipresent street-patrolling policemen.[19] Owing to the forms of social seg-regation occurring in many drinking places, heteroglossia was thereby reinforced, or occupational languages and nonlocal dialects were strengthened and perpetuated. And, at the same time, comradeship, group loyalties, class consciousness, a shared sense of place, a shared sense of history, gender differences, and ideology were all cemented and buttressed by the content of these discourses and storytelling perform-ances (cf. Björklund 1984:65; Thompson 1984:199).

Numerous public bars simultaneously facilitated the reinforcement of heteroglossia and the construction and diffusion of a popular geography because they kept the classes beyond voice reach of one another, because they were subdivided into two spaces, providing separate sections with dissimilar furnishings, even different entrances, for those who could af-ford the cost of finer food or an elaborate smorgasbord along with their aquavit and for those who had to be satisfied with humbler fare.[20] Such proximate segregation was not limited to drinking establishments near areas of intense economic activity, such as Skeppsbron, where the daily paths of dockers, merchants, customs officials, clerks, and others inter-mingled. It also occurred in some predominantly residential areas of Norrmalm and Södermalm, where older, more substantial apartment buildings—like some of their counterparts in Berlin, Paris, and Vienna—were characterized by vertical social stratification: on the lowest floors, large apartments with ornamental facades for the financially powerful or the aristocracy; on the central floors, comfortably sized apartments with less fancy facades for professionals and their families; on the fourth and fifth floors, small units with lower ceilings and plain facades for craftsworkers, public-building watchmen, hat seamstresses, and the like (Gejvall 1954:35, 55–56, 64–69). The famous Berns salonger also opened its doors and Sunday variety show to properly dressed working-class individuals, but it kept them apart from the more well to do, dele-gating its *diplomatläktare* (diplomat gallery) and "large room" to the socially higher and shunting those below to its verandas, to the "little saloon," and to an area referred to as "the shack" for their *punsch*, or arrack liqueur, and coffee sipping.[21] However, while music could be heard and *punsch* acquired under similar circumstances at Strömpis or Strömparterren (The Stream Parterre), the operators of the Grand Hôtel, Hotell Rydberg, Operakällaren (the Opera Cellar), and other of the city's most prestigious and expensive alcohol-serving restaurants provided no second space for those of little means.[22]

Split-space drinking establishments and other public bars further contributed to the preservation of particular occupational tongues, to the deepening of Stockholm's heteroglossia, by drawing customers from a limited number of laboring groups rather than attracting a highly heterogeneous working-class clientele. Thus, to take a handful of examples, Sjele (a corruption of the name Scheele) was frequented primarily by factory workers from Bolinder's Engineering Works and the Pump-Separator factory; Knosan, by ironworkers from the Finnboda and Södra shipbuilding yards; Basaren (the Bazaar), by laborers from the Lundins tannery; Kyrkan (the Church), by dockers and customshouse watchmen; Godhjärtamor (the Good-Hearted Mother), by journeymen craftsworkers and livery stable drivers; Fyran (Number 4), by workers from the Kåbergs wallpaper plant, Barnängens cotton goods facility, and Lännstrands carding comb factory, as well as by dockers who stopped in the morning on their way to work for a shot of bitters, or *en besk*; Timmermansorden (the Carpenters' Order), by employees of the Tanto Sugar Works and livery stable drivers; Brunnsan (the Well's-*an*), by grain carriers, pork packers, wine porters, and other dockers; Mälardrottningen (the Queen of Lake Mälar), by venders, carters, and others connected to the Grain Harbor Marketplace in the Old City; Kilen (the Wedge), by workers from Rörstrand's Chinaware Factory; and Femman (Number 5), by coopers.[23] Cafés and other eating establishments catering to the working classes were often also segregated in the same manner. Stämmar-Kalles kafé (Tuner-Karlsson's Café) drew most of its customers from Ekman's Furniture Factory; Döden i grytan (Death in the Pot), from members of the metalworkers' local at the L. M. Ericsson plant; Mat Lasses (Food Larsson's), from among the employees of nearby retail shops and seamstresses; and Billigheten (the Bargain), from men working at the trolley barns, construction sites, and livery stables in its vicinity.[24]

Other Reference Points and General Designations   Aside from eating and drinking establishments, perhaps the greatest source of popular geographic reference points were places of work, commercial establishments, and schools—locations where considerable amounts of time were spent or where daily paths commonly converged. Places of work were frequently simply abbreviated in a clear-cut or corrupted manner (Atlas for the Atlas Locomotive Works, Korkis for Vijkander's Cork Factory, L.M. for the L. M. Ericson Factory, etc.). In less commonplace instances they acquired folk signifiers because of their architectural characteristics (Pipen [the Spout] for Rörstrand's Chinaware Factory) or the perception—sometimes gender based—of their employees (Snobbfabriken [Snob Factory] for the L. M. Ericson Factory). Owing to the intraurban spatial division of their labor, dockworkers and the drivers of horse-drawn passenger carriages were especially prolific in generating reference point names that occasionally spread beyond their own occupational group (for example, Hövågen [the Hay Scales], Mellantrappen [the Middle Steps], Franska bukten [the French Bay], Rundelen [the Round-about], Järnvågen [the Iron Scales], and Piggtorget [The Spike Marketplace], were docker work locations, while Lergroppen [the Mud Hole] and Guldgruvan [the Gold Mine] were horse-drawn-cab stations). Retail shops, like public bars and cafés, provided detailed locational signifiers based on the names of operators (such as Jonssons), physical appearance (Blådörrarna [the Blue Doors]), actual situation (Körkmurn [the Church Wall]), the quality of goods sold (Billiga priset [the Cheap Price]), or the preservation of older usages (Sockerbruksboden [the Sugar Works Shop]). Schools, also like public bars, could be labeled according to their clientele (Trasskolan [the Rag School]) or antecedent occupants (Malongen [a corruption of Madelung, the name of a man who once operated an apparel factory in the same building]).

The Royal Palace, or Fyrkanten (the Square), was unquestionably the single most imposing reference point in the entire city, occupying about one-fifth of the Old City's land area and being so situated as to present a literally majestic sight to those viewing it across the water from southernmost Norrmalm. Otherwise, residential structures and various types of public institutional buildings and entertainment facilities were, because of direct personal involvement or repeated daily-path exposure, the most numerous and easily utilized of all the remaining orientation-aiding locational signifiers known to have been in use. Mixed-use and purely residential buildings, ranging from old wooden shacks to the newly constructed and ornately facaded five-story buildings of Östermalm, were popularly dubbed, sometimes with much irony, on the basis of their landlord (Backsens [Backsen's house], Looströms [Looström's barracks], etc.), the attributes of their residents (Kolajdargården [Cow Drivers' House], Skojargården [Con Men's House], Mashem [Home for Men from Dalecarlia], etc.), or their physical appearance or location (Mahognyvillarna [The Mahogany Villas], Berghuset [The Hill House], Barackerna [the Barracks], etc.). When no folk-geographic term came to mind, residential structures, of whatever type, were verbally indicated by the definite form of their street address—that is, by adding the -*an* ending to their indefinite form.[25] Thus, for example, residential buildings along Götgatan (Goth Street), Södermalm's main north-south thoroughfare, were referred to as 6:an, 10:an, 22:an, 31:an, 39:an, 41:an, and so on.[26] Less permanent residential lodgings, such of those of the Salvation Army

(Arméns) and the flophouse and prostitutes' hotels of the Old City (Baden [the Baths], Kalmar, etc.), also could be called upon for spatial orientation purposes.

Among the public institutional buildings invoked as reference points were the telegraph office and station (Telegrafen), military housing units (Korvkasern [Sausage Barracks]), police stations (Torpet [the Croft]), workhouses (Träffen [the Meeting Spot], Grubbens gärde [Grubben's Field]), the Royal Opera House (Storan [the Great]), and hospitals and treatment centers for the general public as well as prostitutes (Trumfen [the Trump], Kopphuset [Smallpox House], Grundhäcken [Bottom-, or Basic-, häck]). Churches were similarly invoked with some frequency, owing in some measure to their visual prominence (Tyskan [the German], Katolskan [the Catholic], Beskakyrkan [The Bitter Church], Sirapskyrkan [The Syrupy Church], etc.). Dance halls were also apt to be used as locational designators (Runan [the Rune], Tattarsalen [The Gypsy Hall]), as were theaters (Ladan [the Barn], Hammarska Ladan [Hammar's Barn], etc.), especially if they provided variety shows.

A final important set of precise folk-geographic references referred to monuments (Kungens tandpetaren [the King's Toothpick]) and visually obvious landmarks, particularly windmills (Jan Ers, Grubbens kvarn [Grubben's Windmill], etc.).[27]

When everything else failed, when there was a failure of memory or some ignorance of specific reference-point names, speakers of Stockholm's folk geography could resort to a set of general terms for the type of activity occurring at a particular location. Thus, people might say that on their way to a particular place, they went by a public bar, or *bysa*, two blocks down. Or they might suggest that on the way to an intended destination, you should go past the cigar store, or *snårhäck*, before taking a right at the cheap eating establishment, or *sylta*. In order to pinpoint locations, and thereby provide here-to-there instructions or accounts of paths already taken, these general designations apparently were only supplemented—when necessary—with more conventional functionally descriptive nouns, such as the standard Swedish expressions for hat shop, furniture store, insurance office, trolley track intersection, sewing materials shop, and other phenomena that would have been conspicuous to anybody getting about the streets on foot (cf. Schegloff 1972:122–123).

Streets and Alleys: Lines of Folk Humor   The popular geography of Stockholm would not have been complete without some invented, substitute signifiers for point-connecting streets and alleys, especially since their officially labeled counterparts seem to have been used relatively infrequently, or even avoided, by working-class depictors of late-nineteenth-century daily life in the Swedish capital. Some of the popular street and alley names retrievable from available sources were merely abbreviated or corrupted substitutes for their proper designations (Myntis for Myntgatan, or Mint Street, and Långa gatan for Österlånggatan, or East Long Street). Others simply reflected an activity occurring somewhere along the length of the public way in question (Sopgränd, or Rubbish Alley, for the garbage dump at the end of Västra Vattugränd, or West Hydro Lane). A few, actually referring only to segments rather than to entire streets, indicated physical attributes (Herkulesbacke, or Hercules Hill, for the inclined portion of a street named after the same mythological hero, and Runda hörnan, or The Round Corner, for an unusually shaped intersection). Yet others, significantly, re-presented older appellations that either had been intergenerationally sedimented for more than two centuries (Pelarbacken, or The Colonnade Hill, for Kappellgränd, or Chapel Lane) or were holdovers from before 1885 (Landbyska verken, or the Landsby Works, for a portion of Engelbrektsgatan [Engelbrekt's Street], and Besvärsbacken, or The Troublesome Hill, for a portion of what had recently been Besvärsgatan [Troublesome Street]).

More commonly, however, the folk-geographic signifiers of streets and alleys were expressions of folk humor, of folk humor often laden with symbolic discontent over the everyday circumstances and living conditions of a city being transformed by new forms of capital. Some of this humor joyfully mirrored the spatial concentration of drinking activities (Fyllbacken, or the Booze Hill, for a segment of Götgatan) or built upon what appears to be comparatively innocent wordplay. (Skvallbänken, or the Gossip Bench, created an association between the plank sidewalk along Sveavägen [Mother Svea Road] and a wooden bench found outside cottages and houses in some rural parts of the country, between the summer stink of the open sewer beneath it (Sjöström 1937:33–34) and the foulness of gossip. At the same time, the term exploited the phonetic resemblance of *skvall*—a shortening of *skvaller*, or "gossip"—and *skvala*, "to swash or gush," as sewer water might). The wordplay embedded in Linkstret may or may not have been more socially pointed; for, while it obviously involved a corruption of the English name Link Street (Hamngatan, or Harbor Street, was the principal east-west link in downtown Norrmalm) and a reference to the prostitution occurring along part of its length (*link* was Stockholmska for "pimp"), it possibly further alluded to "hobbling struggle," to the difficult realities of making an economic go of it in the industrial and financial core of the city. But there is little question about the ironic sarcasm and social inversion built into Svältholmen, Lessammagatan, Rännan, and Horstret. Svältholmen, or Starvation Islet, was used to signify not only the island of Kungsholmen but also Hantverkargatan, or Craftsman Street, one of the poorest thoroughfares in that part of the city. Lessammagatan, which conjured up an image of a boring or unpleasant street owing to its corruption of *ledsam*, actually referred to Västmannagatan, a name that, if it represented anything to the middle and upper classes, represented national unity and

Stockholm's growth and progress; for its name was derived from the province of Västmanland, its length was newly extended to the city's northern limits, and its flanks underwent construction through much of the 1880s and 1890s. Rännan (the Gutter) and Snobbrännan (The Snob Gutter) unambiguously flipped the social hierarchy, referring as they did to the streetwide eastern promenade of the Royal Gardens (Kungsträdgården) plus the half-kilometer route to Sture Square (Stureplan), along which the city's most well to do and fashionable, especially women, paraded in their finery. Horstret (Whore, or Fornication, Street), the popular label for the newly incised Birger Jarl's Street (Birger Jarlsgatan), cast the social order upside down because it simultaneously alluded to the isolated pockets of prostitution along its extent (in connection with the back rooms of cigar stores and retail establishments and the nearby Löjtnants kuporna [The Lieutenants' Hives] of Lutternsgatan) and to the officially recognized outer boundary of the district which from 1885 onward was known as Östermalm. This district was by then regarded by its inhabitants as Stockholm's "newest and most well-built section" and was well on its way to becoming the bastion of the city's high bourgeoisie (Stahre et al. 1984:292, quoting from a petition submitted to the City Council).

Streets and alleys were, of course, not the only groups of folk-geographic terms riddled with the humor of bitter or biting irony and social inversion. The renaming of Stadsgården, the turf of dockers, with an expression that invoked finery (Stassgården) clearly involved an elevation of the socially low, as did the labeling of a neighborhood of run-down, wooden residential buildings as Mahogany Villas (Mahognyvillorna). Terms pregnant with resentful or light-hearted ironic commentary on the collective lot of various working-class groups included those pertaining to the marginal living conditions of Norrmalm's Sibirien, or Siberia; the lack of economic resources of people residing on Södermalm's Pankberget, or Broke Hill; the lice-ridden clothing or rooms of the chimney sweeps and others who collected in the vicinity of Luseken (The Louse Oak) on Sundays; the consequences of visiting specific public bars, such as Målarfördarvet (the Painters' Ruin) or Tullfördarvet (the Customs Workers' Ruin); the questionable quality of food served at particular establishments, such as Soplådan (the Garbage Box), Konstgödningen (the Artificial Fertilizer), and Döden i grytan (Death in the Pot); and the cobblestoned Lergropen, or Mudhole, cab station on Skeppsbron, from which prostitutes and drunks were transported away on police orders by the drivers of horse-drawn carriages.[28]

Folk humor in the form of comic irreverence and lewdness also permeated Stockholm's popular geography. Public-bar names such as Kyrkan (the Church), Himmelriket (the Kingdom of Heaven), Kristi lidande (the Passion of Christ), and Lilla helvetet (the Small Hell) were all terms that rejected the sanctity of churchly categories, terms that made little of the

bourgeois other's sense of propriety, terms that via conscious and subconscious devices said no to "'the language of honor and heroes' that the
school-grind of the times so mercilessly hammered in with the long catechism and biblese."[29] ("Hell" was extremely high on the unspeakable
invective list of the fully socialized and properly "civilized" among the
middle and upper classes.) The wordplayful renaming of two places of
worship—Beska Kyrkan (The Bitter Church) and Sirapskyrkan (The Syrupy Church)—shamelessly joked in much the same manner while also
debasing a particular ecclesiastical figure. (The *Bitter Church* was a play
on the name of the evangelical minister, Beskow, who had presided there
since the late 1860s, drawing crowds with his "sugar sweet" sermons.)[30]
The transformation of an obviously phallic obelisk proximate to the
Royal Palace into the King's Toothpick (Kungens tandpetare)—only
that, no more—was a verbal act combining politically laden irreverence
with at least subconscious obscenity, a camouflaged verbal act that had
its counterpart in more overt acts of disrespect for the Crown. In one
such instance, two workers in a bicycle factory tore up a portrait of the
king and demonstratively drew the pieces across their backsides, saying
with their bodies what they thought of Oscar II's aversion to the labor
movement and its objectives, his vigorous opposition to the extension of
voting rights to the wealth-lacking "underclass," and his intervention in
local politics by way of the governor of Stockholm, who was his personal
appointee (Rydberg 1986:118). More unambiguous, unruly ribaldry,
more direct comic celebration of the body's "lower stratum" burst forth
from a trio of lusty locational referents that, like other words of their ilk,
would unquestionably have appeared "embarrassing and improper in the
drawing-rooms" of Oscarian "better folk"[31]—Mother up the Ass (Mor i
arselet), Three Cunts (Tre fittor), and the Loud Fart (Brakskiten).

Popular Geography and the Evasion of Ideological Domination

Why was the vocabulary of Stockholm's folk geography so extensive during this breakthrough era of industrial capitalism? Why were official
street names employed to such a relatively small degree, or perhaps even
totally rejected by some? Why was the folk humor of irony, irreverence,
social inversion, and bawdiness so much a part of the city's working-class
popular geography?

A Response to the Melting into Air of All That Was Solid   It is highly
probable that the answers to the above questions lie partly in the rapidity
of Stockholm's physical expansion, areal reconfiguration, and architectural transformation; in the construction and reconstruction of housing,
workplaces, and infrastructure that accompanied the 80 percent population increase occurring between 1880 and 1900. It might be argued, not

unreasonably, that a rapidly changing environment, and therefore a highly disorientating environment, demanded an elaborate language of spatial orientation.

For all but those whose daily paths were confined to some small area of unusual stability, the—sometimes accelerated, sometimes somewhat slower—physical changes were inescapable. From the early 1880s onward, when there was a high-tempo speculative investment of overaccumulated capital in the city's construction sector, Stockholm was more than figuratively a place where all that was solid melted into air. The rural idyllic qualities of many parts of the city disappeared in wave upon wave of creative destruction, as tile-roofed wooden buildings were torn down to make room for more substantial horizon-erasing structures, as dynamite explosions leveled hills of moraine and bedrock or produced excavations, as land was filled in where water had flowed, as previously open landscapes became populated with buildings, as once-earthen streets were laid with stone. Ladugårdslandet (the Barn, or Cowhouse, Land), an area where a hodgepodge of stalls, cow barns, hovels, and outhouses had lined the streets and old boathouses had fronted the water, quickly became Östermalm, much flattened, traversed by broad esplanades, and with streets now bordered by a growing number of palacelike mansions and apartment buildings, many of which were equipped with elevators that made upper-floor dwelling units attractive to the rich and thereby further hastened a spatial segregation of the classes. The core of Norrmalm was increasingly given over to industrial rather than residential land uses. In then-remote areas of Norrmalm, Kungsholmen, and Södermalm, large working-class tenement buildings, with their typical one-room-plus kitchen flats, replaced small, ramshackle wooden dwellings, and new blocks shot up out of the ground amidst recently planned and newly etched or extended streets. Sheer cliffs were blasted away on the northern side of Södermalm, allowing both for the eastward elongation of the strip along which Stadsgården's docking activities took place and for the further development of Söder Mälarstrand, where some of the vessels arriving from Lake Mälar ports were loaded and unloaded. Portions of the arm of water separating Norrmalm and Kungsholmen were filled in with industrial waste for plant expansion and other economic purposes. New monumental buildings and signifiers of technology triumphant were erected—among others, the new opera house and Telefontörnet (The Telephone Tower) in Norrmalm, the market hall in Östermalm, and the Katarina elevator in Södermalm. Imposing banks and insurance offices were planted in downtown Norrmalm, while new schools and hospitals were scattered more widely over the city and additional trolley tracks were laid down. In short, when almost daily confronted by the sound of pole-driver songs,[32] hammer blows, and the blast of explosives and the sight of "half-torn-down houses, dug-up streets and blown-up rock knobs,"[33] and when exposed to the eye-catching successive importation of neo-Renaissance and Jugend-style architectural features from Berlin, Vienna, and other continental centers, most residents could not help but witness how Stockholm ceased being an overgrown small city and became a modern European capital, both physically and otherwise.[34]

The rural backgrounds of many reinforced the need for a language of spatial orientation to deal with these transformations, reinforced the need for a language of spatial orientation to cope with the recurrent disorientation, bewilderment, and confusion produced by these fleeting spaces of modernity. The cultural baggage of most people arriving from the countryside, including those who had been landless or had operated small subsistence-production farms, contained a well-developed ability to negotiate their local environs with the help of a fine-grained vocabulary of landscape details, with the help of words for specific meadows, cultivated fields, groves, dells, marshes, lake points, islands, houses, cottages, huts, and entire holdings (Frykman and Löfgren 1979:72). In some parts of the country, cottage and hut names were based on biblical references, such as Jerusalem, Bethlehem, and the Joy of Paradise, or on the biographical way stations of urban-oriented craftsworkers, such as London and Paris, rather than on adjacent physical features or functional descriptions. (Rehnberg 1967:118). Cast adrift in an environment with no physical resemblance to the one they had departed, thrown into an environment where so much was unfixed, and finding themselves, like Baudelaire's "archetypal modern man," frequently jolted by the "moving chaos" of city traffic (Berman 1982:159) on lower Götgatan, Österlånggatan, and other major arteries, such people, if not desperate for a popular language of local spatial orientation, presumably found it imperative either to latch onto such a vocabulary and syntax or to contribute to its continual invention and renewal.

Strategies of Street Name Revision, Street Control, and Ideological Domination   To argue that frantically paced creative destruction, the fluidity of circumstances, and biographical background helped shape the need for a comprehensive and nuanced popular language of spatial orientation is not to account either for the relative paucity of official street names and other proper locational signifiers in that language or for the pervasiveness of its unrestrained, un-self-censored humor. Although not definitively demonstrable, these latter puzzling attributes of Stockholm's folk-geographic discourse were almost certainly primarily a form of symbolic discontent—a form of conscious and subconscious resistance to the attempt at ideological domination embedded in the street name revisions of 1885 and the street-naming policy of subsequent years.

In 1885 the nomenclature of the city's streets was radically revised as the result of actions initiated by the Stockholm City Council in response to the large-scale construction occurring along thoroughfares first

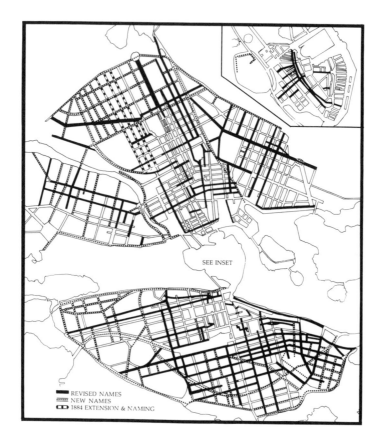

Fig. 5.2 Street Name Revision and the Naming of New and Extended Streets in Stockholm, 1884–1885

Sources: Stockholm's local government 1887; Stockholm City Council 1885, 1886; and Stahre et al. 1984.

planned between 1878 and 1880. In effect, the capital's traditional street names were struck by a state-spread "Black Death" (Ståhle 1981:14), and a new official geography was conferred upon the entire city (see Figure 5.2). Not only were 70 recently plotted or previously unlabeled streets and squares given new names, but 109 preexisting street names were completely erased or shifted to different locations (Stockholm Local Government 1887:74–78; Stockholm City Council 1885, 1886). At the same time, official park names were given to seventeen open areas (many of them atop hills that were not easily built upon), the water flowing between Norrmalm and Kungsholmen became Claraviken (Clara Bay) rather than Clara sjö (Clara Lake), and, to match its physical metamorphosis, Ladugårdslandet was nominally transformed to Östermalm. One year earlier, in a rush to deal with the rapid advance of residential construction along some new thoroughfares in northern Norrmalm, the Standing Committee of the City Council and the Office of the Governor of Stockholm had given early approval to an additional four street names (Stahre et al. 1984:277, 290). Prior to that, only two other new street names had appeared in the city during the 1880s (Stockholm Local Government 1882).

A few of the alternative street names may have caused some minor confusion, or perhaps even gone unnoticed, owing to the subtle modifications involved. On Kungsholmen, for instance, a widened Mariebergs-vägen, or Mariebergs Road, became Mariebergsgatan, or Mariebergs Street, and on Södermalm, a broadened Rosenlundsvägen became Rosenlundsgatan. A small number of other changes were almost certain to cause some amount of spatial disorientation, head spinning, and loss of bearings. In the vicinity of the Royal Library and the Hop Garden Park (Humlegården) surrounding it, what had been Biblioteksgatan (Library Street) became Floragatan, while what had been Norrmalmsgatan became Biblioteksgatan. On Kungsholmen, Arbetaregatan (Workers' Street) was replaced by St. Eriksgatan, while a new street two blocks to the west was labeled Arbetaregatan. On the eastern end of Södermalm, Barnängsgatan (Children's Meadow Street) was changed to Barnängstvärgatan (Children's Meadow Cross-Street), while a newly laid street intersecting it became Barnängsgatan. The extreme case occurred elsewhere on Södermalm, where Fatbursgatan was renamed Fatbursgränd and thereby demoted to alley status, where a portion of nearby Tantogatan became Fatbursgatan, and where another section of Tantogatan became Sköldgatan (Shield Street), while *Tantogatan* was set aside for a street that was as yet only planned. By generating a perplexed state of mind among some, such changes may have further contributed to the need for popular verbal substitutions. However, such instances appear far too exceptional to account for the full extent and character of the folk-geographic vocabulary, especially if it is recognized that other changes reduced the potential for orientational confusion by eliminating those situations in which different lengths of the same street bore a succession of distinct names and by eliminating like-sounding or identically named arteries in different parts of the city. In one instance, two separate Toll Gate streets (Tullportsgatan), one in Norrmalm and one on Södermalm, both disappeared.

The vast majority of new and altered names selected by the City Council—that municipal body put into office by the many-voted economic elite (see Figure 5.3)—were not random, without pattern or purpose. Instead, those 1884 and 1885 choices fell into one of five intentionally designed categories that were heavily laden with the ideology shared by elements of the financially powerful and the well-to-do middle classes: "patriotic and historical names"; "Nordic mythology"; "famous places near the city"; "the southern provinces"; and "the northern provinces"

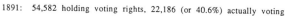

1881: 45,629 holding voting rights, 21,562 (or 47.3%) actually voting

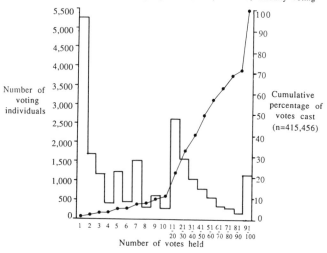

Number of voting individuals

Cumulative percentage of votes cast (n=415,456)

Number of votes held

1891: 54,582 holding voting rights, 22,186 (or 40.6%) actually voting

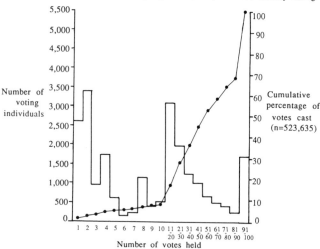

Number of voting individuals

Cumulative percentage of votes cast (n=523,635)

Number of votes held

Fig. 5.3 The Concentration of Voting Power in Stockholm Municipal Elections, 1881 and 1891

As these two graphs indicate, Stockholm truly possessed a ruling elite—a group with concentrated political power—because both the right to vote and the number of votes commanded were determined by annual income and property held.

Sources: Stockholm's local government 1887, 1897.

(Stockholm City Council 1885:1–3; Stahre et al. 1984:14–15). Throughout the remainder of the nineteenth century, newly created streets at the margins of the city were named either according to the same principles or on the basis of two additional ideologically pregnant categories that were a variation on "patriotic and historical names": "famous Swedish authors" and "prominent men within technology and engineering" (Stahre et al. 1984:15). And, not accidentally, the clarity of the messages conveyed by the categories of 1885 and the years thereafter was enhanced by the spatial clustering of names of the same type.

This ideological strategem, this impression of ideological expressions upon the expanding street network, was not an isolated phenomenon. It was part of a larger interwoven context, part of a set of variously scaled, ongoing structuring processes in which concretely situated practices, power relations, and individual and collective forms of consciousness were dialectically intertwined with one another.

Both in Stockholm and in Sweden as a whole, the youthful surge of industrial capitalism during the 1880s and 1890s brought in its wake an increase in the class antagonisms and social tensions that had only sporadically manifested themselves in the immediately preceding decades. Although the trade union movement did not really burgeon until the century's final decade, its first rustlings in the 1880s, its organization of strikes and demonstrations, and its call for voting rights and other "radical" changes were enough to create some uneasiness and anxiety among the middle and upper classes, enough to renew the fearful specter of the lower orders in revolt that was born with the French Revolution and revived with the upheavals of 1848 and the Paris Commune. Traditional norms pertaining to hierarchy and loyalty were crumbling, and, in the eyes of an observer of the late 1880s, the capital already had become "a metropolis where bosses and workers stand on different sides, suspiciously observing each other's movements" (Lundin 1890:648). To many of the bourgeoisie, viewing their local world from an economically and socially protected vantage point, the demands and threats being voiced by the working classes, the demands and threats produced from below, the demands and threats generated by what they termed the "underclass," were demands and threats coming from what they regarded as virtually "another race," a less developed "crude," "coarse," unclean, and dangerous people, "a seething mass, a formless . . . rabble," with many features that seemed to unite "them with the primitive, the animal in the world"—"insufficiently controlled impulses, less elevated wants, simpler pleasures, and so on" (Frykman and Löfgren 1985:129).

Nowhere did many of the bourgeoisie sense more heightened apprehension or greater threat than amidst the welter of activities and bustling movement of the city's streets. There one might be cast adrift in a social hodgepodge, in a sea of pedestrian promiscuity, where the banker and the bum, the wholesaler and the whore, the retailer and the ragpicker, the respectable and the disrespectful, the high and the low, the clean and the dirty, flowed and jostled, side by side, over the same spaces. There, common laborer and drunken "ruffian," poor worker and criminal, were not necessarily distinguishable.[35] There, one might unwillingly witness a drunken brawl or men urinating against the side of a building, be pestered by ill-clad urchins wishing to sell one item or another, or have one's ears assaulted by swearing and "uncouth" language.[36] There, one was subject to contamination; there, one might be infected by the disease-carrying, unsanitary, morally impure, proletarian Other.[37] There, horse spillings or other inadequately looked after filth might besmirch one's shoes or offend one's nose, provoke nausea, arouse disgust. There, disorderly, undisciplined conduct and uncontrolled passions reigned and might be encountered despite precautions. There, the gathering of a crowd, in connection with a strike or some other event, might result in a calamity. (The last-named source of anxiety was considerably magnified in September 1885—the year of street-name revision—as a result of one of "the more violent disorders in the history of Stockholm . . . [which occurred] when a crowd of thousands assembled in front of the Grand Hotel to hear a free concert by the popular singer Kristina Nilson. . . . As the audience began to move away from the hotel at the end of the performance, new crowds approached. Many people had been misinformed about the time of the concert and were just arriving. Confusion turned into panic: nineteen people were trampled to death and 100 were injured" [Graborsky and Persson 1977:263]).

Practical measures and intentional or unintentional ideological antidotes were necessary if order was to be imposed upon both a threatening "underclass" and the streets that it walked. Control and discipline, if not self-control and self-discipline, could be brought to the streets through new (re)forms of power, through the local-state management of space and application of knowledge supposedly beneficial to entire subpopulations (through the local-state application of "bio-power"),[38] through the imposition of a new grid of bureaucratic rules, through the creation of a new matrix of police enforcement. At least according to the more idealistic, progress-believing, and missionary elements of the bourgeois population, those lacking "culture" could be "cultivated" or "civilized," infused with ambition-chaneling, unrest-defusing middle-class ideals regarding respect for authority and the centrality of one's home and family, and thereby lifted above their condition of "backwardness" (Frykman and Löfgren 1985:60, 129; Frykman and Löfgren 1979:117–119). Or, if unreceptive to this patriarchal and self-legitimating take-yourself-by-the-collar-and-become-as-us message, those beneath could be subjected to "an appeal" concerning the existence of "a national community transcending class gulfs," to a campaign promoting national romanticism and solidarity (Löfgren 1984:18).

By the late 1870s, initial steps already had been taken to bring greater order to the streets. Measures to curb public drunkenness had been taken in 1877, with the introduction of the Göteborgssystemet (Göteborg System), and its attendant private sales monopoly, the Stockholm Liquor Retailing Corporation, and with the addition of successively stricter rules in 1882 and 1885 as to the time, place, and manner of alcohol sales (Key-Åberg 1902:197–201). From 1875 onward, rules began to take shape governing who could drive passenger cabs under what circumstances and designating which critically located cab stations were to be staffed at specific hours,[39] thereby assuring those with sufficient means that they could move rapidly or avoid the unpleasantness of the streets almost whenever and wherever they wished. Throughout the 1880–1900 period, there was a multiplication of municipal rules pertaining to the sale of foodstuffs and other goods at open-air marketplaces and other street locations; to the placement of signs, advertisements, and posters on the city's buildings and streets; to the driving of livestock to slaughterhouses or other destinations; and to the transportation and removal of animal and human excrement, industrial waste, garbage, and snow. There was also a burgeoning of rules regarding the responsibility of property owners for keeping their adjacent sidewalks, gutters, and streetways clean; regarding the speed of vehicle movement on specified streets and the impermissibility of vehicular traffic on the sidewalks; and regarding such potential minor pedestrian inconveniences as downhill sledders, dogs being taken for a walk, and, after 1894, velocipede riders.[40]

The police department, which was responsible for the enforcement of all these rules, as well as for governing the street behavior of prostitutes and for upholding more long-standing laws, had its numbers expanded substantially (from a force of 324 in 1880 to one of 582 in 1900).[41] It also underwent a number of organizational changes, including the formation of a mobile riot squad in 1887 (Graborsky and Persson 1977:271). Increasingly, the police officer assumed the role of street disciplinarian, of wandering watchful eye, of roving reminder of the consequences of transgression, of patrolling protector of public order—seemingly ubiquitous, present on every major thoroughfare and at every marketplace, theater, steam launch landing, and densely trafficked point of convergence—attempting to ensure the unencumbered movement of trolleys, cabs, and wagons, the free circulation of pedestrians to and from stores, service establishments, and places of work; preventing the progress of vehicles at speeds that would endanger those on foot; walking beats that were covered around the clock; making sure, insofar as possible, that the wrong people were not at the wrong locations at the wrong times; seeing to it that no labor movement demonstration occurred within city limits (cf. Franzén 1982:10–13). In a setting where "forestalling all that disturbs [the] calm, order and safety" of the streets was something of an obsession, even the patrolling constables were themselves subject to surveillance, their whereabouts and performance being controlled day and night by higher-level officers who roamed throughout each of the city's nine precincts (Sydow 1897:286–292; Lundin 1890:548–549). (Beat constables, like industrial laborers, construction workers, and dockers, were known to struggle over their working-hours use of time and space, to drink on the job, and to employ a variety of tactics to avoid their responsibilities, which had to be met seventeen out of every eighteen days.[42])

Further measures designed to keep life on the streets orderly and secure included the introduction of an afternoon woodworking program for older primary-school boys, who might otherwise get into mischief or collectively act in publicly unsettling ways. Exemptions from this extra class at essentially working-class schools were allowed to those whose parents could demonstrate that they would be usefully employed rather than idling about on the streets (Sandin 1984:124). The so-called muzzle law (*munkorgslagen*) and other legislation enacted by Parliament between 1887 and 1890 sought to discourage organized and spontaneous public protests, in some cases empowering the authorities of Stockholm and other cities to arrest speakers and to disperse crowds even in the absence of disruption (Gaborsky and Persson 1977:267).

The *rotemans*, or district registrar, system was put into in effect in the downswing year 1878 by a City Council wishing to prevent Stockholm from being "overrun by a population of drifting riff-raff" and to keep municipal authorities abreast of exactly when, where, and how to intervene in civilian life. The operation of this system more than indirectly contributed to the long-term maintenance of public order by repeatedly reminding inhabitants that they were under surveillance, moral supervision, and control in a bureaucratically constructed, closely knit spatial mesh. The system required all those making an intraurban residential shift or an initial move into the city to provide the appropriate district registrar's office promptly with an address and information regarding date and place of birth, occupation, marital status, prior education, "character," and any previous military service, smallpox infection, or receipt of poor relief. More important, the registrar, who organized his materials by block, property unit, and household, was to keep his district population under microscopic observation. Not only was he to gather information annually about births, deaths, marriages, divorces, school attendance, and vaccinations; he was also to serve as a clearing house for those in search of social welfare and continuously assemble knowledge regarding the joint residence of unmarried couples, the spending behavior of poor-relief recipients, the conduct of foster parents, arrests, court judgments, personal bankruptcies, changes in religious belief, hospital stays, and the like. As a bureaucratic patriarch, who was exposed to much gossip, each of the sixteen to twenty-five registrars was to be alert to anything that might adversely affect the "general order" and to inform the police when necessary (Jakobsson 1977; and Matovic 1984: 171, 241, 272–273). The expansion of the number of *rotar*, or registration

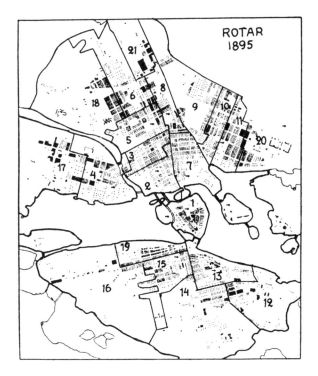

Fig. 5.4 The *Rotar* (Registration Districts) and Population Distribution of Stockholm, 1895

Source:William-Olsson 1937:18.
Note: Each dot represents twenty-five persons.

districts, from sixteen in 1880 to twenty-five in 1899 (largely through the repeated subdivision of preexisting units), plus the modification of some district names, (Jakobsson 1971:93–101), may well have provided a weak secondary source of spatial disorientation, another minor impulse to the formation or use of a popular geography (see Figure 5.4).

  The city planning that created the seventy streets and squares initially named in 1885 also involved efforts to solidify order, to eliminate chaos and potential anarchy, to reform the threatening "underclass." Authorities responsible for designing Stockholm's physical expansion and spatial organization revealingly spoke of *g,aturegulering*, or "street regulating"—of governing the streets by rule—rather than of planning (Selling 1973:26, 55). For them, and for their counterparts in Paris, London, Berlin, and elsewhere, the ordering of space and the ordering of people were to be combined, the rationalization of the street network and the normalization of the population were to be united, the regulation of previously unregulated public spaces and public behavior were to occur

jointly, and the planning of urban space and scientifically informed political control were to be articulated with each another (cf. Rabinow 1983,
1989). The members of the Municipal Finance Committee, civil engineers, surveyors, and others who were empowered to deal with planning
issues from 1874 onward were much influenced both by Haussmann's
radical restructuring of Paris and by English town planning. Albert Lindhagen and lesser figures therefore gave priority to circulation and hygiene
as well as to elegance, working on the assumption that straight streets
and broad boulevards would do away with those odious and repugnant
aspects of urban life—"darkness, crowding, unclear air and the unnatu-
ral." Or, straight streets and broad boulevards would not only facilitate
the economically essential movement of goods and people but, in yielding
light and fresh air, would also make for subpopulations of sound body
and mind, rather than ones who were diseased with dysentery, tuber-
culosis, diphtheria, scarlet fever, measles, or whooping cough, who had
very high death rates, and who were mentally "dirty and stupid," consequently morally decadent, and thereby dangerous.[43] If perhaps not sharing a fear of outright proletarian insurrection with their Parisian
counterparts, it would appear that administrators within Stockholm's
planning apparatus who were familiar with Hausmann's principles did
know full well that straight streets and broad boulevards, or *esplanader*
(esplanades), greatly eased the summoning of police and locally garrisoned troops, and hence the quelling or inhibiting of disturbances of
whatever size.[44]

Parallel to all of these order-in-the-streets measures and bureaucratic
oversight devices was a backward-turning, status-quo-legitimating, na-
tionalism-promoting, anxiety-reducing, and threat-dampening mythology that began to emerge among the middle and upper classes, gaining
full strength by the 1890s. Broadcast for working-class consumption
through a greater emphasis on Swedish history and geography in the
schools (where children were also socialized for the labor market through
the imprinting of time and space discipline)[45] and publicly represented in
works of fiction, paintings, newspaper commentaries, the reconstructed
rural scenes of the outdoor Skansen museum, and much of the content of
the Art and Industrial Exhibition of 1897, the mythology trumpeted a
tune of national romanticism and solidarity, proclaiming a shared past, a
common cultural heritage, a jointly held love of the nation's undefiled
landscapes and nature. The rural "past" was not merely to invoke the
once-existing past but was now to signify "the good old days," an age of
unity to be recaptured, a time when life in agricultural villages "was
simple and harmonious," an epoch free of speedy technological change,
an era when the everyday was uncomplicated, straightforward, and fric-
tionless, a period when "people knew their place and relations between
high and low were marked by paternal care and attention on one side and

contentedness on the other."[46] Untamed nature and unspoiled landscapes were no longer symbolized by the drama of "mountain tops and storm-whipped seas" but by "the whispering spruce forest, the starlit winter night, the birch grove and the hillside flowering with wood-anemone," or by that which was quintessentially Swedish in its sentimentality and melancholiness, and that which was grounded in a community of experience transcending all class boundaries and political differences (Frykman and Löfgren 1987:58).

During the mid- and late 1880s, the early stages of this myth building intermingled with the ideological preoccupations of an older generation of the economically and socially dominant. Those holding to this *"punsch* [arrack liqueur] patriotism" waxed enthusiastic about ancient Scandinavia and made much of national honor, historical battlefield heroics, and the power-wielding giants of the past.[47] The street name revision of 1885 and subsequent artery-naming policies were thus based upon elements from older as well as emergent forms of dominant ideology. The emphasis on "patriotic and historical names" and "Nordic mythology" was in keeping with *"punsch* patriotism." The recourse to names of "the southern provinces" and "the northern provinces" was a harbinger of national romanticism and the myth of solidarity: the Swedish word for "province," *landskap*, also means "landscape" and is filled with connotations of a regionally characteristic landscape. The invocation of "famous places near the the city" was in each particular instance always compatible with one of the two ideological forms.

As a strategem to help bring order, control, and discipline to the city's streets, the imprinting of dominant ideology upon the topography of Stockholm through street name revision cut two ways. As an on-the-ground effort to impose ideology, as an attempt at making cultural hegemony concrete, street name revision involved both the emplacement of new signifiers and the displacement of old signifiers. Many preexisting street names were deeply sedimented usages, once spontaneous on-the-spot popular creations resulting from events, persons, physical features, or economic activities associated with the street in question or its immediate vicinity. The erasure of former names, in other words, often involved the censuring of an intergenerationally transmitted folk geography that dated back decades or centuries and that had begun to obtain legitimacy in 1763, when a royal proclamation went into effect requiring the placement of name signs at the corners of important streets.[48]

The flavor of this administratively terminated popular geography is suggested by a handful of 1885 eradications. On Södermalm, what since 1661 had been known as Pilgatan (Willow Street) because of its parallel tree rows became Folkungagatan, after the aristocratic Folkunga family that ruled in Sweden from 1250 to 1363. In the same part of the city, Holländaregatan (Dutchmen Street), which since the seventeenth century had borne names relating to the Dutch windmill situated upon it, was transformed into Ölandsgatan, after the Baltic island and southern province of Öland. A Norrmalm thoroughfare referred to as Trebackarlånggatan (Three Hills Long Street) for about 150 years was renamed Tegnérgatan in honor of the bishop and poet Esaias Tegnér (1782–1846). On Kungsholmen, Reparebansgatan (Ropewalk Street), a name stemming from a ropemaking facility established there in 1689, was set aside for Flemminggatan, an appellation exalting Klas Fleming, an early-seventeenth-century admiral. Glasbruksgränden (Glassworks Lane), another designation on Kungsholmen, derived from a two-centuries-old production unit, was obliterated in favor of Owengatan, after the immigrant industrial hero Samuel Owen, who had launched the country's first steamboat at the foot of this street (Ståhle 1981:12, 16; Stahre et al 1984:96, 109–110, 177, 222, 272–273).

Ideological Resistance and Arsenalsgatan: Turning the Local Wor(l)d on Its End

Given the context of street-discipline and population-control strategies,
given the resistance simultaneously expressed in the multitude of
    discipline-avoidance and retaliatory tactics employed on the job by in-
        dustrial laborers, dockers, and construction workers,[49]
given the localization of the most thorough revision of thoroughfare
        names to a portion of eastern Södermalm containing a rather
        high working-class population density (compare Figures 5.2
        and 5.3),
given the unmistakable thrust of street-naming policies and their resul-
        tant expunging of long-standing folk usages,
it is difficult not to connect the apparent reluctance to utter official street
        names and the heavy reliance upon an extensive, humor-filled
        geography with ideological resistance,
difficult not to see the lost worlds of footing about Stockholm,
        the lost words of spatial orientation and popular geography,
    as in some measure subsuming
a lost world and language of resistance to ideological domination.

If working-class popular geography was not merely a response to disorientation and the melting into air of all that was solid, if it to a considerable degree represented resistance to the forms of ideological domination associated with industrial capitalism, it represented resistance in a particular multidimensional form. It was resistance that was neither concerted, nor organized, nor intentionally coordinated even in the most informal sense. It was resistance composed of individual acts, innumerable individual acts that cannot be dismissed because, through their very volume and repetition, they contributed to the establishment and reproduction of a collective consciousness, to the construction of a local class culture, to the formation and perpetuation of a symbolically embedded, practice-based sense of community and sense of place, to the shaping and strengthening of cultural boundaries.[50] It was cultural resistance by those hemmed in by power relations at work, by those reined in by power relations on the streets, by those over whom the iron cage of bureaucratic rationality was being dropped, by those trying to get around the space-constraining rules instituted by others. It was resistance by symbolic means, resistance that was consciously or subconsciously aimed at those who not only controlled the new physical means of production and distribution but the means of symbolic production as well. It was resistance that, in rejecting the perceptions and calming platitudes propagated from above, rejected the established social order. It was resistance that, with all its humorous resort to irony, sarcasm, ridicule, and social inversion, demonstrated the ability of the otherwise trammeled to penetrate and demystify the word of the elite Other by falling back upon the myriad lessons learned on the ground through routine practices and the daily experience thereof.[51] It was resistance that, unlike the blatant rhetoric of labor movement leaders regarding the "capitalist system" and the interests of "municipal authorities," involved the pulling of verbal tricks, the use of cunning linguistic ploys to counter Oscarian prudery and sexual hypocrisy. In its employment of linguistic manipulation, it was resistance—like the ideological resistance and symbolic discontent of subordinate groups in so many other historical and geographical settings—that exhibited much "imaginative capacity" and relied upon the "weapons of the weak" to conduct a kind of "sniggering guerilla warfare" "from a position of social inferiority" (Scott 1985:331; de Certeau 1984:23; Löfgren 1985:99). It was resistance that occurred largely outside of public view, uttered for the most part behind the scenes, beyond elite earshot, in those "social sphere[s] where the powerless [could] speak freely" (Scott 1985:330). And yet, despite its lack of visibility, it was a type of resistance that, by struggling over naming and meaning, attempted to prove who it was that really reigned in the streets.

Resistance to control of the streets and its related forms of ideological domination was not, of course, confined to the language of popular geography. Occasionally, resistance was given more overt expression as a consequence of sheer necessity, group daring, taunting playfulness, unfettered rebelliousness, or drunken cantankerousness. Survival tactics and resistance merged when, despite police efforts in the streets, horse-drawn cabs were driven about the city illegally at night, young boys hawked newspapers and goods after permitted hours, alcohol was vended illicitly from doorways and alleys, and prostitutes ignored time, place, and manner rules.[52] In the late 1890s, milk wagon drivers who lacked the funds to hire a meeting hall held their weekly trade union gatherings outdoors, disregarding the requirement to seek a police permit because they did not wish to "beg for permission," but keeping men on watch in case any *byling* (cop) should appear.[53] *Utridargrabbar* (ride-out boys) responsible for bringing fresh horses out to in-service trolleys not infrequently tried to make their deliveries at a gallop, at speeds deemed legally reckless.[54]

Adolescent street gang members often shouted *"gris"* ("pig") or more scabrous jeers at patrolmen from a judicious distance or, much more rarely, even jumped lone officers when the safety of numbers, darkness, and isolation produced the right chemistry for action.[55] Intoxicated laborers, when halted in the Old City or elsewhere for disturbing the peace, were not always content to follow passively to the nearest precinct station but sometimes chose instead to resist vehemently, arms flailing uncontrollably, kicking wildly, screaming insults, throwing well aimed-blows, or rolling in the street in such a manner as to require the summoning of additional police.[56]

The language of popular geography itself contained another tactic of ideological resistance—the practice of oral recalcitrance, the persistent utilization of deeply sedimented terms, of terms officially recognized prior to 1885. In short, the use of naming to recover memory and meaning. If Trebackarlånggatan had been transformed into Tegnérgatan, and Holländaregatan into Ölandsgatan, then people could still rely upon Trebackarlång and Holländaren as locational indicators for public bars situated upon their respective lengths. If, for the sake of simplicity, Västra Kapellgränd, Norra Kapellgränd, and Östra Kapellgränd (West, North, and East Chapel Lane, respectively) had been combined into one zigzagging Kapellgränd, then the older folk unifier Pelarbacken (The Colonnade Hill) could still be retained. If, in deference to a "famous place" near the city, Besvärsgatan (Troublesome Street) had lost its official identity to Brännkyrkagatan, then working-class residents of Södermalm and other parts of the city could still refer to its steeply inclined segment as Besvärsbacken. If Arbetaregatan (Workers' Street) had been elevated to St. Eriksgatan, then it apparently could still be spoken of as Arbetaregatan despite the conciliatory creation of another nearby street with the same name.[57] Moreover, characters in Henning Berger's novel Drömlandet (The Dreamland), verified by scholars as extremely accurate in its depiction of Stockholm in the late 1880s, by "custom" referred to Östermalm's Karlavägen (relabeled in homage to Kings Karl X Gustav, Karl XI, and Karl XII) as Esplanaden. And they also reminded themselves that what they spoke of as Norrmalmsgatan had become Biblioteksgatan and what they referred to as Ålandsgatan had been nominally incorporated into its westward continuation, the previously existing Mäster Samuelsgatan (Berger 1927:48–49; Lagerstedt 1963:120; Stahre et al. 1984:163–164, 300).

While these and other undocumented instances of street name persistence eventually faded away among generations born into the post-1885 nomenclature, gradually relinquished without clamor or protest, there were a few cases in which, right from the outset, a political battle was waged in order to preserve traditional usage. Backed by building owners, residents of Parisgränden (Paris Lane, after a seventeenth-century occupant of the area) fruitlessly petitioned the Standing Committee of the

City Council not to alter their street name to Observatoriegatan (Observatory Street) (Stockholm City Council 1886:14–15). The City Council claimed to be making the change because the street, situated in what was then Norrmalm (now Vasastaden), had an identically named counterpart in Södermalm. However, this argument was not particularly convincing, as the latter street also had its label altered at the same time. It has been conjectured that council members remained obstinate because they wished to eradicate all "incorrect" and "undesirable" mental associations, especially when generated from below, and since *paris*, when pronounced with an accent on the first syllable, was a lower Stockholmska (Stockholm dialect) pejorative for policemen patrolling in pairs (Stahre et al. 1984:223–224, 282). In the absence of any ideologically objectionable double meanings, the residents of Klara Östra and Klara Västra Kyrkogatan (East and West Klara Church Street), also aided by their landlords, successfully fended off their replacement by Axelsgatan and Kjellgrensgatan. Furthermore, despite opposition from a Standing Committee minority, who favored a more patriotic alternative, an unusual concession to previous popular usage was made when the name Strandvägen (Shore Road) was given to what was developing as Östermalm's most prestigious and palatial residential street (Stockholm City Council 1886:15–17, 21–22).

Perhaps the most gleefully fiendish resistance to the ideological heavy-handedness of 1885, the ultimate act of off-stage verbal truculence, the mentally boldest rejection of the (street) sign, the most cunning linguistic flip-of-the-tongue gambit for skirting domination, involved not the substitution of folk-geographic signifiers for official street names, not a Tokyoization of orientation in Stockholm,[58] but the ascription of a meaning of mocking obscenity to a "proper" street designation. At some indeterminate point during the late nineteenth century, *Arsenalsgatan* began to be used in some male working-class circles as a signifier for the "space" running from a woman's asshole-"anus" to her cunt-"pudenda."[59] In all likelihood, this usage was not merely a matter of simple ribald punning, of raucously flouting the taboos of "standard" Swedish, of countering the Oscarian proclivity for mentioning "indecent" body parts and functions only with circuitous and "cautious euphemisms" (Frykman and Löfgren 1985:69–70), of turning a local word on its end by playing upon the English "arse" and the English-Swedish "anal-" (*analöpping* = anus). At a deeper level, there appears to have been a slyer, more subtle semiotic sl(e)ight of mouth involved, an enlisting of forbidden body parts and functions to debase the affluent Other, an erection of a degrading, sexually laden link between local topography and those locally on top, a drafting of the tabooed in order to effect an "arsy-versy," "bass ackwards" inversion of social hierarchy, a turning of the local social world on its end by playing upon the geography of Arsenalsgatan (see Figure 5.5).[60]

Fig. 5.5 Arsenalsgatan from Gustaf Adolfs torg to Kungsträdgårdsgatan, or Snobbrännan (The Snob Gutter)

Source: Lundgren 1886.

At its western end, Arsenalsgatan merged into a large opening, Gustaf Adolfs torg, a square adorned at its midpoint with an equestrian statue of its namesake, King Gustav II Adolf, who had ruled Sweden from 1611 to 1632 and had maneuvered the country to its temporary position as a "Great Power." Flanking the three built sides of this opening in the central body of Stockholm were the Royal Opera House (whose reconstruction in the mid-1890s resulted in an especially grandiose and offensively dominant symbolic form), the Hereditary Prince's Palace (Arvfurstens palats), which housed the Foreign Ministry, and the Hotel Rydberg, one of the city's two most fashionable hotels, regarded then as a must for visiting wealthy travelers as well as discriminating late-evening diners (Lundin 1890:67–69). It would have been from these edifices that the wastefully dressed and the filthy rich, or those shitty with money, exited, from these edifices that the posh and powerful, including those directly responsible for street name revision, poured out into the city via the anal terminus of Arsenalsgatan. Period photographs indicate that Gustaf Adolfs torg also might have served as the "shitty," "asshole" end of Arsenalsgatan by virtue of the volume of horse droppings scattered there by passing and waiting passenger cabs; but this reference would not have been primary to the word game, as such sights—and smells—were common throughout Stockholm.

About two hundred meters to the east, after passing through the Royal Gardens, Arsenalsgatan intersected with Kungsträdgårdsgatan (Royal Gardens Street, less glamorously known as Östra Trädgårdsgatan, or East Garden Street, until 1885). We have already encountered this crossing thoroughfare in its folk-geographic version, Snobbrännan (The Snob Gutter).[61] As a "gutter," a dirty groove, a flowing channel, a rut for the morning display of feminine elegance, a vegetation-bordered furrow belonging to the city's finest, most splendidly dressed women,[62] this in the eyes of working-class males would have been the "cunt" to which Arsenalsgatan ran. Such a simultaneous turning on end of local word and local world, such a double cartwheel of meaning, would have been in keeping with the perceptions of those who were not blind to Oscarian hypocrisy, of those who knew full well of the contrast between the stiff demeanor and facade of respectable propriety worn by male Oscarians and their forced lia(y)isons with maidservants, their escapades in bordellos and the cigar store and laundry backrooms where women beneath them were the article of consumption (cf. Frykman and Löfgren 1985:72–73).

Postamble

The centrality of space to capitalism's repeated reconfigurations,
       restructurings,
       and self-reinventions,
is not confined
    to an association with time-space compressing episodes of new
        transportation
        or communications technology,
   to new landscapes of accumulation,
   to a new, large-scale, political and economic geographies,
   to shifts in the national and international division of labor,
   to new articulations of the local and global.
With the local transformations wrought by new forms of capital
there come new local spaces of modernity,
   new articulations of local space
     in the sense of new locational interdependencies,
       of new configurations of local difference and connectedness,
       of newly linked specialized areas,
       of newly joined sites of production, consumption, and residence,

and new articulations of local space,
  in the sense of newly authored daily paths of movement,
  in the sense of newly spoken languages,
    new discursive mediations of everyday life,
    new utterances for negotiating and representing local spaces,
    new expressions appropriate to the experiencing of those spaces,
    new meanings of the local map,
      that are parts of larger "maps of meaning,"
        of new symbolic topographies.[63]

Outside(rs) In and Inside(rs) Out: South Korean Capital Encounters Organized Labor in a California Industrial Suburb

It is ironic that 35 years ago we went over there to fight for them [in the Korean War] and now they're trying to put us in the god-damned poorhouse.
                                   Ken McGrew, unionized construction worker

A few years ago skeptics were predicting the demise of the steel industry in the United States. Fortunately, the pessimists were totally wrong. . . . We hope this [the USS-POSCO plant in Pittsburg, California] will be an inspiration—a blueprint for others to follow.
                                                   Gerald Ford, former President

A FINAL SHIFT IN FOCUS brings us to contemporary California and the traditional on-the-ground foe of capital in long-industrialized countries. In this closing (geographical-hi)story, the local appearance of newly guised capital elicits symbolic discontent—and political resistance— among two groups of organized labor. Here we witness the cultural and political responses of people who are already organized adversaries of capital, of people who—unlike Gambian peasants, most late-nineteenth-century working-class Stockholmers, or Islamic fundamentalists in northern Nigeria—are already institutionally joined to defend or assert themselves against the exploitative strategies of their actual or potential employers. Here, as globally triggered local restructuring unfolds, as a steel plant is re-modern-ized, as those included (and excluded) thereby experience yet another shock of modern-ity, we discover not a one-dimensional reworking, not a single, fixed focus of contestation, but a shifting terrain in which labor issues, over time, become issues of nationalism, moralism, and identity, only to become labor issues yet again.

On December 16, 1985, a joint-venture agreement was announced between USX Corporation, formerly known as U.S. Steel, and Pohang Iron & Steel Company Ltd., or POSCO, a company based in Pohang, South

Fig. 6.1 The Situation of Pittsburg within the San Francisco Bay Area
Metropolitan Complex

Korea, and nearly 70 percent owned by the government of that country
and its Development Bank. A seventy-eight-year-old steel mill operated
by USX in Pittsburg, California, an industrial town within the San Francisco Bay Area metropolitan complex (see Figure 6.1), was, by virtue of a
ninety-million-dollar payment, to become 50 percent owned by Pohang
and to function under a new name, USS-POSCO Industries. A pattern
was to be reversed. The plant was no longer to be threatened repeatedly
by layoffs or permanent shutdown. Instead, the facility that once provided jobs for more than five thousand steelworkers was to be renovated,
modernized, and expanded, at a projected cost of $350 million, thereby
making it the largest-ever South Korean investment in the United States.
Although the latest round of cutbacks had permanently deprived 665
steelworkers of their jobs between 1980 and 1985, the remaining 1,100
production laborers, office workers, sales workers, and managers could

now view their employment future with some degree of security. The mill that had made the cables for the Oakland-Bay Bridge, and that had been a long-time producer of tinplate for the neighboring Continental Can Company plant and other Bay Area can manufacturers, was to become, in the eyes of experts, "the world's most advanced cold steel finishing facility,"[1] employing computer-steered "continuous annealing lines" to turn out rolled products of various dimensions in an uninterrupted flow, rather than using older methods that required different customer specifications to be met one at a time.

With a projected annual capacity of 1.4 million tons, the revitalized mill was not only to manufacture an improved grade of tinplate for food and motor oil cans, but also high-quality cold-rolled sheets for office furniture and household appliances, as well as galvanized sheets for use in highway culverts, gutters, and other construction products. At the outset the Pittsburg mill was annually to rework four hundred thousand tons of steel coil imported from Pohang's South Korean facilities, with its remaining raw steel inputs coming from U.S. sources.[2] However, it was anticipated that the USS-POSCO plant would be able to obtain its unfinished steel entirely from South Korea beginning in the fall of 1989, when President Reagan's "voluntary" trade restraint agreement was due to expire. (This was not to come to pass, because of President Bush's decision to extend the steel import limits on twenty-nine nations until March 1992). The Pittsburg mill also was to be integrated into global networks of capital on the export side. Whereas its output had been previously marketed virtually exclusively to customers in the Western states, its new efficiency, flexibility, and high quality of production would permit competition with Japanese and other foreign steels in countries all around the Pacific Rim as well as elsewhere in the world.[3] (The production of better-quality steel would also permit the recapturing of some West Coast markets previously lost to the Japanese.)

The theoretical question of what the USS-POSCO plant was to become shifted to a matter of practice when, on April 6, 1989, former President Ford, with much ceremony and symbolic legitimation, threw a switch to launch full-scale operation of the facility's new production equipment. In so doing, in moving a lever from "off" to "on," he was figuratively closing one chapter and opening another in a tale of place-bound political struggle and cultural conflict precipitated by a particular articulation of the local and the global under conditions of late-twentieth-century capitalism. Although certain peripheral issues remained to be settled in the courts, although bitter memories were to linger, and although there were to be echoes elsewhere, completion of the mill's modernization in effect marked the end of a prolonged confrontation between discontented local building and construction trades workers and the agents of two corporations with global interests. At the same moment, the initiation of computerized milling equipment, and thereby the setting into motion of a newly defined labor process, marked the beginning of a new set of every-day contestations between on-the-line steelworkers and their South Korean and U.S. employers.

In some regards this two-part tale is characteristic of the local shocks of new experience associated with the highly dynamic universe of late-twentieth-century capitalism. In some regards this tale is characteristic of the episodes of practical and symbolic resistance associated with that highly unstable universe. But this tale is not in every sense characteristic of the locally particular political and cultural responses engendered by that universe of economic ephemerality and material flickering; by that universe of "flexible accumulation," rapid product change, and market uncertainty; by that universe of hypermobile money and continually churning and shifting investments; by that universe of geographical patterns of production, employment, and consumption in fitful flux. It is also an atypical tale to the extent it involves neither the movement of capital within and between the nations of the "First World" nor the dis-place-ment of "First World" capital to the "Third World" and "New Industrializing Countries," but a reverse flow, from an Asian "NIC" to a "First World" power.

If the Pittsburg-centered labor conflicts and their associated struggles over naming, meaning, and identity are especially distinctive because of the involvement of South Korean interests, because of a world of capital mobility turned outside in and downside up, then any interpretative un-packing of those contests first requires some historical-geographical con-textualization, some depiction of how local transformation came to be embedded in more far-reaching processes, some sketch of how foreign investors came to find an opportunity within a San Francisco Bay Area industrial suburb. Such a contextualization most appropriately begins with a brief account of the U.S. iron and steel industry in general and of the strategic behavior of the U.S. Steel Corporation under conditions of sectorwide crisis in particular.

Steeling Up after the Worst:
The Road of Joint-Venture Capital to Pittsburg

Global Crisis and the
Decline of the U.S. Iron and Steel Industry

In the aftermath of the severe recession of 1974, the steel industry was beset by a worldwide crisis, which deepened in the 1980s, following the tightly sequenced recessions of 1979–1980 and 1981–1983, and which took a particularly heavy toll on U.S. production. Raw steel output in the United States, which had reached a peak of 136.8 million metric tons in 1973, oscillated downward to 109.6 million metric tons in 1981, and then collapsed in 1982 to 67.7 million metric tons, never to fully recover throughout the remainder of the eighties.[4] This extended decline brought massive unemployment and attendant suffering to steel producing cities and towns across the country; between 1980 and 1987 alone, branchwide employment fell by nearly 60 percent, from 399,000 to 163,000.[5] There were, as well, tremendous capital losses incurred: "Over the five year period from 1982 to 1986 the industry lost $12 billion . . . [while more than] 25 steel companies, including large steelmakers like LTV and Wheeling-Pittsburgh, filed bankruptcy proceedings" (Howell et al. 1988:501).

As most analysts would have it, the dramatic downfall of the U.S. iron and steel industry was closely intertwined with ongoing global developments within the industry.[6] Steel production capacity outside the United States had been increasing precipitously for some time prior to 1974. Non-U.S. capacity had grown almost 500 percent between 1950 and that date,[7] in no small measure because often-overoptimistic or -unrealistic governments in Japan, Europe, and elsewhere had implemented policies providing investment incentives, subsidies, and tariff protection for domestic steel producers in order to promote national industrialization schemes and economic growth. Thus, "with far too many steelmaking facilities . . . built for national markets, or the world market, to support," the global crisis that developed in the steel industry after 1974 "was fundamentally a crisis of overcapacity, a gross imbalance between supply and demand. . . . When world steel demand fell off sharply after 1974, prices plummeted as steel producers desperately sought to maintain their operating rates and to find outlets for their surpluses. Facilities on which construction had begun prior to 1974 continued to come on stream for the remainder of the decade, and altogether new capacity was added, compounding an already serious overcapacity problem" (Howell et al. 1988:2). Remarkably, yet further capacity was brought into operation in Brazil and other "developing" countries with assistance from the World Bank, the Inter-American Development Bank, and, especially, major private banks of the industrialized world, who were feverishly seeking outlets for overaccumulated petrodollars.[8] As new steel plants began functioning within their borders, "developing country governments established import restrictions to protect them, with the result that traditional export outlets for mills in the [U.S. and other] industrialized countries were progressively foreclosed at the very moment that other world markets were contracting. At the same time, developing country suppliers, eager to establish themselves in international markets, launched vigorous export drives" (Howell et al. 1988:5).

Already engulfed in an overcapacity crisis of global proportions, and having to compete against foreign manufacturers who used more technologically advanced plants and efficient equipment to turn out superior products, the U.S. steel industry was brought to its knees during the early eighties by the rapid appreciation of the dollar's value. Reagan's successful push for large tax cuts and greater military spending had significantly increased the federal budget deficit, thereby forcing the government to borrow large sums, consequently further driving up interest rates (already made high by oil-based inflation and Federal Reserve policies) and making the dollar extremely attractive to international currency speculators. With the value of the dollar thus forced upward, the profitability of U.S. producers was negatively hit in at least four ways. First, world export prices, when converted to dollars, fell sharply, thus easing the entry of foreign steels into U.S. markets.[9] Second, as labor costs abroad fell sharply in dollar terms, automobiles, a wide range of machinery, and other steel-intensive goods of foreign origin also were able to make huge inroads into U.S. markets, thus reducing domestic production in those branches and further diminishing demand for the output of U.S. steel mills. Domestic demand shrunk further as automobile manufacturers— caught up in a global overcapacity crisis of their own—increasingly turned to the production of fuel-efficient vehicles, and thereby increasingly substituted aluminium, plastics, and other lightweight inputs for steel. Third, high interest rates and an expensive dollar magnified the indebtedness of "Third World" countries and enormously reduced their capacity to import steel-based manufactures from the United States or anywhere else. Finally, with additional equipment idled for all of these reasons, the cost-competitiveness of U.S. producers was further undermined—until drastic measures were taken—since production costs per ton in the steel industry are significantly dependent upon the level of capacity utilization.

The difficulties experienced by the U.S. steel industry's major producers during the early and mid-eighties were not only intensified by the dumping tactics occasionally employed in U.S. markets by manufacturers based in Japan, Argentina, Spain and elsewhere. They were further exacerbated by the competitive position of domestic minimills and by frequently poor, if not derelict, management.

Minimills neither require the use of coking coal and iron ore nor demand the presence of coke ovens and blast furnaces, as they melt scrap in an electric arc furnace to yield molten steel, which is then usually processed into standard bar products, small structural shapes, and wire rods. Such mills, which initially mushroomed from 1968 to 1977 and then continued to increase in number during the persistent crisis,[10] could sell high-volume products at lower prices,[11] not only because of their much lower level of investment per ton of capacity[12] but also because they had been principally located at sites in Florida, Texas, and elsewhere in the South and Southwest, where local demand was high and where, in the face of feeble union strength, labor costs could be kept at levels sometimes less than half those of the older, larger-scaled, integrated iron and steel mills operated by the major steel corporations (Bensman and Lynch 1988:86; Barnett and Schorsch 1983:83–103).

There appears to be a consensus among experts that the leading U.S. steel-producing corporations have been plagued by mismanagement and executive incompetence throughout the post-1974 era and the years immediately preceding it. Typically, older, inefficient plants were either starved of the capital necessary for modernization, or funds were so (mal)invested as to create mediocre facilities rather than truly cost-competitive mills. Shortsightedness resulted in an initial gross underestimation of the competitive potential of the minimills. And, the introduction of technological innovations to counter foreign competitors was frequently incompatible with a management philosophy that emphasized short-term financial dealings much more than the long-term production of goods. Management in U.S. Steel and the other leading corporations was extremely hierarchical, both inside and outside the plant, and so authoritarian, so often patronizing and arrogant to those at the bottom, so demanding of strict adherence to rules and regulations, so fixed on employee control, so protective of its unilateral "right" to run production, so intent upon minimizing any form of local-level consultation with union officials, so wedded to Tayloristic "scientific management" and "the theory that employees don't want to be involved in their work," that it was unable "to see that labor could contribute ideas and commitment that might arrest . . . decline," that it was unable "to involve the union officials, much less the workers, in cooperative efforts to improve the work process."[13] Moreover, the headquarters executives of U.S. Steel and some other "Big Eight" firms "allowed nepotism, poor coordination, and corruption to flourish under their supervision because, in the days when the American steel oligopoly dominated world markets, U.S. Steel [and other corporations] could afford to be lax."[14]

Cutting Back and Cracking Down:
The Strategic Responses of U.S. Steel

During 1982 U.S. Steel had lost $154 for each ton of output it had shipped (Hoerr 1988:426). By the time these extreme conditions came to prevail, it was obvious that corporate survival called for drastic measures. It would no longer suffice merely to press authorities in Washington for import restrictions, as had been the case in 1968 and 1976, when firm representatives led the industry's efforts to prevent the further dumping of Japanese and European steel in U.S. markets. Although, in 1982, U.S. Steel's chairman, David Roderick, once again helped to spearhead lobbying efforts that resulted in a three-year import-control agreement with the European Community, two other major strategies had already been set in motion. Roderick stepped up the company's shift of investments into nonsteel activities, which had begun in 1976, raising funds by taking advantage of tax code provisions, and using write-off incentives to shut sixty-three production units between his assumption of office in 1979 and the end of 1982. Having pronounced that "U.S. Steel is in business to make profits, not to make steel" (Bensman and Lynch 1988:88), he launched an intensified diversification scheme—emphasizing oil and gas, chemical industry, and real estate investments—which peaked with the $6.4 billion purchase of Marathon Oil Company in December 1981 (a move that helped justify the eventual renaming of U.S. Steel to USX Corporation).

Roderick's other strategic thrust, that of, in his own words, "cracking down on labor," was in keeping with his corporation's deeply sedimented antiunion pattern of behavior, and was soon encouraged by Reagan's firing of the air traffic controllers and the quick emergence, under his administration, of a Labor Department and National Labor Relations Board that were openly antagonistic to organized labor.[15] By virtue of several decades of strong organization and the previous global hegemony of U.S. steel firms, members of the United Steelworkers were able to conclude a series of three-year industrywide settlements during the 1970s that made them "the highest paid industrial workers in the United States, if not the world" (Hoerr 1988:15). But in 1982, U.S. Steel—burdened by interest payments on its Marathon Oil purchase as well as huge operating losses—joined other producers in demanding wage concessions. The concessions, when eventually granted in early 1983, still left its employees at wage-and-benefit levels more than twice those of Japanese workers.[16] To further reduce costs, plant supervisors were ordered to lower the number of labor hours per ton of steel from 7.5 to 4.0. Superintendents were to achieve this goal in part by intensifying labor through combining what had been narrowly defined job crafts and cutting crew size, in part "by contracting out as much work as possible," not only in the realm of equipment maintenance and custodial services, but also in the province of temporary and part-time shop floor jobs.[17] The pressure exerted on labor was further increased in 1983 when, because postrecession steel demand was only recovering weakly, the management of U.S. Steel decided to write off more major assets, decided to eliminate the financial hemorrhaging associated with the maintenance of unused and underutilized facilities, decided to dramatize the need for further import restrictions by resuming plant closures and massive job layoffs before the end of the year. While plant closure decisions were to depend on such purely economic considerations as market accessibility, degree of obsolescence, and estimated modernization costs, they also were to depend upon the "cooperativeness" of labor, or the willingness of union locals to accept crew size modifications, the combination of previously separate crafts, new job assignments, other work rule changes, early retirements, and the eventuality of further wage and benefit reductions (Hoerr 1988:437–443).

It was in this "labor crackdown" climate, in this threatening atmosphere where, effectively, locals were pitted against one another, in this environment of fear where U.S. Steel plants were actually permanently shut down near Cleveland, in Trenton, New Jersey, and at several Pennsylvania locations, in this confrontational setting where recalcitrant locals were attacked in pungently worded newspaper advertisements,[18] that the leadership of Pittsburg's Local 1440 proved sufficiently pliable to preserve the jobs of 1,100 of its members, sufficiently pliable to leave management open to the possibility of modernizing a mill whose deepwater port location and market accessibility advantages were being severely undermined by Asian steel producers, not the least of whom was Pohang Iron & Steel Company.

The Outsider Gets Inside:
The Genesis of POSCO's Investment

The South Korean corporation that placed its capital in Pittsburg was not a long-established and managerially conservative behemoth like its joint-venture partner, but a young, quickly rising, and innovative force in the arena of global steel competition. In conjunction with an ambitious, export-oriented, heavy-manufacturing-emphasizing industrial expansion program developed by South Korea's military dictatorship, the Pohang Iron & Steel Company, or POSCO, was established in 1968 as an entity more or less under the complete control of the state.[19] Run throughout its twenty-two-year history by Park Tae Joon, a retired general plucked from relative obscurity, its first plant, a state-of-the-art integrated facility situated at the east coast port of Pohang did not go into operation until 1973, when it began producing at a rate of 1.0 million metric tons of raw steel per year.[20] Fueled, against World Bank advice, by preferential loans at low interest rates, the Pohang plant underwent a series of expansions, which brought its production capacity to 9.1 million metric tons in 1983, the same year in which construction of a second plant was initiated at Kwangyang, a small south coast settlement with a superior harbor. When the second unit of the extensively automated and computerized Kwangyang plant was completed in August 1988, Pohang's total capacity of 14.5 million metric tons made it the second largest producer in the world. In mid-1988 it was anticipated that once additional Kwangyang mills came on line, POSCO, still 70 percent controlled by the state, would be on a par with the current global leader, Nippon Steel.[21] POSCO benefited from its highly productive and efficient technology (much of which was improved upon after being aggressively transferred from Japan and Europe), from government-restricted wage levels that gave it "one of the lowest labor costs per ton of any integrated steel mill in the world" (Howell et al. 1988:299), from an extraordinary emphasis on worker training and the imposition of militarylike discipline on its employees, and from "special treatment on price and credit terms for its raw materials" (ibid.:298), as well as from a repeated broadening of its product line and the expansion of protected domestic shipbuilding, automobile, and construction markets. It further benefited from complete income tax exemption until 1982 (and special favorable rates thereafter), from government subsidization of its capital costs and infrastructure investments, from various government export-promoting financial incentives, and from determined, zealous management, which, among other things, placed a great emphasis on quality control. Consequently, by the time of its joint-venture involvement, POSCO was one of the world's lowest-cost steel producers and was able to sell at prices 15 to 50 percent below those of its major Japanese, Taiwanese, and U.S. competitors. It was thereby able to capture many of Japan's key Southeast Asian outlets and to make dramatic incursions into markets in the Western United States, Canada, Australia, and elsewhere around the Pacific Rim.

POSCO's mercurial ascendance during an extended global slump in demand, its aggressive maneuvering in the face of oversupplied markets, did not fail to arouse concern or elicit opposition. In 1982 Canadian manufacturers filed dumping charges, protesting that South Korean–welded steel pipe was being sold under the cost of production; and one year later, "the Canadian government found that 100 percent" of the wide-flanged beams being imported from South Korea "had been dumped at margins averaging 34.9 percent." Between 1982 and 1985, U.S. producers had submitted "a spate of antidumping and countervailing duty complaints against Korea," having become especially annoyed after 1984, when the share of the total U.S. market for pipes, tubes, and wire nails held by POSCO and secondary South Korean firms "reached a startling 34 percent" (ibid.:304). With the South Korean government's—which still owned 69.1 percent of POSCO—having been forced into an agreement in February of 1985 to limit exports to the United States for five years, retroactive to October 1, 1984, and with the very real prospect of further acts of protectionism by both the United States and the European Community; the management of POSCO was driven to consider measures that would place it inside, rather than outside, the wall of trade restrictions.[22] An unintegrated, or cold-finishing, facility of the type existing at Pittsburg was especially attractive because, in the long-run at least, it appeared to guarantee a U.S. market for 1.4 million metric tons of POSCO's annual raw production. Through providing a sizable infusion of capital and technology, through publicly proclaiming its welcoming of the opportunity "to help America retool its aging steel industry," through repeatedly pronouncing a desire thereby "to support the U.S. in its leading function in the Free World," POSCO further entertained the possibility of future favorable trade arrangements with respect to other of its products.[23] Moreover, although POSCO would have to pay at least $180 million of the bill for plant renovation and expansion, the joint venture in Pittsburg also was appealing because it provided recruitment-free access to skilled, experienced steelworkers and it allowed entry without the problems of site selection and land procurement.

The Renovation and Expansion of the Pittsburg Facility: A Construction of Struggle

This is the biggest job ever to go non-union in our own back yard. It sent a shock wave through organized labor . . . but this woke labor up. What they did is they woke the sleeping giant.

Nathan Koburn, unionized construction worker

In the months following the formation of a joint venture between Pohang Iron & Steel Company and USX Corporation, the new entity, USS-POSCO Industries, set about designing the Pittsburg plant's modernization and putting the construction project out for bids.[24] When it was revealed in January 1987 that the project contract had been awarded to an "open shop" firm, BE & K Construction Company of Birmingham, Alabama, a foundation was laid for conflict with local unionized construction workers and their umbrella organization, the Contra Costa (County) Building and Construction Trades Council (hereafter referred to simply as the Contra Costa Council).

The selection of BE & K, which had obtained the contract by submitting a bid forty-five million dollars lower than any of its five competing unionized contractors, was especially provocative because of the company's previous performance and reputation. BE & K was not just another "open shop" employer. Specializing in construction and maintenance-service provision primarily for the pulp and paper industries, and secondarily for the oil-refining, petrochemical, and power industries, BE & K had taken only fifteen years to develop an annual business volume of about one billion dollars and become the country's thirty-second ranking construction company as well as its largest strictly "open shop" building contractor.[25] The founder and president of BE & K, Ted C. Kennedy, had served as president of the Associated Builders and Contractors (ABC), which, with its nineteen thousand members, was the most politically influential association of nonunion contractors in the United States. Very shortly after securing the USS-POSCO contract, Kennedy took on the chairmanship of a new ABC "emergency panel," which was to counter initiatives recently undertaken by various building trades unions concerned about their diminishing share of the nation's construction activity.[26] BE & K had not only gained a widespread "union-busting" reputation within organized labor circles but also had become notorious as a "strikebreaking" firm because of its provision of largely out-of-state equipment-maintenance workers to strikebound pulp and paper plants. In the spring of 1987, BE & K was providing about 250 such workers to the International Paper Company's strike-afflicted Androscoggin Mill in Maine.[27]

BE & K submitted its significantly lower bid with the intent of paying wages considerably under the union rates then prevailing in northern California. One estimate puts the average hourly construction wages actually paid during 1987 by BE & K and its eventual partners at $12.39, including benefits. The corresponding average figure arrived at for an area within a seventy-five-mile radius from Pittsburg was $27.97.[28] Given the publicity surrounding the USS-POSCO joint venture, as well as the expected magnitude of union reactions, BE & K spokespeople were quickly forced to defend the company's hiring and payment practices. They immediately asserted that, as a "merit shop" (or open shop) company, which awarded subcontracts to the lowest bidder, BE & K had never failed to use at least one union subcontractor on any of its major jobs.[29] The company soon further contended that it "provide[d] employment opportunities for workers who otherwise would be locked out of the construction industry by providing jobs to unskilled people and offering training along with the work experience." Kennedy himself claimed that BE & K "trainees move through skills much faster than union apprenticeship programs allow," that the firm's "Wheels of Learning" scheme was "a more efficient method of training craftsmen than union programs," and that "when we leave we will leave behind a better trained work force." Most chillingly to union members, he rationalized that BE & K planned "to bid on other projects in the area and the people being trained now will provide a qualified work force for future projects."[30]

USS-POSCO also had to explain its selection of BE & K to the public. E. A. Roskovensky, the USS-POSCO president, maintained that "every effort" to select an all-union contractor had been made. He further noted: "We tried to work with them [the building trades council]. But this particular industry is not one that can afford to spend any extra money on anything. Look at the steel companies now in bankruptcy."[31] It was suggested, in essence, that both the plant's ability to compete in national and international markets and the job security of hundreds of steelworkers would be jeopardized unless the modernization project was completed at the lowest possible cost.

Regardless of the precise content of the public statements made by BE & K and USS-POSCO representatives, a vigorous response by the leadership and rank-and-file members of local construction unions was virtually ensured by the very dimensions of the Pittsburg-project award— at $350 million it represented the highest nonunion construction award in California history. Fearful of the implications of the contract for future large-scale projects in the area, intent upon preventing its local commercial construction market from being substantially eroded by nonunion contractors in the same manner as its residential construction market had been, and shored up by the recent successful efforts of its counterpart in adjacent Alameda County, which had undermined the nonunion assignment of the state's largest-ever highway contract,[32] the Contra Costa

Building and Construction Trades Council soon adopted a number of practical resistance tactics, which were supported morally and in more substantial ways by the California Building Trades Council. What quickly became at issue in the deployment of these tactics was not only the forfeiture of most of the projected eight hundred to nine hundred construction jobs to nonunion men and women, but also the surrender of a substantial share of those work opportunities to out-of-state and other distant residents. Almost from the outset, the building trades unions affiliated with the Contra Costa Council had grounds to suspect that BE & K would not hire about 85 percent of its employees from eastern Contra Costa County as it had publicly promised[33]—that it would instead import people willing to work at its low wages from beyond California, and especially from the Gulf Coast and Southeastern states in which the firm was already most active.

The Practical Tactics Assembled

The terrain of practical, political struggle for the Contra Costa Council and its rank-and-file members encompassed two fronts. At a commanding position stood USS-POSCO, which somehow was to be maneuvered into terminating its original contract and picking another contractor who willingly would pay union-scale wages. Off to one side stood the assigned contractor, whose operations somehow were to be hindered—BE & K, or AMK International as it came to be known legally once BE & K took on two smaller project partners in May of 1987.[34] (In the public and private discourses associated with the struggle, which went on for over two years, the term of reference for the contractor was most often BE & K rather than AMK International, or simply AMK.) The tactics eventually deployed on that terrain for the most part fell into three, sometimes overlapping, types: the mobilization of elected officials and other political figures; the identification of regulatory violations and the initiation of legal challenges; and the recourse to conventional picket line protests and larger-scale demonstrations.

The Mobilization of Elected Officials   With the aid of the California Building Trades Council and two well-connected Washington and Los Angeles political consulting firms retained by that parent group, members of the Contra Costa Council very rapidly found themselves supported by powerful politicians. (Such support was in keeping with the influence exerted in Democratic party circles by the unusually strong county-level central labor councils of the San Francisco Bay Area.) On February 27, 1987, eighteen members of the California congressional delegation, including Senator Alan Cranston, dispatched a letter to USS-POSCO in which they observed that the BE & K contract will "seriously undermine local wage rates among members of the construction trades" and thereby urged the drafting of a replacement contract "consistent with the best economic interests both of local residents and the joint venture."[35] In the state legislature, Senator Dan Boatwright soon introduced a joint resolution imploring President Reagan and Congress to reconsider trade agreements with South Korea in retaliation for the contract award to BE & K. At the first major rally called in support of unionized Contra Costa construction workers, the chairman of the State Assembly's Labor and Employment Committee, Richard Floyd, put in an appearance to decry the BE & K contract as not in keeping with a California "where you get a fair day's pay for a fair day's work."[36] Before 1987 was out, Floyd also was persuaded to have his committee hold a hearing in Pittsburg where the safety record of BE & K was "assailed by union officials and former . . . employees."[37]

Support from political heavyweights in Washington and Sacramento provided backing that was high in symbolic value and low in concrete yield. The Contra Costa Council therefore sought to achieve more substantial results through intervening with less exalted local political figures, through inserting itself into the "politics of place" with actions aimed at the County Board of Supervisors, and by exploiting the fact that the organization directly above it—the Central Labor Council of Contra Costa County—was in many ways the backbone of the county's Democratic party.[38] Already in 1986, before BE & K was even chosen to oversee the Pittsburg modernization project, the Contra Costa Council attempted to influence the county supervisors' deliberations over new land-use controls for plant expansions, pressing for stricter rules and thereby signaling to USS-POSCO that failure to select a unionized contractor could prove troublesome, could lead to confrontation, and could precipitate project-delaying obstructionist tactics.[39]

Less than two months after the contract award to BE & K, a majority of the Board of Supervisors appeared to be taking sides. Expressing a concern that foreign industrial investments might constitute a threat to local workers, the board designated a committee to study the impact of such investments on the Contra Costa County labor market and, in addition, specifically requested BE & K "to explain if it plans to hire from the local labor force."[40] Apparently not insensitive to the construction-labor sympathizers who packed their meetings in Martinez (the county seat), the full board and its various committees, or the agencies they had called upon, were by early summer investigating a number of union allegations regarding BE & K and the USS-POSCO project. These included charges that inadequate worker benefits were being paid by BE & K, that pickets were being assaulted, that there were various instances of worker-safety neglect, that the welding performed at the construction site was inadequate, largely as a result of the use of insufficiently experienced labor, and that drug testing was being used to discriminate against local job seekers.[41]

It was especially around the issue of distant labor recruitment that the Contra Costa Council was able to mobilize visible support from the Board of Supervisors. By June of 1987 the board's Internal Operations Committee began holding a series of meetings on wages and hiring practices, at which testimony was presented by both union representatives and managers from BE & K and USS-POSCO. At the first session a spokesperson for the carpenters union claimed that only 33 percent of those on the job were local residents. On the basis of a count made by picket line participants, and a check of Department of Motor Vehicle records, he asserted that 122 of 280 nonunion employees driving into the plant construction site had cars with out-of-state license plates and another 52 had cars with California plates but came from more than one hundred miles away.[42] Nine months later, after repeated charges, the committee recommended that the full board request the California Highway Patrol "to step up ticketing of out-of-state license plates," and, in so doing, expressed a concern that out-of-state workers were not immediately registering their vehicles as state law required, thereby "depriving the county of its share of registration fees." At the same session the committee also recommended that "the Health Services Department begin investigating complaints that [out-of-state] workers without homes are sleeping at job sites and [thereby] violating county health laws."[43] Although the highway patrol had previously cited individual BE & K-employed license-law transgressors, it went about matters much more methodically once the board took action. During July and August of 1988, the highway patrol first posted an undercover surveillance van to observe cars and trucks entering and leaving the Pittsburg plant premises, then established a surprise registration checkpoint at the plant exit, which netted 160 delinquent construction workers in 1.5 hours, and finally conducted another two thunderbolt operations, which trapped an additional 76 violators.[44]

Not too long before the highway patrol measures, in apparent response to pressures regarding the issue of out-of-state workers, BE & K attempted to recruit local high school seniors. This elicited "alarm" from at least one member of the Board of Supervisors, Sunne McPeak, who publicly referred to the labor practices of BE & K as "despicable" and added that it was "very, very disturbing that they're going to younger and younger people while many trained union laborers are jobless."[45]

Legal challenges

We're in a no win situation. The building trades union is going to stage public relations events; they're going to trump up legal challenges they know won't go anywhere. It's guerilla public relations—it's hit-and-run and they keep doing it.
                    Scott Robertson, BE & K Construction Company spokesperson

Every time something goes wrong it's: "The building trades did this, the building trades did this." Well, they broke the law. We didn't make the rules. Those are rules everybody plays by.

Greg Feere, business manager of the Contra Costa Building and Construction Trades' Council

From the very opening of the Pittsburg-centered struggle, the Contra Costa Council sought to discourage USS-POSCO and encumber the progress of BE & K through a steady series of legal challenges, developed with the assistance of lawyers provided by the California Building Trades Council.[46] The intent was not, as Robertson's remark suggests, simply to prove a short-term nuisance and to drive BE & K to distraction with chanceless challenges. Tom Adams, an environmental lawyer assisting the Contra Costa Council, from the outset indicated that he was "prepared to tie up the project for years with lawsuits on land use, water quality, and hazardous waste permits."[47] Within fifteen months of the contract assignment, more than forty lawsuits and unfair labor practice charges had been made against the contractor and the joint venture, resulting in, among other things, a subsequently appealed sixty million-dollar arbitration award based on the exclusive use of nonunion labor by Eichleay Corporation, one of BE & K's two junior partners, in violation of a national agreement to hire solely unionized cement masons.[48] If BE & K could not actually be hindered from completing its obligations, a clearly discouraging message regarding legal difficulties, delays, and daunting expenses was to be sent to other would-be participants in the local commercial construction market.

With respect to land use, lawyers appealed to the Board of Supervisors to halt construction until a land use permit application was submitted by USS-POSCO, as a recently passed ordinance stated that industries using or generating a given quantity of toxic chemicals were required to obtain such a permit before initially building or expanding. Having failed at this, they filed a suit on June 7, 1987, contending that the county was legally bound to regulate the Pittsburg modernization project.[49]

Legal actions taken on the environmental front included the filing of a suit alleging that workers were being illegally exposed to various toxic substances. In the wake of that suit, and the building permit commotion, the U.S. Environmental Protection Agency (EPA) initially cited USS-POSCO for violating the Clean Air Act by not applying for a permit from that agency. According to the EPA notice, a permit was required since the modernized and expanded plant would "add at least 15 million tons of particulates per year to the air" as well as "soot and other pollutants that can cause respiratory problems."[50] Shortly thereafter, following a "random" surprise inspection, the EPA fined USS-POSCO twenty thousand dollars, primarily for improperly handling the PCBs (polychlorinated biphenyls) contained within some of the steel plant's transformers.[51] Legal moves by union lawyers also helped to entangle USS-POSCO with both the Bay Area Air Quality Management District and the California Regional Water Quality Board. In the latter instance, Contra Costa Council lawyers hired an environmental management consultant who testified that the waste discharges made by USS-POSCO into an adjacent portion of the Sacramento Delta were very probably "responsible for [the] elevated levels of chromium and other heavy metals" found in shellfish there.[52]

When precarious working conditions at the construction site became evident almost immediately, safety issues were converted into another avenue for legal troublemaking. In May 1987, following the filing of the toxic substance exposure suit and an incident in which a laborer burned his feet by stepping in a hole containing acid-contaminated water, the workers of two of BE & K's unionized subcontractors were pulled off the job for seven working days after a lawyer asserted that "concrete pilings were being driven into ground containing high acid levels."[53] In the ensuing nine months, one employee was killed after being run over by a truck carrying steel reinforcing rods, another construction worker lost his life when an electrical shock forced him to fall ninety feet from an overhead crane, and two other workers were hospitalized when a cable on a radio-operated crane snapped. Although the two fatal accidents helped convince the State Assembly's Labor and Employment Committee to hold its aforementioned Pittsburg hearing (and thereby provide a public forum for union lawyers), and although those same tragedies led to citations and fines from the federal Occupational Safety and Health Administration (OSHA), it was the submission of a formal complaint to OSHA after the cable-snapping incident that proved most irksome for BE & K and its nonunionized subcontractors. This legal challenge prompted a "comprehensive investigation" that ultimately resulted in fines of at least $21,200, as well as citations requiring the correction of sixty-nine "serious" violations, regarding, among other things, electrical hazards; the provision of guardrails, safety nets, and scaffold-access ladders; the face and eye protection of welders; the use of safety belts and lifelines; lead-contamination exposure; and the operation of heavy equipment beside inadequately shored-up, worker-occupied excavations.[54] Soon afterwards, two members of the Board of Supervisors were finally moved by Contra Costa Council arguments to call for a "full-blown investigation" by OSHA into a 1985 roof fire, which apparently had exposed steelworkers to asbestos and had not been reported to state and federal authorities as required by law.[55]

Other legal challenges included a suit brought on behalf of out-of-state workers who were allegedly "persuaded or induced" to come to Pittsburg through "false or misleading representations." BE & K was specifically charged with "misrepresenting its wages, hours and benefits and not disclosing there was a labor dispute at the facility."[56]Yet another suit charged that pickets had been intentionally struck by certain cars.[57]

Cementing Solidarity: Picket Line Protests and Public Demonstrations   Before BE & K and its associates were able to get plant modernization under way, a crowd of five hundred to seven hundred workers affiliated with the Contra Costa Council and other Bay Area unionized construction groups gathered in an organized, but boisterous, rally outside the Korean Consulate in San Francisco to protest the hiring of the Alabama-based open shop contractor. This extensively planned February manifestation—primarily aimed at the Korean half of the USS-POSCO joint venture—was highly successful in the sense that it was endorsed by the California Federation of Labor, it brought out several prominent labor movement speakers, and it attracted major media attention throughout the state. All the same, it was a tactical gesture that did not easily lend itself to repetition; among other reasons, there were logistical problems in assembling large numbers of Contra Costa County workers at the consulate's location. Closer-to-home, and for the most part more modestly scaled, protest actions soon came to dominate direct rank-and-file participation in the political struggle against the new, nonlocally centered form of capital that had appeared in Pittsburg. However, a large number of Contra Costa Council members did again congregate in San Francisco on March 7, 1988, in order to join five thousand Bay Area construction workers demonstrating—raucously and otherwise—outside the annual convention of the Associated Builders and Contractors, the major "open shop" contractor organization previously led by BE & K's Ted Kennedy.[58]

Some weeks after the April 1987 commencement of construction, groups of at least twelve to twenty weekday pickets normally gathered at the gates of the USS-POSCO facility, with their numbers sometimes increasing to fifty or more on Saturday afternoons, when workers who were alternatively employed or had other Monday-to-Friday commitments were able to donate their time and physical presence.[59] In a strictly practical, as opposed to symbolic, sense these picketers occasionally exercised agency by collecting out-of-state license plate data (subsequently brought before the Board of Supervisors[60]), by distributing handbills to BE & K employees, and by attempting orally to persuade those same individuals that their conditions of work were extremely unsafe as well as unjust to others. Contra Costa Council representatives claimed that partly as a result of the latter two tactics, there were single days when as many as seventy-five BE & K workers quit. Members of Cement Masons Local 825 initiated the first picket line and were especially active thereafter, being fired up by their understanding that one of BE & K's two minor-interest partners was party to a national collective bargaining agreement that obligated the firm solely to hire union workers.[61]

In conjunction with special circumstances the number of men and women demonstrating outside the USS-POSCO gates swelled considerably. About 100 protestors moved to the plant from a City Hall ceremony marking a sister-city agreement between Pittsburg and Pohang. A moral support rally drew 250 to 400 building trades workers from throughout the Bay Area. A "birthday party" held to commemorate one year's construction activity drew large numbers of demonstrators, as did a pre-Christmas food giveaway at the site for the unemployed and needy arranged by the Contra Costa Council and a pre–Labor Day barbecue at the picket line location.[62]

Because of their convenient evening hours, and because of the political centrality of specific agenda items, certain meetings of the County Board of Supervisors brought out large numbers of the rank and file. When the board held hearings on the possibility of interrupting construction until USS-POSCO submitted a land-use permit application, over 500 persons were in attendance and "more than 200 people had to leave the crowded board chambers before the county fire marshall's office gave approval for the meeting to go on."[63] Attendance levels also were particularly high when the wages and hiring practices of BE & K were up for discussion. On more than one occasion a police presence was necessary to prevent any physical confrontation between protesting construction union members and those local interest representatives who saw considerable economic promise in the plant modernization project.[64] As time went on, and as the political struggle to undermine BE & K intensified, members of the various Contra Costa Council unions also became accustomed to making demonstrative appearances at relevant meetings of the Bay Area Air Quality Management District, the Regional Water Quality Board, and the Pittsburg City Council.

The most media-visible and grandly scaled demonstration mounted by the local building trades unions and their rank and file centered around a March 19, 1988, campaign speech delivered by Jesse Jackson at the football field of Pittsburg's Los Medanos College. Following the speech—which was co-sponsored by the Contra Costa Council, the East County Rainbow Coalition, and several other groups collectively known as the Labor Community Coalition for Peace, Jobs and Justice—a crowd estimated at ten thousand participants marched to the USS-POSCO plant to voice their collective dissatisfaction with the presence of BE & K. This peaking of publicly visible protest activities, which came less than two weeks after the huge anti–Associated Builders and Contractors demonstration in San Francisco, was coordinated with sympathy actions elsewhere in California, including smaller protests at other locations, the leafleting of customers and passersby at selected Hyundai auto dealerships, and a work stoppage by four thousand or more longshoremen at a number of California ports from Eureka to the Mexican border.[65] The supportive action by the longshoremen, the first of its kind in thirty years, was motivated by a concern that unfinished steel destined for the USS-POSCO plant would be unloaded by nonunion laborers once a planned deep-water addition to port facilities at Pittsburg came into operation, thereby leading to a deterioration of wages and benefits.[66]

The last gasp of public protest occurred on April 6, 1989, as a morning prelude and afternoon accompaniment to corporate ceremonies celebrating completion of the modernization project. About four hundred construction union members and Korean War veterans rallied at the main gate of the USS-POSCO plant, yet again to hear union officials and local politicians decry the use of low-paid, out-of-state labor. Far from being totally dispirited, speakers did not only assert, "They've [USS-POSCO] given us the will, the means and they have shown us what to do to protect our rights." They also held out the hope that USS-POSCO would award a seventy-five-million-dollar contract to union-hiring construction firms for the renovation of a galvanizing line that was to commence in 1990.[67]

From beginning to end, the participation of the construction unions' rank and file in picket lines, in appearances before the Board of Supervisors, and in demonstrations and rallies obviously involved something more than their mere physical presence, than their mere bodily engagement in a political struggle, than their mere corpo-real insertion in a localized clash between capital and labor. Through their physical involvement, their concrete practices of protest, and their hearing accounts of actions undertaken by comrades, they accumulated a stockpile of more or less common experiences and more or less identical knowledge; they assembled elements of a collective memory; they internalized a highly similar perception of the USS-POSCO/BE & K enemy. Through their physical presence they, in short, built up a particular form of collective consciousness, constructed a particular, place-bound form of power-relation consciousness (or a particular, place-bound form of class consciousness),[68] and erected a particular "culture of solidarity," or a particular ensemble of oppositional practices and meanings, "a new repertoire of behavior, associational ties, and valuations" of the type that emerges in "those moments when the customary practices of daily life are suspended," that emerges in times of crisis (Fantasia 1988:14).

Certain protests and demonstrations appear to have been especially important to the constitution of collective memory and consciousness because of the extraordinary or dramatic events surrounding them, because of the rush of adrenalin and intensity of experience they brought to direct participants, because of the vivid, excited manner with which they were recounted to others, because of their amplified echoing of already negative dispositions toward USS-POSCO and BE & K, because of their accentuation and reinforcement of us-versus-them attitudes. Among such solidarity-cementing episodes was a June 1987 incident in which a picketing cement mason was struck by a car with Louisiana plates only minutes after an Alabama-plated car had swerved toward the pickets as it approached the steel plant. The symbolic significance of this event was magnified over the ensuing weeks as two other picketers were hit by vehicles, as a provocatively held picket sign was pushed aside by a car, as California Highway Patrol officers refused to report two of the three "hit-and-run" occurrences, and as accounts of cars driven by nonunion workers and supply trucks entering the plant at unsafe speeds were repeatedly passed on. Finally, moved to rage, about one hundred pickets gathered at 6 P.M. on July 29 to block the USS-POSCO entrance as BE & K-hired construction workers attempted to leave for the day. As resentment boiled over, rocks were thrown, several cars were kicked and three automobiles were damaged: their windshields and side windows broken, or their headlights smashed.[69]

Struggles over Naming,
Identity, and Meaning

Juxtaposing the Building Stones of Political and Cultural Struggle

For the construction-union rank and file, at least, engagement in the practices of political struggle unavoidably had its cultural counterpart; its symbolic side; its contiguous struggles over naming, meaning and identity; its dimension of significant reworkings. These war-of-words aspects of struggle went beyond the hurling of derogatory names, imaginative insults, and pinpointed profanities at BE & K employees entering the work site; beyond the off-stage expression of dismay, disgust, and disease; beyond the out-of-earshot verbal aggression aimed at USS-POSCO and BE & K power holders. In their lived experience of picketing and demonstrating, in the course of their formally meeting or informally socializing to plan such protest actions, in the process of unintentionally developing a collective consciousness, there emerged a small set of targets of contention that were central to their culture of solidarity, a small set of issues that served as foci for their repeated expressions of symbolic discontent.

Naming the Villain: The (Non)Employer/Enemy as Foreigner

Unionized construction workers who had been foreclosed from earning money at the Pittsburg modernization project chose to label their (non)employer enemies with their own words, to reject the self-designating names offered by those enemies; and, in so doing, to draw boundaries and make distinctions that solidified their collective identity. BE & K could not transform itself into AMK International, could not alter its strikebreaking, union-busting reputation by altering a few letters, could not suppress negative imagery by an act of acronymic legerdemain. In everyday parlance, BE & K usually remained BE & K, although the otherwise neutral component letters of that acronym could be made congruent with the anger they evoked, could be recharged with unambiguous antagonism, as when a picket sign was made to read "Bad for Economy & worKers."[70] Likewise, the joint venture, which labeled itself USS-POSCO, was usually spoken of simply as POSCO. This widespread refusal to utter an official designation, this persistent stripping away of USS, served at one and the same time

to confine the enemy to the invading outsider and the foreign,
    rather than the resident familiar (U.S. Steel had been in Pittsburg for
    decades),
to emphasize that the contract award to BE & K was un-American
    insofar as it violated an unwritten code of fairness,
        ripped up the fabric of everyday life and
        threatened future prospects,
to preserve a (collective and individual) self-image of the construction worker
    as patriotic and "conservative" (of that which is).

By reducing the enemy, the villainous "they," to the Korean, one could oppose both USS-POSCO and BE & K and still bear a bumper sticker that read, "Build, Buy and Be American," still carry a picket sign that stated, "Wake up America, after they break unions you're next."[71] Or, by converting the partially foreign to the entirely foreign, one could resist and still remain loyal to the existing (ruling) order.

The succession of rallies, picket line activities, and miscellaneous protest activities in which unionized Contra Costa construction workers became involved provided frequent out-in-the-open opportunities for cultural expressions of dissatisfaction to be voiced on-stage, and yet somewhat anonymously, from amidst the safety of numbers. The February 1987 rally at the South Korean Consulate in San Francisco lent itself especially well to an open symbolic focusing on the foe as foreigner and to a simultaneous reaffirmation of patriotism. Buttons proclaiming "Unemployment—Made in Korea" were worn with glad defiance by workers who at the same time protected themselves from the rain with union caps and held small American flags. When shouted, common obscene nouns were given a loaded particular meaning by preceding them with the adjective *Korean*. When orally tossed, common obscene adjectives were given an explosive meaning by succeeding them with the plural noun *Koreans*. A picket sign acclaiming "Réagan—The Best President for Korea" linked the adversary, the agent of foreign capital, with the domestic personification of antiunionism. Vilification of the Korean (non)employer was rationalized by the summing up of past sacrifices. One picket sign announced, "We Saved Your Ass, Now You Want to Break Ours." The same unionized speaker who angrily observed, "It's ironic that 35 years ago we went over to fight for them and now they're trying to put us in the goddamned poorhouse," later added, "As a taxpayer I resent it, as a labor union member I resent it and as an American I resent it." The then–secretary treasurer of the Contra Costa Council, another rally speaker, poured additional fuel on the fire of resentment by underlining that the "average construction wage in [South] Korea is $1.41 an hour."[72]

The demonstration held in protest of the Pittsburg-Pohang sister-city agreement ceremonies also provided an obvious focus for the public display of discontent, for an open symbolic assault on the foreign-based depriver of local union employment. At this July 1987 demonstration, the verbal tarring of the enemy combined elements of outrage at the Korean government's repression and solidarity with Korean labor, plus elements of xenophobia, union pride, and personal distress. Among the picket sign messages were "Free S. Korean Labor Prisoners," "If I were in Korea I would be in jail—Unions are illegal," and "Sister city is not so fine—it put me in the unemployment line." While union members jamming City Hall booed South Korean and local officials, and chanted, "Go home," and "Union, union," so loudly that ceremonies had to be abbreviated, others who overflowed outside made a number of wrath-filled statements for media and general public consumption. One exclaimed: "No government that treats people the way the South Korean one does should be even mentioned in the same breath as an American city, period." Another echoed similar sentiments, stating: "I think it stinks to get a sister city in a country with so much turmoil. You can't even speak your piece over there." He later self-reflectively added: "I don't like the Koreans coming here. They're taking food out of my and my family's mouth." Yet another let off steam with this outburst: "It's bull. We don't need the Koreans over here. Before long they're going to own this city." And, when the Pittsburg police chief warned the crowd that arrests would be forthcoming if the shouting didn't stop, one protestor yelled, "Just like in Korea."[73]

The flying of the South Korean flag side by side with the U.S. flag at the USS-POSCO mill entrance, which began on April 1, 1986, eventually served as a magnet for disgruntlement, as a new sign that could be equated with a new set of antiunion conditions, as a reductive indicator that the target of struggle was foreign, as an everyday object of contempt for picketers. Hence, when the modernization project was a completed fact, when this particular job opportunity battle was irrevocably over, more than two years of symbolic sparring could be summarized by a public flaunting of disrespect, by the burning of some two hundred small South

Fig. 6.2 BE & K as Depicted in a Union-Circulated Handbill

Korean flags at the protest that accompanied former President Ford's appearance at the switch-throwing ceremonies.[74]

Not all of the gestures and representations directed at the (non)employer/enemy as foreigner were as symbolically straightforward as those thus far reported. In at least one instance there was a slyer, more many-meaning-filled, naming depiction of the enemy, a depiction that multiplied its messages through superimposing different symbolic spaces. In a union-circulated handbill[75] proclaiming that "We Say No! BE & K Must Go!" BE & K was simultaneously cartooned as the Ayatollah Khomeini, a devil, and a rat (see Figure 6.2). The first two dimensions of this portrait were prompted by the following statement made by a BE & K spokesperson exasperated by union countertactics and charges in a Maine labor dispute: "We're [perceived as] a devil, like the Ayatollah's devil."[76] Through adorning the face of the Ayatollah's devil with the Ayatollah's own beard and eyebrows and stamping the figure with the BE & K acronym, the Alabama firm was equated with the ultimately evil foreigner of the U.S. mass media. Through transforming the unmistakably American BE & K into a foreign devil, through symbolically reworking BE & K to be congruent with the principal foreign devil (POSCO), through cross-categorizing the Iranian with the Korean, a particularly strong we (good)–they (evil) opposing and identity-confirming image was projected.[77] The solidarity-reinforcing character of that beyond-the-boundary image was further intensified through a clever mixed visual metaphor, through likening the facial features and tail of the BE & K/(POSCO) foreign devil to those of a rat. This hybridization of binary opposites, or ascription of animal qualities to a human figure,[78] was a particularly telling representational tactic, for the rat is, in the popular mythology of American organized laborers, the union-buster or strike-breaker incarnate. Long prior to the distribution of the handbill in question, rank and filers were referring to BE & K as a "rat contractor." Pickets commonly shouted, "Rats!" as they heckled BE & K employees entering the USS-POSCO premises. And the somewhat tumultuous mass demonstration at the Associated Builders and Contractors convention had been designated Rat Monday.[79]

Whether presentations of the (non)employer/enemy as foreigner were symbolically straightforward or cloaked in layers of semiotic disguise, the extent of such imagery clearly suggests that for many unionized construction workers it obscured or dis-placed the fundamental economic issues involved in their struggle against BE & K and POSCO, that it defused or obfuscated the labor-versus-capital issues that were central to their struggle. It is equally clear, however, that matters were far from totally opaque for large numbers of unionized construction workers. Their vociferous focus on the foreign often was not simply a matter of transferring (hegemony-challenging) anticapitalist sentiments into the (hegemony-supporting) realm of xenophobic/patriotic sentiments. Their expression of symbolic discontent often rested upon a perception that POSCO was the principal mover, that USX was somewhat of a passive agent, that POSCO was doing them in in a way that USX would not have (if acting on its corporate own). The cartoon of BE & K (Figure 6.2) may well have directly appealed to readily accessible xenophobic/patriotic sentiments; but in making that appeal, and in invoking the image of the rat, it allowed union leaders to play upon anticapital sentiments that were sometimes slumbering, repressed, less accessible.

Insiders Turned Out:
Out-of-State Workers and Local Labor Identity

If the collective identity of organized construction laborers was fortified by representing the enemy as a foreign outsider who had entered into the local picture, then BE & K's use of out-of-state workers and other nonlocal workers gave construction union members a sense of being insiders who had been turned out, and thereby led them to erect a triple-strength boundary around their identity. The playing out of the politics of struggle, the practical engagement in group(self)/other relations, resulted in a construction of identity along a local-versus-nonlocal axis as well as along labor—versus—(foreign) capital and union-versus-nonunion axes.

In the course of events following the contract award to BE & K, there grew an increasingly strong awareness that those who were taking jobs away were not only nonunion "scabs" and "rats," but imported "scabs" and "rats" who ought to "go home." Collective identity was reconstituted as a new category of exclusion became central to collective consciousness, as it became perceived that those employed by BE & K were not only willing to work for lower wages, not only willing to work without pension contributions, vacation pay, or sick pay, and not only willing to live in campers and otherwise accept a lower standard of living, but also inclined to "take the money and run," to "send it back to Texas or wherever they're from."[80] The detestable otherness of the job stealers taken on by BE & K was magnified and reinforced by statements repeatedly heard and made associating them with the ruining of local family life, with causing local children to starve and face a "cold Christmas." The local versus nonlocal distinction was further intensified by the picketers' experience of counting out-of-state licensed cars as they approached the Pittsburg plant gate, by the occasional chanting in unison of the names on out-of-state plates: "Texas, Illinois, Florida, Utah, Louisiana, Alabama, Wyoming, Arizona, South Carolina, Oregon," and so on.[81] That distinction was also reimprinted and given even sharper contours by the instances in which out-of-state drivers either struck or recklessly swerved at picketers.

The local aspect of we-ness was greatly buttressed by the responsibility-shifting, self-serving public stance of BE & K and USS-POSCO representatives: by repeated, press-publicized assertions that the blame for the hiring of out-of-state construction labor was to be placed on local union-affiliated workers themselves. Recurrent pronouncements and redundant messages such as the following, spread out over months of struggle, could not fail to reaffirm the local/nonlocal dimension of collective identity (as well as the labor/capital and union/nonunion dimensions of that identity):

Because of terrorist-like activities by union members [we plan] to recruit workers farther away instead of using local labor.

Normally we hire a lot of union people. But if unions restrict their members from working for AMK, it may be impossible for the company to fulfill its stated goal of having 640 of 800 total workers from the local area.

More would have been hired locally, except for the building trades trouble.

Our [local hiring] objectives were being attained in the early stages of construction. But as the intimidation increased, it discouraged local people from wanting to seek employment.

With the gauntlet that the unions established there [at the USS-POSCO gate] it was intimidating the local people, plus the unions put out the word for their people not to apply. So at that point, our recruiting began to encompass a wider area and we quit keeping numbers as to where people were coming from."[82]

In the face of all this, in the face of local-identity-strengthening gestures, such as the formation of a rank-and-file Work Preservation Committee by one construction union local (Steamfitters Local 3422), Greg Feere, a leader of the Contra Costa Council, eventually was able to state: "We've realized that organized labor is not a special interest group. It's a community."[83]

The Contesting of "Merit": A Simultaneous Struggle over Meaning and Identity

In its effort to escape opprobrium, to avoid a term that carried strong pejorative undertones among unionized laborers, to somewhat defuse the resistance-inciting potential of its mode of operation, BE & K had, even prior to winning the USS-POSCO contract, begun referring to itself as a "merit shop" company, rather than an "open shop" company, just as some other construction firms were doing. In the eyes of BE & K's own "skilled management," its "merit shop" policies, its countering of the "artificially" high wages created by limited-membership unions, its willingness to enter into agreements with unionized as well as nonunionized subcontractors, and its awarding of each contract to the lowest bidding subcontractor, all resulted in "workmanship second to none" and "a high quality, low cost end result" (BE & K 1986).

BE & K's adoption of the term *merit shop* placed the self- and group-worth, the self- and group-esteem, and thereby the identity of local union-belonging construction workers at risk. What the word *merit* might suggest—at least subconsciously if not consciously—was that those employed in the USS-POSCO modernization project were in possession of "merit," while those on the picket line and otherwise left outside were without "merit." If left uncontested, the BE & K meaning of *merit* could stimulate doubt, could put individual and collective identity in question.

Those engaged in the political struggle against BE & K and USS-POSCO were not readily duped culturally, did not allow the job-robbing other to be symbolically elevated at their own expense. *Merit* was too transparent an attempt at obfuscation. BE & K was, after all, a firm that had been publicly condemned by the AFL-CIO as a "strikebreaking service, attractive to companies willing to engage in unfair labor practices."[84] *Merit* was, then, a euphemism. One was not to be fooled by BE & K's taking on of two secondary subcontractors who together employed forty members of Pile Drivers Union Local 34 and Operating Engineers Local 3. The only "merit" of those employed in Pittsburg by BE & K was their acceptance of low wages.

Although *merit* was a transparent euphemism, the use of "merit shop" workers, in conjunction with developments on the residential construction labor market, did force concessions on the part of some Contra Costa union locals, and thereby threatened some reduction of their member's self-value. Pointing to two hundred unemployed members, one hundred of them resident in Pittsburg and adjacent Antioch, and singling out the nonlocal hiring practices of BE & K, Local 302 of the electricians union decided to roll back its wages by four dollars an hour as of June 1, 1987).[85]

In order to compensate, in order to defend against such image diminishment, in order to displace any degree of uncertainty, the "merit" of BE & K employees had to be further contested. What was perceived to be their obvious lack of "merit" had to be given voice. Thus, in daily discussing the employer/enemy and the state of the struggle, questioning references apparently were often made regarding the lack of skill and experience of those taken on by BE & K, regarding the inadequate competency of those who were part of the "Wheels of Learning" program, of those who had to go to after-work classes to develop welding and other skills. Pickets were constantly reminded that BE & K personnel were subject to such training by the seemingly gate-of-hell-like message— "Free to Earn, Free to Learn"—conspicuously displayed by the contracting firm on a sign at the USS-POSCO entrance gate. How could people who were not experienced specialists avoid unnecessary accidents? How could anybody without "proper training" do anything right? How could quality work be achieved by green workers who were often expected to perform as jacks-of-all-trades on the job?[86]

From Conflict Bystander to Submersion in a Labor-Process Struggle: The United Steelworkers and Plant Modernization

Caught between USS-POSCO and the Unionized Construction Workers

We're definitely in the middle. I sympathize with them, they are our brothers, but then again . . .

Tony Cifaldi, unionized USS-POSCO steelworker

I understand the building trades unions, but we've got 1,100 people working here who have children who might want to work here.

Dan Malone, unionized USS-POSCO steelworker

On February 24, 1987, just when the struggle between USS-POSCO and unionized construction labor was heating up, the members of United Steelworkers of America (USW) Local 1440 voted, by a narrow margin, to accept a new contract from their joint-venture employers.[87] Well aware of the recent closing of Bethlehem Steel's American Bridge plant and other, less important steel-producing facilities in the Bay Area and somewhat persuaded by USS-POSCO that sacrifices were necessary in order to remain competitive with the Japanese- and Brazilian-owned steel-producing facility in Fontana, California, the steelworkers simultaneously conceded a 4.3 percent wage cut, a freeze in cost-of-living allowances until 1991, a reduction in vacation and holiday benefits, and a suspension of their right to strike during the agreement period.[88] The agreement also stipulated that some cost savings would be channeled into a labor retraining and education program, thereby presumably ensuring that USW members would be prepared to work under modernized conditions. That the majority of Local 1440 members understood that pliability was in order for the moment—that they were fearful of eventual plant closure and unemployment, that they did not wish to see plant modernization (and their jobs) jeopardized by unacceptable wage demands—is further reflected by the fact that they had not gone out on strike when their previous contract had expired on July 31, 1986, but instead had accepted a series of temporary extensions, thereby disregarding orders of USW's national leadership. This stood in strong contrast to the situation of twenty-two thousand USX Corporation steelworkers, who, upon failing to accede to company demands, were unable to return to work for six months after July 31.[89] It stood in even greater contrast to the plight of USW members at the USX Geneva Works in Provo, Utah, who saw their plant put on "indefinitely idled status," or shut down, after the six-month confrontation, in no small measure because the Pittsburg mill was no longer to use the semifinished steel they had been producing (Hoerr 1988:561).

Throughout the period during which the Contra Costa Council and its rank and file conducted their struggle, relations between Local 1440 and USS-POSCO remained relatively peaceful, although far from friction free. Following the June 1988 election of Joe Stanton, who was clearly more skeptical about his employer than the preceding local president had been,[90] there were expressions of concern about both the use of nonunion employees to substitute for those steelworkers who were training-program participants, and the believability of company claims that no layoffs would be necessary after the modernization project's completion. At this time the joint venture also was strongly requested to make a psychiatrist available for union members who were under mental strain because of working conditions: one steelworker had lost an arm in a work-related accident, and there was growing fear that poor safety could lead to job-ending mishaps; another ex-steelworker, apparently devastated by an involuntary medical retirement, had recently shot the company doctor to death at the plant.[91] Finally, in December 1988, there was some protestation and a day of picketing stimulated by the company's resort to planted informers in an internal investigation of on-the-job drug use and thefts. Demonstrating steelworkers were joined on the picket line by members of at least four building trades unions.[92]

When juxtaposed with the efforts of locally organized construction workers, the atmosphere of relative calm engulfing relations between Local 1440 and USS-POSCO placed those steelworkers who thought of themselves as loyal unionists and champions of solidarity in a dilemma, in a situation where a core element of their individual and collective identities was threatened. On the one hand, unionized steelworkers frequently visualized themselves as coming from a more activist, militant, assertive tradition than that of their local construction-worker "brothers." On the other hand, they saw the modernization of the Pittsburg facility as their salvation, as the creation of a "massive plant able to compete on any level," as a project whose completion would bring an end to "rumors that we were closing down"; therefore they were made uneasy, displeased, or angry by any political, legal, or protest action that appeared to endanger the progress of that project.[93] In the face of the construction workers' tactics, rank-and-file steelworkers, as well as their union officials, repeatedly were driven to express contradictory wishes: to wish that the construction contract had gone to a union contractor instead of BE & K, and to wish that BE & K could proceed without obstacles. Sometimes referring to the Catch-22 qualities of their situation, comments such as the following were made: "As trade unionists, we support [the Contra Costa Council] and wish them luck in their endeavor. [But], of course, [we are] opposed to any attempt to stop the modernization." "We have no choice, really. I could be a hard-core advocate of union at any cost, but we have to be realistic—where are you going to find 1,000 [steel-production] jobs?"[94] Such identity-clouding sentiments were propped up early on by a USS-POSCO threat to drop the modernization project if the Contra Costa Council succeeded in persuading the County Board of Supervisors to request a land use permit application of the joint-venture firm. Such attitudes of ambivalence were sometimes further shored up by self-serving statements from USS-POSCO to the effect that it could not "in good conscience" satisfy the wage expectations of the Contra Costa Council after having extracted concessions from its steelworkers.[95]

As the tactics and actions of locally organized construction labor piled up on one another, the caught-in-the-middle stance of steelworkers sometimes slid over into a position of querying resentment and transferred guilt. 'Why," it was asked, "do they start bringing this [environmental issue] stuff up now if it's been going on for years?" Why are they giving us "an unfair bad rap" regarding air quality and other matters? Why are they putting us "in an awkward position?" After all, "we've got one chance in a lifetime to be back in the race. God don't [let them] take that away from us."[96]

Putting It on the Line:
A New Labor Process and a New Focus of Struggle

Once the modernization project was completed, once computerized milling equipment went into operation during the spring of 1989, many steelworkers quickly found themselves confronted by an identity crisis of a rather different sort, found themselves directly submerged in a struggle of their own, found themselves articulating symbolic discontent of their own, found themselves again regarding their employer as an adversary, found themselves reconstituting their place-bound consciousness of employment-centered power relations, or class.[97]

The technology of the modernized mill demanded a thorough restructuring of the labor process, a radical rearrangement of the concrete activity of producing cold-rolled and galvanized steel sheets for a variety of purposes. The technical capabilities of the new computer-steered equipment simultaneously called for a reorganization of individual and group tasks, a revision of the detail division of labor, a reconfiguration of the temporal and spatial details of everyday mill-floor practices, a new choreography of worker/machine and task interactions, and, consequently, new on-the-job social relations and a reshaping of worker skills, discipline and autonomy (cf. Walker 1985:esp. 179–182). The technology of the new "continuous-annealing lines" enabled "flexible production," enabled rolled products of unlike dimension to be manufactured without interruption. With computerized production lines it was no longer necessary to halt the flow of materials and recalibrate, substitute, or adjust equipment every time different customer specifications were to be met, and a much wider range of finely differentiated products became possible. As with the use of other automated "continuous-processing" manufacturing technologies, everyday work became nonroutine work and "a high degree of responsibility, alertness and adaptability [became required] to minimize down time and deal with unforeseen circumstances" (Storper and Walker 1984:34–35).

In order to implement the restructured labor process, in order to provide their steelworkers with the new, higher levels of technical skill necessary for continuous-line operations, in order to prepare those workers to labor under more team-oriented circumstances, USS-POSCO had to re-move people from still-functioning older production lines in order to pro-vide them with four months of operations and maintenance retraining either in South Korea or in locally run classes. The training program placed considerable emphasis on the inculcation of new forms of task flexibility and the adoption of new forms of regimentation. In this sense it was in keeping with earlier moves by U.S. Steel to reduce costs and reas-sert its control over work practices by combining different narrowly de-fined job responsibilities, by erasing highly restrictive shop floor rules and job-classification manuals, by doing away with old craft distinctions and combining them into "supercrafts."[98] However, the training program de-parted from U.S. Steel practices by encouraging worker involvement in the improvement of production line defects, by in other new ways pro-moting employee identification with the company, by in other ways insisting that employee interests and employer interests were identical.

As Piore and Sabel (1984) would have it, the replacement of mass, standardized production routines by flexible production routines should result in a greater realization of human potential. That may well be the case in some instances, but the introduction of flexible production on USS-POSCO's continuous-annealing lines brought with it an immediate awareness of "many problems"[99]—problems that were not confined ei-ther to the discovery of computer-program imperfections and other tech-nical "bugs," or to the difficulties of often working with inferior-grade steels from Gary, Indiana, rather than with high-quality steels from Pohang. These problems also extended to frequent worker dissatisfac-tion, to what was often sensed as a frustration of self-potential, to an undermining of identity, to the drawing of legalistic and cultural battle-lines. In the Pittsburg mill, at least, new conditions of work, a new form of technical organization, meant new conditions for resistance, new grounds for the development of militancy and solidarity among some workers.[100]

In accord with the contractual agreement between Local 1440 and USS-POSCO, the assignment of individuals to specific tasks and job re-sponsibilities within the modernized mill was to be determined by the testing of skills. Under these circumstances many veteran steelworkers found that they were being bypassed for important assignments by workers of little mill experience, by younger workers who had never pos-sessed the skills in which they had long taken personal pride, by relatively recent hires who did not share their store of no longer valid shop-floor knowledge. Finding themselves declared "unqualified," or "incompe-tent," they initiated a practical, legalistic struggle against their employees by filing numerous grievances and simultaneously submerged themselves in a cultural struggle, contesting the meaning of *qualified* and *competent*, and thereby defending their self-identity as skilled, accomplished craftsworkers. It was argued that duty assignments were biased, that the test results which shunted them aside were subject to a rather different interpretation. It was contended that the company had not adequately built upon the acquired talents of more senior employees, had not properly fulfilled its training obligations.[101] What was at issue was not only the long-standing question of whether it is labor or the employer who really controls the steel mill floor, of the extent to which steel mill employees would retain an essential degree of control over the conception and performance of their work.[102] There was also the parallel, immediate question of who is in control symbolically.

Symbolic discontent among those working on the continuous-production lines during their first months of operation was not confined to individuals suffering job assignment dissatisfaction. With four hundred million dollars of investment now in concrete form beneath their feet and in front of their eyes, with computerized equipment actually running, with the possibility of plant closure removed into the reasonably distant future, with related pressure now removed, some steelworkers apparently allowed elements of residual distrust and re-pressed antiemployer hostility to resurface under their new conditions of employment.

Confronted by new labor-process practices (and the new foreign language of technical terms necessary to implement them),
confronted by new forms of practical knowledge and experience,
confronted by a new set of workplace rules and payoff promises,
confronted by new team-oriented, allegiance-demanding criteria of performance,
confronted by a new rhetoric of cooperation and mutual objectives,
confronted by a new call for participation in management's production goals,
confronted by new forms of interaction with both their peers and their superiors,
confronted by a new social order within the workplace, or new "relations in production,"

the steelworkers did not merely cope or resist by attempting to discover ways of bending the rules of the "labor-process game," ways of skirting subordination that may have unintentionally diverted attention from the surplus-labor-extracting, profit-gaining purposes of USS-POSCO's production.[103] Instead, a vocabulary of relation-unveiling resistance appears to have come into use by some under off-stage, beyond-the-earshot-of-management, circumstances.

The use of everyday language as a vehicle for symbolic discontent was reinforced, if not directly encouraged, by the circulation of a printed glossary of company-objective-rejecting, company-ideology-rebuffing terms originally developed within another United Steelworkers local. Three consecutive issues of the *Rank & Filer*, the monthly newsletter of Local 1440, contained a glossary of twenty-six interrelated expressions that were unambiguously subversive in their call for workers "not to Care," not to toe the company line regarding production-line behavior, not to accept the propaganda of "the forces who control our working lives."[104] To have given the glossary such distribution at this early stage of modernized operations, Local 1440 leaders must have regarded the meanings assigned to the words and phrases in question as striking a responsive chord with those subjected to the new routines and pressures of team-focused, responsibility-heightened, supervision-intensified work. The following sample of terms and definitions amply captures the pun-ishing and ironic discontent embedded within the glossary as a whole.

CARE: this is a psychological disorder which leads to feelings of pride, loyalty, and accomplishment in the face of injustice, abuse and/or indifference to a worker's needs.

CARE PUSHER: a supervisor at any rank.

CARE-ESS: ego stroking performance by a Care Pusher to reinforce Care.

CAREBARIAN: a sworn enemy of the insidious Care Factor, ...

CAREBERIA: a psychological Siberia to which Carebarians are banished for showing a lack of Care. Often takes the form of a Care Pusher threatening to "write up" a Carebarian as an inducement to Care. Not only ineffective but counter-productive as well.

CARE-O.T. (pronounced "CARROT"): an offer dangled before workers to raise their Care Factors by making them think that the company is making them rich.

CARE STARE: an apparent attempt to introduce Care through mental telepathy, as Care Pushers attempt to induce employees with low Care Factors to work simply by staring at them. Usually unsuccessful.

CAREWALA BEAR: a worker stricken with Care, they are conspicuous by their odd dedication and fawning around Care Pushers. Approach these individuals with caution because, although they are in dire need of help, they are unpredictable in their actions. They will not likely attack you openly, but may betray you to Caring ears behind your back.

F.A.C.E. (F---[uck]-All Co-Efficient): a healthy reaction to industrial and political exposure. Inversely proportional to the Care Factor, it offers a measure of balance . . . .

PUBLIC RELATIONS: the propaganda used to convince the community at large that the workers are all happy and Care, and that they do not therefore need any further inducements, such as wage increases.

This vocabulary is typical of the linguistic weapons deployed by "weak," power-relation-ridden groups in its many-faceted cleverness, in its usage of multiple entendres, its mocking tone, its bitter irony, its lowering of those who surveil, control, or are otherwise situated above, and its lifting of those who are surveilled, controlled, or otherwise situated below. Its cleverness is illustrated by its construction of an identity-reinforcing social distinction that simultaneously builds on the "Care" theme, small spelling shifts, and the imagery of geographical difference: they, the bad, supervising others, con-sign us to the freezing gulag-islands of Careberia-Siberia; we, the good guys, in naming ourselves as-sign ourselves to the warm, sun-drenched islands of the Carebarian-Caribbean. Its clever sl(e)ight of mouth is further illustrated, for example, by its well-chosen ascription of animal qualities to those taken in by company objectives and inclined to sycophantic behavior, by its equating of such "Carewala Bears" with koala bears, with creatures who signify an inert, placid, helplessness, a motionless—but content—stupidity, an inability to attack anyone or anything directly.

This vocabulary of resistance, however, is one that is not blind to fundamental relations; one that is not merely confined to cute wordplay, to the tossing of clever cultural barbs, to the verbal release of pent-up hostility regarding past events, to the voicing of frustration with immediate labor-process circumstances. That this vocabulary is also one that places the employer/worker power relation beneath a merciless spotlight, which involves a class-ic war of words, is underscored by a series of quotes, attributed to the "Carebarian Council," that accompanied the initial vocabulary installment.[105] Among the more telling of these quotes are the following:

The Company's point of view is known as "information" whereas anybody else's point of view is known as "propaganda."
Why is it that when the rich want more money, it is referred to as "capitalism," but when a worker wants more money, it is referred to as "communism"?
The Company claims it is not in business to make steel; it is in business to make money. Well, what's good for the goose . . . we are not at work to do whatever we do there; we are there to make money. And just as they feel justified in cutting their expenditures at all costs, we have the right to conserve our own expenditures of health and energy as much as possible.
Why is it that the Company can continually afford to spend enormous amounts of money on improving their equipment to improve productivity, but they are always broke when it comes to spending money in the form of pay increases to boost the morale of the people who keep this same Company running, in order to improve their productivity?

Some students of bureaucratic organizations might dismiss any usage of the above vocabulary as nothing more than a symptom of the "retreatism" typically resorted to by employees unable to influence decisions, as nothing more than a personal choice "to reduce their involvement and to commit themselves as little as possible to the organization" (Hoerr 1988:316, citing Crozier 1964:199). Such a dismissal would appear ill-founded because of the vocabulary's collective overtones, its political combativeness, its conversion of alienation into aggressive attitudes. The symbolic discontent expressed by the vocabulary, as well as the "Carebarian Council" quotes, clearly appear better characterized as a tactic of militant, collective withdrawal than as "personal retreatism," especially in the light of accompanying comments that speak of a growing "cause" and of pressing for policy changes.[106] Whether or not that nonretreatist symbolic discontent will eventually serve as a tinderbox for protracted forms of local organized political resistance remains to be seen.

Rearticulations

The political and cultural struggles in which Contra Costa County's unionized construction laborers and steelworkers became engaged were a consequence of a particular articulation of the local and the global under conditions of late-twentieth-century capitalism. This particular articulation of large-scale structuring processes involved, on the one hand, practices and power relations associated with iron and steel industry overcapacity and international movements of investment capital and, on the other hand, practices and power relations associated with local production and employment. The unfolding conduct of political and cultural struggle was repeatedly constrained and enabled by already existing social and spatial structures that were themselves being constantly reproduced or transformed; by the exercise of parent-company power already established in Pohang, South Korea, and Pittsburgh, Pennsylvania; by the parent-company-influencing exercise of power by corporate and state organizations already based in other distant locations; by the exercise of power by already existing local authorities; by the simple fact that the steel mill was already present in Pittsburg. Or, in exercising individual and collective agency, in conducting their political and cultural struggles, locally unionized construction laborers and steelworkers did not make history and produce human geographies under circumstances of their own choosing, but in the context of already existing social and spatial relations.[107]

Because BE & K is a construction company that operates on a nationwide basis, because the interdependencies existing within the iron and steel industry in general—and within USS-POSCO's production system in particular—are geographically extensive, and because the building trades and steelworker locals of Contra Costa County are affiliated with nationally operating unions, the political and cultural struggles considered here should directly or indirectly rearticulate with the lives of women and men elsewhere, with structuring processes that locally manifest themselves elsewhere, with the distant, nonlocal making of histories and construction of human geographies, with other political and cultural struggles. Such a rearticulation was already in process by the fall of 1989 in Minnesota, where a major dispute was focused on BE & K's use of out-of-state labor at low wage rates on a $535 million plant expansion project at Boise Cascade's International Falls paper mill, and where the protesting construction workers involved were not unaware of preceding events in Pittsburg. On November 9, in the wake of a riot that resulted in "more than $1 million in property damages," in the wake of a growing public concern for the job-loss and income consequences of BE & K's employment practices, the Minnesota House Economic Development Committee ordered the Minnesota Department of Jobs and Training to conduct "a study on the economic impact of [BE & K's] hiring out-of-state construction workers" ("Minn. Legislature Panel . . ." 1989). The inquiry's methodology was to be modeled after that of the study carried out under the auspices of the Contra Costa County Board of Supervisors in response to pressures brought by local building trades unions. The impending study was no mere political gesture without potential practical consequences, as its predecessor contained rather negative conclusions,[108] as state money had been used as an incentive for Boise Cascade's mill expansion, and as the legislature was considering not only how it should eventually handle the conflict, but how economic development dollars were to be allocated in the future.

What other rearticulations will occur?

In what other unintended and unanticipated ways will the modernization of USS-POSCO's Pittsburg plant result in "a blueprint for others to follow"?[109]

What other labor actions will be sparked elsewhere?

What other dramas of political and cultural struggle, of new-found solidarity and symbolic discontent, will unfold in connection with similar local appearances of such new forms of capital?

As investment capital relentlessly shifts, as new mammoth construction projects become necessary, what new (counter)strategies will be developed by employers elsewhere?

Coda

I first saw Elvis [Presley] live in 1954. It was at the Big D Jamboree in Dallas and first thing, he came out and spat on the stage. . . . I didn't know what to make of it. There was just no reference point in the culture to compare it.

Roy Orbison, rock musician

[T]here's no such thing as "England" any more . . . welcome to India brothers! This is the Caribbean! . . . Nigeria! . . . There is no England, man. This is what is coming. Balsall Heath is the center of the melting pot, 'cos all I ever see when I go out is half-Arab, half-Pakistani, half-Jamaican, half-Scottish. . . . I know 'cos I am [half-Scottish, half Irish] . . . who am I? Tell me who do I belong to? They criticize me, the good old England. Alright where do I belong? You know I was brought up with blacks, Pakistanis, Africans, Asians, everything . . . who do I belong to?

White reggae fan from Birmingham

IN A CURIOUS WAY, this book is rooted in the same ground as Roy Orbison's reflections on one of rock and roll's iconic figures, namely, the dislodging effect of cultural practice, and more precisely of seeing culture as a sort of reference point, as a set of markers, as a map of meanings.[1] We have addressed these questions, however, from a particular vantage point, specifically, of trying to understand what metamorphoses capitalism is capable of, of endeavoring to grasp its seemingly infinite capacity for reconfiguration and recombination, its desperate propensity for destruction, and its relentless drive toward the commodification of virtually everything. In short, we have examined both the deeply radical character of capitalism and also the complex articulations of capitalism, modernity, and culture understood as a field of struggle, what Fredric Jameson has called the "attempt to theorize the specific logic of the cultural production of [late capitalism]" (1989:33).

In attempting to breach the hard edges and contours of capitalist accumulation *culturally*, we have focused on, as it were, commodity culture rather than the commodity circuit. In this sense there is much in common between our theoretical approach and cultural studies (on both sides of the Atlantic), as is implied by Renato Rosaldo in *Culture and Truth*:

Whether speaking about shopping in a supermarket, the aftermath of nuclear war, Elizabethan self-fashioning, academic communities, tripping through Las Vegas, Algerian marriage practices, or ritual among the

Ndembu of Central Africa, work in cultural studies sees human worlds as constructed through historical and political processes, and not as brute timeless facts of nature. (1989:7)

Contained within Rosaldo's vision, and within cultural studies more generally, are, in fact, at least four interrelated claims about cultural diversity and creativity, cultural construction and symbolic contestation, and the relations between cultures, especially between mass and popular cultures.[2] First, culture in general is seen to be political, and popular culture in particular is substantially more than "flying ducks on the wall and garden gnomes" (Hall 1979:234). Rather, culture and the vernacular specifically, in its multiplicity of guises, was a field of struggle, an arena that necessarily engaged dominant and powerful subcultures; *that* is why, Hall stated with admirable frankness, popular culture matters, and "otherwise, to tell you the truth, I don't give a damn about it" (1979: 239). Second, culture is framed dialectically in terms of the delicate polarities of containment and resistance, reification and utopia. Rather than capitulating to a blunt view of culture as something that is simply a form of class control or alternatively as an authentic form of subversion—in other words, in terms of unified, coherent oppositions and voices—Denning (1990) to take simply one exemplary case, relocates these polarities by suggesting that cultural creation under capitalism was divided against itself. Alongside the prosaic and the banal of commercial culture lay "elements of recognition and identification . . . to which people are responding" (Hall 1979:223); in the same way that works of mass culture cannot be ideological without being utopian, "they cannot manipulate unless they offer some genuine shred of content as a fantasy bribe to the public about to be so manipulated" (Jameson 1979:144). In this sense the question is not so much whether culture is authentic as much as the complex interpenetrations, dependencies, contests, and negotiations between consent and conflict. Third, and relatedly, culture is active, not merely marking or living out wider social contradictions but, as Paul Willis put it, working upon them "to achieve partial resolutions, recombinations, limited transformations" (1977:124). Culture is a form of symbolic creativity, and a part of *necessary work,* as Willis (1990) himself says, which contains its own "grounded aesthetic."[3] And finally, there is a sensitivity to what Jameson (1979) called the false problem of value, the modalities by which culture is distinguished from nonculture, how cultures are themselves separated, evaluated, judged, and classified. Boundaries represent, then, an exercise in cultural power, which itself should be an object of scrutiny (Denning 1990:6).

If an early concern of cultural studies was to link culture and class, its horizons have been enlarged (challenged?) by what one might call the new pluralism. In fact, the growth and proliferation of gender, sexuality, race, and ethnicity within wide-ranging theoretical and cultural debates actually rested upon a meltdown of—or at least a growing skepticism toward—the class reactor. Culture was in some sense impoverished if it was linked to a notion of class as a master narrative, which typically produced a revolutionary subject (the white working-class male), who always showed up at the right historic moment, if sometimes temporarily delayed, but rarely duped, by the trappings of false consciousness. This grand view of class has been replaced, in some quarters at least, by the multiplication of sites of struggle, by a scattering of antagonisms, indeed, by a fragmentation of the political itself. Blown in part by the Gallic winds that rejected the idea of totality, and placed difference and hetero-nomy very much on the agenda, cultural studies became in multicultural and postcolonial advanced capitalist societies, a safe harbor for all sorts of emergent discourses.

Broadly speaking, Aronowitz (1991) is quite correct in his assessment that cultural studies in this expanded sense contributed to, and have radically challenged, three primary domains: *epistemic* (including forms of knowledge and facticity, and the constitution and limits of conven-tional disciplines), *discursive* (how social identity is constructed by communities and how communities are constructed discursively), and *aesthetic* (the historical context of the aesthetics of everyday life). Defined in this way, cultural studies were an intellectual and academic expression of new social movements, what has come to be labeled "identity poli-tics." In sum, what began tentatively as an interrogation of culture has led to a concern with what Cornel West calls "the new cultural politics of difference": "Distinctive features of the new cultural politics of differ-ence are to trash the monolithic and homogeneous in the name of diver-sity, multiplicity and heterogeneity; to reject the abstract, general and universal and pluralize by highlighting the contingent, provisional, vari-able . . ." (1990:93). If these gestures are not new, what makes them distinctive, according to West, are the weight and gravity lent to *repre-sentation,* and how and by what *difference* is constituted.

We have suggested that this concern with difference is echoed in the geographic arena where the relations among space, place, and globaliza-tion are central. More concretely, we have posited the need for a sort of mapping of cultural forms onto certain spatial, social, and class identities in the context of global capitalism. The common ground, then, is funda-mentally about space, identity, and the politics of difference, but most especially about cultural meanings and social identities. In this regard, the recent analyses of modernity provided by Anthony Giddens in his *Consequences of Modernity* and by Ed Soja in his *Postmodern Geog-raphies* are both singularly lacking. In Soja's marvellous description of the "extraordinary crazy quilt [and] dazzling patchwork quilt" (1989: 245) of Los Angeles, or in Giddens's (1990) invocation of the disso-nances and heterogeneities that compose a larger structure of modernity, there is little consideration of how people define themselves, how these identities are cobbled together and contested. In the hyperspace of post-modernity, space is not irrelevant but rather has been reworked; as Gupta and Ferguson (1992) note, this forces a radical rethinking of community, solidarity, identity, and cultural difference. How are places forged from spaces, who has this power to forge, how is it contested and fought over, and what is at stake in these contestations?

Living in a global economy necessarily blurs the distinction between "here" and "there." This is necessarily so for the millions of refugees, migrants, and displaced persons. But the experience is more general. We inhabit a world of diasporic communities linked together by a transnational public culture and global commodities; not only has the old international division of labor been realigned but so have the some of the older identities between people and places (Rouse 1991). Prerevolutionary Iran arises in contemporary Paris and Houston; "Pakistanis" in northern England and Pakistan simultaneously engage in the book burning of Rushdie's *Satanic Verses;* Third World simulacra appear in the First World, and vice versa. Furthermore, not only the displaced experience displacement. Identities within the "periphery" are as surely reworked as they are in the "metropole" and for similar reasons. There is an erosion of the spatially circumscribed homeland or community and a compensatory growth of the imaginary homeland from afar, an imaginary always shaped however by specific political-economic determinations (Gupta and Ferguson 1992).

Amidst the shards of modernist disengagement, fragmentation, and difference, what types of identity can be, and are, constructed? As Clifford (1988:275) says, at the end of the twentieth century, "what processes rather than essences are involved in present experiences of cultural identity?" How can we approach the experience of the Korean Buddhist chemical engineer, recently arrived from three years in Argentina, who becomes a Christian greengrocer in Harlem? Or the New Yorker, from Guyana, who served on the Howard Beach trial jury? Or the life on the border, as Guillermo Gomez-Pena describes the state of being Mexican-American: "Who are we exactly? The off-spring of the synthesis, or the victims of the fragmentation; the victims of double colonialism or the bearers of a new vision. . . . What the hell are we? DeMexicanised Mexicans, pre-Chicanos, cholopunks, or something that still has no name" (1986:1). And perhaps the border is the appropriate metaphor for the postmodern subject, the site of what Bhabha calls hybridity, a place of "incommensurable contradictions within which people survive, are politically active and change" (1989:67). The borderland becomes the home of the postmodern. But what can this mean when only a protean self can seemingly occupy this space?—Proteus was, after all, divine (Sennett 1991:6).

Our case studies point to the importance of understanding these processes of interpellation, of how the geographer's concern with the nexus of the global and the local can be explored by "mapping" the labile, sliding identities that are forged in specific yet globalized sites. Stuart Hall has problematized this mapping process as follows:

I use the term identity . . . precisely to try to identify that meeting point where the processes that constitute and continuously reform the subject have to act and speak in the social and cultural worlds. . . . I understand identities therefore as points of suture, points of attachment, points of temporary identification. . . . [O]ne only discovers who one is because of *the identities which one has to take on in order to act* . . . always knowing that they are always representations [which] can never be adequate to the subjective processes which are temporarily invested in them. . . . I think identity is sort of . . . like a bus, you just have to get from here to there, the whole of you can never be represented in the ticket you carry but you just have to buy a ticket in order to get from here to there. (Hall 1989: n.p., emphasis added).

Accounting for the processes by which we acquire our bus ticket(s)—not least, in a world in which the routes are many and global—is a worthy and complex important project. How exactly are individuals interpellated by multiple and often contradictory cultural and symbolic practices rooted in historically constituted communities and places? What are the processes by which a sense of self-construction is shared with others? Why and in what ways are such representations made more or less appealing, and how are they contested (Radway 1990:24)?

In posing these questions, two points need to be made. First, to the extent that identity is constructed across difference and in relation to other identities, then we are necessarily brought back to the question of mass, popular, and dominant cultures in something like a transnational public sphere. In the same way that hegemony is hard work (the adage is Stuart Hall's) and always subject to negotiation, so personal and community identities are malleable (but not infinitely so) and flexible because of the failure to exhaust the meanings of popular experience from below (cf. Anderson 1990; Ryan 1989). And second, identities are complex sorts of "holding operations," stories told by ourselves about ourselves and therefore fictions, if *necessary* fictions (Hall 1989). As such, they are imaginary, straddling, so to speak, the Real and Desire, from which, it seems to us, they derive their weight and effect.

We have tried to explore some aspects of these lofty issues across the last century and across the First and the Third World. Under an increasingly "planetary capitalism" (the term is from Gayatri Spivak [1990]), every national society now creates and debates its own modernity (Paz 1990). A central question, then, concerns the trajectories that shape modernization and the modalities by which some voices "get to play with modernity" (Appadurai 1990). It is this public culture, as Appadurai calls it, a zone of globalized cultural debate, encounter, and interrogation that arises in all of our case studies. In this, we are following Spivak

(1990:94) in her request that "what goes on over here be defined in terms of what goes on over there."

To return to one of our cases studies—the Muslim revolt in Nigeria—a thread linking our narrative has been what Raymond Williams (1961) called "the structure of feeling" under various forms, and at various moments, of capitalist development. Our argument, as the Maitatsine case revealed, is that such a feeling, a particular social and personal identity, was revealed through what one might call the local hermeneutics of Islam. Rather than being rigidly prescriptive, Islam is a text-based religion that is made socially relevant through enunciation, performance, citation, reading, and interpretation. It is this dialogic and interpretive tradition around a central text that is fundamentally enigmatic and that necessarily leads to questions of how and which texts are used, by whom, and with what authority (Fischer and Abedi 1990). In this sense, Maitatsine was renegotiating and contesting a certain sort of Muslim tradition, building certain identities through idiosyncratic interpretations and readings. He focused solely on the Qu'ran and gave a literalist reading—certain Arabic characters, for example, resembled a pictorial representation of a bicycle and hence spoke to Maitatsine's antimaterialism—in a way that cobbled together both a particular sort of Muslim and ethnic identity, and a wish image of a Benjaminian sort (a future community that, like the Angel of History, was being propelled backwards by looking to the past). Maitatsine drew upon the global resources (and commodities) of capitalism and the Muslim diaspora to assemble, in local terms, a *bricolage*, which derived its power in part from the historical tension between the community (*umma*) and the state in Muslim discourse. To this degree, Maitatsine was part and parcel of wide-ranging global debates within Islam over modernity.

What can one derive from the Maitatsine insurrection, or our case studies from The Gambia, Stockholm, and California, in relation to modernity and identity? Let us begin, with what we are not saying. We are not simply suggesting that we need willy-nilly more studies of "subaltern resistance," more studies of the culture of the poor and powerless, who are always assumed to speak with one unified voice. We have some grave misgivings about the conceptions of power in some of these studies, and in any case, in the wake of an imperialist Gulf war, we surely need more work on the rich and powerful. Neither are we appealing in an unproblematic way to religion or space as a basis for understanding identity politics.

Rather, we want to stress the importance of understanding the historical production of difference within a unified system. Difference and identity are produced and reproduced within a field of power relations rooted in interconnected spaces linked by political and economic relations. Maitatsine's appeal can only be grasped in relation to the Muslim diaspora, world commodities, and the oil-based political economy of Nigeria, just as U.S. workers in California were framed by similar cultural and world systemic processes. In addition, there are fundamental relations between identity and the contesting and negotiating of difference in cultural terms. Maitatsine's community and popular geographies in Stockholm do say something about both the symbolic materials and the symbolic creativity through which, to return to Stuart Hall, one gets from here to there. The symbolic contestation of modernity is instantiated in shifting identities rooted in enunciation, dialogue, and what Paul Willis (1990), in another context, calls the symbolic creativity of "mismatching." Insofar as these sliding identities are narratives, they invoke and draw sustenance from the imaginary, the wish images that recapitulate the ceaseless configuration and reconfiguration of the old and the new in a commodity society. Cultural and symbolic struggle, the contesting of meanings, is the means by which identities are given shapes that allow us to act.

And finally, there is the matter of difference and politics: how identity, which rests on difference and division, can produce a political common ground. How, as Hall (1989) says, can we think about forms of political action that enable us to understand these processes of identification rooted in difference, rather than try to transcend them? And it seems to us that this project requires not a retreat from class but a desperate need to retheorize where class has gone to, and to rethink, and reassert it in nonessentialist terms.

These are bold claims, and we are making even bolder assertions— namely, that these questions strike to the heart of certain experiences of modernity here, and can be discussed (to return to Spivak's injunction) in terms of what goes on there as much as in terms of what goes on here. "There" is to be understood as both a historical and geographical other. In the dialectical images thrown up by African modernity, in the fantastic intermingling of the old and the new in fin de siècle Sweden, among struggles over gender identity in The Gambia, there resides the possibility that "our own expectations and understanding [be brought] to a momentary standstill" (Taussig 1990:224).

Notes

CHAPTER 1 *Capitalisms, Crises, and Cultures I*

1.   Despite this claim, in his effort to focus on local knowledge, to explain social phenomena "by placing them in local frames of awareness" rather than by "weaving them into grand textures of cause and effect," Geertz (1983:6) tends to get lost in a thicket of difference and variance. He eschews both explicit theory formulation and the idea that difference can be produced from within a unified system, in other words, how processes of local knowledge formation and political economy play upon one another.

2.   For excellent discussions of the meteoric rise of the Silicon Valley, see Saxenian (1990), Keller (1981), and the work of the U.C. Santa Cruz Silicon Valley Research Group, and Hayes (1989).

3.   This literature is, of course, huge, subsuming debates over development theory, uneven development, the role of multinational capital, the rise of the NICs and much more. For important encapsulations of these debates, see Peet and Thrift (1989), Lipietz (1987), and Froebel et al. (1980).

4.   On this point, I am grateful to discussions with Dr. Paul Lubeck, whose forthcoming work on Malaysia documents these changes.

5.   This term first appeared in the October 1988 special issue of the British Left journal *Marxism Today,* and also was used by Jacques and Hall (1989). It subsequently came to represent a particular theoretical and political position on the real meaning of Thatcherite Britain (see also Sivanandan 1989).

6.   Harvey (1989) uses the work of Lash and Urry, Halal, and Swyngedow to capture the variety of transitions envisaged in post-Fordist literature. One might just as easily include work by Claus Offe and some of the regulationist school, such as Lipietz and Aglietta.

7.   See, for example, Sayer 1989; Gertler 1989; Harvey 1989.

8.   This restructuring program has focused on (i) the way enterprises respond to competition, especially through product lines and work organization (for example, the rise of flexible accumulation), (ii) the creation and destruction of spatial divisions of labor associated with new conditions of profitability (the rise of new industrial spaces and production complexes), and (iii) the links between uneven development and social relations, typically expressed through locality studies (see Lovering 1989; Cooke 1990a).

9.   As Jessop (1988), points out there are substantial variations within and among the Parisian, Grenoble, German, and Dutch regulationists, athough they share a realist epistemology, a Marxian heritage, and a concern with the changing forms and mechanisms by which expanded reproduction of capital is secured. See also Walker 1989.

10.   There is, of course, a substantial debate over the periodization, including Schumpeterian innovation cycles, the product cycle, Kondratieff's long

waves, and so on. For our purposes, we note a broad distinction between extensive (1820–1920) and intensive (1920–present) systems of accumulation differentiated in the following way: commercial capitalism (1820–1870s); competitive industrial capitalism (1873–1896); early monopoly capitalism (Taylorism) (1896–1929); crisis period (1929–1945); second phase of monopoly capitalism/Fordism (1945–1966); crisis/neo-Fordism (1966–present). This is similar to the periodization offered by Soja (1989), though he refers to mercantile, competitive industrial, corporate monopoly, and state-managed Fordism.

11.   Anthony Giddens's notion of space-time distanciation is also relevant here.

12.   Soja does argue rhetorically that that there is always room for resistance (p. 235), but the broad thrust of his argument is toward "the numbing depoliticisation of social life" (p. 219). It is the unity of perspective and voice, the totalizing vision, that is so striking.

13.   There are, for example, few studies of the everyday life of flexible accumulation, or indeed, sensitive studies of the cultural politics and historical struggles associated with the making of the Third Italy or Orange County.

14.   The important and relevant books by Beneria and Roldan (1987) on subcontracting in Mexico City, by Kondo (1990) on power and gender in the Japanese workplace, and by Pauline Peters (forthcoming) on property rights in Botswana illustrate this point.

15.   See also Pred (1989, 1990a) for an elaboration of this perspective drawing in part upon structuration theory and time geography.

CHAPTER 2 *The Shock of Modernity*

This essay was originally delivered as the Attwood Lecture to the Graduate School of Geography, Clark University Worcester, Mass., on October 24, 1989. I am especially grateful to Billie Turner and to the faculty and students of Clark for their kindnesses and hospitality. In tracing the connections between oil-based capitalism, Islam, and social protest in Nigeria I am, as always, deeply indebted to my fellow *ba'haushe*, Paul Lubeck of U.C. Santa Cruz, whose writings on culture and class, and on Maitatsine, have beeen inspirational. I have been especially privileged to read the brilliant historical writings of Bala Usman, who, long ago, spoke with extraordinary clarity on the intersection of class and religion in Nigeria. Hans Panofsky of the Herskovitz Library at Northwestern University provided me with rare and obscure documentation of one sort of another. At various points over the last few years, John Pickles, Arjun Appadurai, Carol Breckenridge, Peter Stallybrass, Mary Beth Pudup, Michael Burawoy, Allan Pred, Dick Walker, Michael Fischer, Dick Peet, Jack Goody, Dick Werbner, Ivan Karp, Gunnar Olsson, Paul Rabinow, and Janet Roitman have offered advice and criticism, and a wonderful cohort of ornery graduate students, including Karen Lewis, Katharyne Mitchell, Eric Hirsch, Rod Neumann, Michelle Cochrane, Susanne Friedberg, Patrick Heller, Rick Schroeder, Libby Wood, and Lucy Jarosz, have always been there to challenge my unfashionable structuralism. This chapter first saw the light of day in an undergraduate class at Berkeley, which perhaps says a great deal about teaching at that institution. I dedicate this essay to the memory of my father, John Watts, with whom I shared some precious moments in Nigeria.

1.   Maitatsine's diaspora extended across much of northern Nigeria and into southern Niger Republic, a region sharing a cultural kinship with the Hausa heartland in Nigeria. These networks provided fertile recruiting grounds for *al-majirai* and *gardawa*. Witness #49 before the official tribunal (Nigerian Federal Government 1981a:58), one Uzairu Abdullahi, was one such Hausa disciple, recruited from Niger eleven months prior to the insurrection.

2.   The Aniagolu Report (Nigerian Federal Government 1981a) notes, however, that while there were a number of complaints over Marwa's activities and clashes with police throughout the period 1974–1979, there was a marked escalation of complaints in 1980. Eleven in all, these complaints pertained to heretical preaching, violent personal attacks on local residents, the popular appropriation of a public bathroom, and the unlawful expansion of Marwa's compound onto other private lots, including the blockage of a major drain. The brotherhoods are social organizations with West African Islam, which emerged as institutions of refuge, but now serve as the religious and political vehicles for particular interpretations of Islam and for the promotion of specific Muslim practices.

3.   This section is drawn from the following works: Christelow 1984, 1985; Clarke 1987; Nigerian Federal Government 1981a; Hiskett 1987; Lavers 1982; Lubeck 1981, 1984, 1985, 1987; Na-Ayuba 1986; Nicolas 1981; NIPSS 1986; Omoniwa and Abu 1986; Yusuf 1988; "Maitatsine Had 10,000 Men," *New Nigerian*, February 5, 1981, 7; ibid., December 23, 1980, 1.

4.   Total manufacturing output, in any case, increased at 13 percent per annum during 1972–1980, even though the industrial sector accounted for only 6.7 percent of GDP in 1979–1980. The marginal propensity to import was extremely high (67.7 percent); consumer durables and nondurables increased by over 700 percent between 1973 and 1980.

5.   For similar arguments within Muslim discourse in relation to capitalism, see Ong (1990) and Lambek (1990).

6.   Benjamin 1973:159. I am especially indebted to the brilliant work of Susan Buck-Morss (1989), whose study of Benjamin's Arcades Project is enormously helpful in clarifying his thinking.

7.   There is a substantial literature on the First Republic and the civil war. See Sklar 1963; Post and Vickers 1973; Kirk-Greene 1971; Graf 1987; Akpan 1976; Diamond 1983.

8.   Nolutshungu 1990:89. The work of Watts (1983), Lubeck (1986), Laitin (1986), Joseph (1987), and Usman (1980) have explored the imagining and construction of Nigerian ethnicities.

9.   Laitin (1986) shows how British indirect rule in Yorubaland constructed Yoruba ethnicity as such in its reincarnation of the ancestral city as a basis for local political rule. Lubeck (1986) and Watts (1983) show how the class alliance between Lugard and the Hausa-Fulani aristocracy in the north limited missionary incursions and vastly expanded the powers and autonomy of Muslim patrimonial rule and a deepened sense of "Hausaness" more generally.

10.   There is a huge literature on the so-called oil syndrome. For a representative literature, see Commander and Peek (1983), Crystal (1985), Gelb

(1981), Hausmann (1981), Petras and Morley (1983), Pesaran (1982), Pollard (1985), Roemer (1983), Seers (1964), and Imam-Jomeh (1985).

11.   Absorptive capacity is the capacity to absorb oil revenues locally as productive capital (as distinct from the capcity to import). See Gelb (1981) for a discussion.

12.   The relevant literature for Nigeria, which provides statistical estimates of these aggregate growth trends as a function of oil revenues is as follows: Bienen 1983; *The Economist* 1984; IBRD 1985a, 1985b; Kirk-Greene and Rimmer 1981; Onoh 1983; *Oil, Debts, and Democracy in Nigeria* 1986; Watts 1984; Usman 1980; Wright 1986.

13.   This has been explicitly addressed by a scholar of Iran, Hamza Katouzian: "[O]il revenues accrue directly to the state . . . [which] does not have to depend on the domestic means of production. . . . Once these revenues rise to a high level . . . they afford the state an unusual degree of economic and political autonomy. . . . [Therefore] the entire system . . . depends on the size and strategy of state expenditure" (1981:34). See also Evans and Reutschmeyer (1985) on the relative autonomy of the state.

14.   In Kano itself, car assembly (Fiat), chemicals (ICI), textiles (CFAO), batteries (Union Carbide), and a host of other manufacturing establishments were established in the 1970s.

15.   The indigenization issue is explored in detail in Bierstecker (1988) and also in Lubeck (1987).

16.   By 1980 agricultural exports constituted only 2.4 percent of GDP by value.

17.   Novelist Chinua Achebe observed that Nigeria is "without shadow of a doubt one of the most corrupt nations in the world" (1984:42). For example, the National Petroleum Company lost twenty-five billion U.S. dollars over a four-year period as a result of smuggling and contract malfeasance. Records in state ministries were regulary torched in "accidental fires," and the culture of not "being on seat" was the lodestar of Nigerian bureaucratic machinery.

18.   Nigerian contracts (for example, for house, road, or office construction) were typically 200–400 percent higher than in comparable African states (*The Economist* 1984:17).

19.   In his monumental study, *Global Rift*, Stavrianos cites a UN survey that estimated that a civil servant in oil-rich Kuwait worked an average of sixteen minutes per day (1981:664). My suspicion is that many Nigerian civil servants, for ostensibly similar reasons, logged in a similar "workday."

20.   One of my most vivid impressions of the commodity boom in Nigeria was of a child trader standing in a traffic jam on Lagos Island, selling Father Christmas paperweights containing snow-filled wintry scenes, reindeers and all.

21.   Port Harcourt, for example, increased by 400 percent between 1969 and 1977.

22.   By 1981 the staple food import bill stood at three billion U.S. dollars, roughly 17 percent of total domestic consumption. Nigeria was self-sufficient in the mid-1960s. The major change here was, of course, in taste, specifically the emergence of white bread, what Andrae and Beckman (1985) call the "wheat trap," as a staple of the urban poor. Interestingly, many of the 'Yan Tatsine supported themselves as sellers of tea and bread to the Kano talakawa.

23.   The northern irrigation schemes (1.5 million hectares at N0.5 billion per year) were sources of lucrative contracting in their own right; in addition to their cost (and hence political attractiveness) and inefficiency, the largest project at Bakalori was associated with bloody strife and conflicts over land accumulation and compensation. For discussion of these and other agrarian transformations, including the impact of World Bank–funded Green Revolution programs see the following sources: Adams 1988; Agbonifo 1980; Alkali 1985; Andrae and Beckman 1987, 1985; Iliya 1988; Kimmage 1989; IBRD 1985a, 1985b; Jega 1985; Kaduna State 1981; Ukpolo 1983; Watts 1983, 1987; Williams 1988.

24.   In 1982 the Central Bank of Nigeria could not provide estimates of income, expenditure and external debt. To this day there is still a debate over the exact magnitude of Nigeria's external debt.

25.   Oil production fell by two-thirds between January and August of 1981; oil revenues slumped from U.S. $27.4 billion in 1980 to U.S. $11 billion the following year. The Economic Stabilisation Act of 1982 substantially reduced state expenditures, capital investment, and imports. The boom had finally bust.

26.   See Seers 1964:236; ILO 1981. In 1978, four million households were below the poverty line, an increase of over 25 percent since 1973. For other discussions of the income and equity issue, see Collier (1983), Sanusi (1982), and Jamal (1981).

27.   I follow the lead of Raymond Williams, E. P. Thompson, Paul Willis, and others who posit culture as interwoven with all social practices. As Stuart Hall (1980:26) put it, culture is "*both* the meanings and values which arise amongst distinctive social groups and classes on the basis of their given historical conditions and relationships, through which they handle and respond to the conditions of existence; *and* as they are lived traditions and practices through which those understandings are expressed and in which they are embodied."

28.   Hiskett (1987) is quite mistaken to refer to the 'Yan cin-rani simply as "opportunists and Dick Whittingtons." Many were the casualties of land grabs, of the failure of the state to compensate for land appropriation (cf. the Bakalori scheme), and the victims of generalized rural poverty. Many fled the rural areas under a cloud of shame as destitutes (*yawon dendi*).

29.   An extraordinary series of documents—the twelve-volume Kaduna State Lands Commission study—produced by the PRP provides endless examples of how peasants lost access to land through nefarious land scams, fraud, and state corruption (Kaduna State 1981). See also Swindell 1986.

30.   Hiskett (1987:213) is also wide of the mark, however, when he links the gardawa to an urban subculture of magicians (yan tauri). It should be pointed out, however, that syncretic (pre-Islamic) beliefs have always been a central part of Hausa society at all levels, and Maitatsine clearly had a reputation for magical powers which he successfully welded onto his Qu'ranic exegetical skills.

31.   The infamous Ricegate scandal, in which a cabinet official was directly implicated in rice smuggling and hoarding, is, of course, well known to scholars of Nigeria.

32.   The PRP's ticket proclaimed that it promoted "the freedom and dignity" of the "common people" against "retrograde northern feudalists" and the "hard core of the NPN made up of a tiny oligarchy" (PRP 1982:215). The PRP abolished local rural taxes as semifeudal hangovers.

33.   The governor's aides apparently met (and dined?) with the Maitatsine leadership, and the governor himself visited 'Yan Awaki Ward prior to the insurrection.

34.   I have discussed the moral economy at length in my book *Silent Violence* (Watts 1983: esp. ch. 3).

35.   Gumi is a former Grand Kadi and founder of the Jamaatu Naasril Islam, which attempts to serve as an umbrella organization for Muslim groups. Linked to the NPN and the northern oligarchy, Gumi is a conservative reformist (a sort of mixture of the American evangelical preachers Falwell and Robertson).

36.   The critique focuses especially on certain innovations: the folding of arms while praying, not facing Mecca while praying, collections of fees by mallams, and the wearing of amulets. The last is especially interesting because it speaks to the popular belief across many segments of society in non-Muslim spirits and powers. It is precisely this source of power (often associated in northern Nigeria with non-Muslim Hausa [Maguzawa] and the urban underworld) that Maitatsine drew upon; indeed, Maitatsine was recognised as a sort of sorcerer. Several of Maitatsine's lieutenants carried talismans; one, quoted in the Aniagolu Report, said, "[I]f I were cut into pieces an' die I shall come back to life."

37.   I rely here on the excellent work of Na-Ayuba (1986).

38.   The Muslim Students Society, also in part the product of Islamiyya schools, has also been active, with the 'Yan Izalas, in a quite extremist reading of Islam.

39.   Associated with the brotherhoods, darikat practice involved daily prayer and meditation, strict discipline, and obedience to saints.

40.   See, for example, the widely circulated poem "Waken Karohen Duniya" (Song of the End of the World), which was distributed in northern Nigeria in the 1920s and which attacked "modern ways," "illiterate youth," etc. (see Clarke 1987).

41.   Several of the official and press publications refered to the 'Yan Tatsine as 'Yan Izalas (see NIPSS 1986), which they clearly were not. There is evidence, however, that the 'yantatsine were involved in various clashes between extremist elements of the 'Yan Izalas and security forces.

42.   See Laitin (1986) for a discuussion of the so-called shari'a debate and the writing of the Nigerian constiution in the period prior to the 1979 elections and the return to civilan rule.

43.   By 1980 the residential compound occupied close to three thousand square meters.

44.   Herbst's (1990:197) hopelessly oversimplified explanation argues that the Maitatsine were "outsiders" and that the insurrection was simply a function of the disappearance of "exit options," that they had "nowhere else to go." Because of their heretical ideas and their limited mobility (but the Maitatsine did flee!), Herbst believes that violent confrontation was inevitable (p. 198).

45.   The Kano State Government (1981) response to the Aniagolu Report reveals the extreme tension between the NPN-dominated federal government and the PRP state administration. The former, at one level, did not wish to assist its political protagonists; on the other hand, the political sensitivity of a "Muslim" revolt in the north during a sensitive period of debate over shari'a created some concern among the NPN, which was dominated by the conservative northern oligarchy.

46. Sunni Islam demands that ill-gotten wealth must be distributed to the needy, a sentiment conspicuously absent among the Kano notables.

47. In Nigerian society, wealth is not per se bad or unworthy; rather, it must be acquired according to a cultural blueprint. As Barber (1982) shows, the rise of the petronaira was associated with the notion of "magic-money"—wealth without any evidence of work or dutiful effort. This is a popular theme in Nigerian literature (see Emecheta 1982). I have explored this in depth in Watts (1992).

48. There is a substantial literature, of course, on money in Africa and its relationship to witchcraft and the supernatural, and on rules pertaining to the disposition of illegitimate wealth. See Shipton 1989.

49. One of the most important prominent national figures under detention is Balarabe Musa of the PRP.

50. In April 1990 there was an attempted coup against the Babangida regime by disgruntled officers who complained of northern dominance in the federation.

51. Several public conferences on SAP and its alternatives, featuring such speakers as Soyinka and the prizewinning novelist Festus Iyayi, have been banned by the government, and many participants arrested. See *Bulletin of Concerned Africanist Scholars*, no. 28 (Fall 1989).

CHAPTER 3 *Living under Contract*

Critical comments were provided by Jane Guyer, Gill Hart, Pauline Peters, David Cohen, Louise White, Henry Bernstein, Ben Crow, Maureen Mackintosh, Michael Burawoy, Frank Hirtz, Diane Wolf, and, especially, Mary Beth Pudup. Versions of this paper benefited from discussions at the University of California, Davis, the University of Hawaii, Cornell University, or the Red Lion Seminar, Northwestern University. Some of the research was sponsored by the Institute for Development Anthropology, Binghamton, New York; I am grateful for the assistance and comments of Peter Little, Steve Jaffee, Ivan Karp, David Goodman, Dick Walker, Bill Friedland, Margaret FitzSimmons, and, especially, Judith Carney of UCLA, whose published work I drew upon heavily. Some of this chapter draws upon our joint work (Carney and Watts 1990, 1991). Additional support was provided by the Berkeley Working Group on Contract Farming, including Alex Clapp, George Henderson, Lucy Jarosz, Brian Page, and Jorge Lizarraga. The section entitled "Property, Power, and Politics: A Case Study of Irrigated Rice Contracting in West Africa" relies on the work of Carney (1986, 1988) and also appears in Carney and Watts (1990, 1991).

1. Hog production in the United States was quite resistant to contracting until the deepening of the farm crisis in the 1980s. The fiscal crisis after 1982 created the opportunity for corporate contractors to capture overcapitalized and heavily indebted hog growers. Brian Page, a doctoral student at the University of California, Berkeley, is currently completing a Ph.D. dissertation on this subject.

2. Following FitzSimmons (1986:337), industrialization refers to changes in the labor process and in relations between capital and labor within the firm, by industrial sector and by region. This is akin to the notion of appropriation employed by Goodman et al.

3.   *Corporate* refers not to capitalist industrial enterprise but to the complex institutions that link growers and contractors in dense social networks. The contractor may, indeed, be corporate (in the narrow sense of a foreign or local agribusiness) but quite frequently is a state or parastatal enterprise or some form of merchant's capital (buyers-exporters-traders). See Tchala-Abina 1982; Swainson 1986.

4.   One strand of the literature has focused on the internal organization of the firm; another, on the workings of the labor market and, to a lesser extent, on finance and services (Williamson 1985; Elson 1988). This literature has been central to the new industrial geography (see Scott and Storper 1985; Walker and Storper 1989).

5.   The neoclassical literature on share, labor, and tenancy contracts—specifically focusing on efficiency and risk characteristics and contract specification—is huge, but it generally argues that the choice of contract maximizes the gain from risk dispersion subject to transaction costs (see Binswanger and Rosenzweig 1984). For a different, Marxist reading see Pearce (1983).

6.   Ball (1987) estimates that the number of contractors increased by 50 percent between 1950 and 1985 in British agriculture. In California agriculture, there has been a 74 percent rise in farm labor contractor employment over the period 1978–1987 (Vandeman 1988).

7.   I am grateful to Dr. Mary McDonald of the University of Hawaii, Honolulu, for this information.

8.   Mighell and Jones (1963) provide a simple taxonomy distinguishing between market-specification contracts (future-purchase agreements), resource contracts (growers are provided seed, credit, and technology), and production contracts (in which the labor process is determined, controlled, and supervised).

9.   Vertically integrated corporate agribusinesses account for only 7.4 percent of U.S. farm output.

10.   Some of the earliest contracting in the United States emerged half a century ago in the vegetable-canning industry, as processors mounted a campaign for "orderly marketing" in the face of volatile supply. Commodities such as fresh milk, potatoes, and many horticultural crops are dominated by contract production. See Sporleder 1983; Wilson 1986; Pfeffer 1985; Watts 1990a; Reidmund et al. 1981.

11.   In Japan, for example, 25 percent of all rice production is contracted (see Japanese Ministry of Agriculture, *61st Statistical Yearbook* [Tokyo: Ministry of Agriculture, 1986–1987]), and contractual relations among growers, cooperatives, and business are widespread (see Asano-Tamanoi 1988). On Western Europe, see Marsden et al. (1988).

12.   In 1935 the production of broilers (live weight) was 123 million pounds; by 1975 the figure stood at 11,034 million pounds (USDA 1976).

13.   McDonald's and Kentucky Fried Chicken are, of course, the two primary retail outlets for chicken, two fast food enterprises whose global reach extends from Moscow to Beijing to Mexico City. Tyson Foods, which supplies poultry to Kentucky Fried Chicken, exports more than one hundred million U.S. dollars' worth of prepared chicken products to Asia alone.

14.   The USDA actually sponsored the search for a "perfect broiler" between 1945 and 1955 (see USDA 1976).

15.   In the past fifteen years, two weeks have been sliced off the time to grow a fryer (it is currently about seven weeks).

16.   According to the U.S. Congress, the composite farm wage rate in the southern states was fifty cents an hour (cited in Wilson 1986:60).

17.   In some cases, for example, lettuce production by grower-shippers in California, these agro-industrial complexes are capitalist, corporate, and transnational. In others, for example, sharecropping of rice in California by heavily capitalized family enterprises, capital relates indirectly to production through processes of appropriation (the conversion of rural production processes into industrial products and services by agro-industrial and financial capitals).

18.   This raises an important theoretical point about the persistence of petty commodity production under capitalism. Peasants are not, in the short term, doomed to be capitalism's victims but may fill spaces manufactured in the course of capitalist development. Peasants can be "captured," to use Goran Hyden's language, in a variety of ways—contracting is one form of subsumption or capture by capital—which nonetheless significantly restructure the peasant economy, in spite of the continuity of household forms of production.

19.   Contract farming is not only a "peasant strategy." Contracting is distinguished by a substantial degree of diversity in its social organization, embracing relations between capitalist enterprises (for example, United Fruit contracts with indigenous capitalist banana growers in its Central American operations) at one extreme and contracts between lilliputian growers and a small buyer-processor on the other (for example, peasant women growing green beans on half-hectare plots in Western Kenya for a French company). In this chapter I shall be primarily addressing contracting between state and/or private capital and small-scale commodity producers of an admittedly quite differentiated sort (but not capitalist enterprises). For a discussion of the variety of contract farming forms, see Watts (1990a).

20.   In the early 1980s, USAID commissioned, through its Bureau of Private Enterprise, a study of agribusiness and the small farmer, conducted by the Business International Corporation. Many of its case studies discuss contracting as a glowing testament to the notion of a "dynamic partnership" between capital and peasant producers. See Karen and Williams 1985.

21.   The CDC is a British financial institution, active in promoting contracting since the 1950s. It currently sponsors thirty-four schemes (seven hundred thousand hectare), embracing six hundred thousand smallholder growers of sugar, tea, coffee, and palm oil. Of these, 75 percent involve combinations of centralized estates, peasant outgrowers, and a central processing unit (see Commonwealth Development Corporation 1984). The World Bank has focused on outgrower tree crops (tea, cocoa, oil palm) and new lands settlement projects (van der Laar 1980); 50 percent of the projects are African.

22.   Large public-sector contract farming schemes typically have some equity holding by transnational capital, and the project may be managed by foreign agribusiness. The Kaleva Smallholder Sugar Company in Zambia, for example, is owned by Zambia Sugar (a parastatal), Barclay's Bank, the Commonwealth Development Corporation, and the Development Bank of Zambia and is managed by the British Conglomerate, Tate, and Lyle.

23.   Fresh fruit and vegetables accounted for 12 percent of world agricultural exports by 1985, comprising the fourth-largest commodity group, with a value of twenty-five billion dollars. The Third World accounts for 40 percent of this production.

24.   This ratio is almost identical to the labor demands of millet and French beans in Western Kenya.

25.   See also Palmer-Jones (1978), Daddieh (1987), and Nabuguzi (1987) for discussions of tobacco in Nigeria, tea in Malawi, and cocoa in Ghana. An inventory of contract farming in Africa appears in de Treville (1987).

26.   It has been estimated that in the case of East African tea—like other contracted crops, an extremely labor-intensive crop—the actual grower return to labor input (the latter is estimated at, on average, two thousand hours per acre per year) is *less* than the wage paid to estate laborers, who are seen to be among the most exploited of the rural poor.

27.   Located in MacCarthy Island Division, Wallikunda is some three hundred kilometers east of the capital, Banjul, in the middle river region.

28.   The Gambia covers ten thousand square kilometers and is nominally part of a confederation with Senegal. Its population was 695,000 as of 1983; 40 percent were Mandinka, the most numerous ethnic group.

29.   *Swamp rice* refers to several traditional, nonirrigated rice ecologies regulated by daily, monthly, or seasonal tides and by the presence of salinity, which may extend at least 160 kilometers upstream during the dry season (that is, low-volume) period.

30.   National Archives (NAG), The Gambia, Banjul, File 2/3313, n.d.

31.   This project, jointly funded by a foreign donor and the state (U.S. $16.53 million), developed pump-irrigated double-cropping of Green Revolution rice varieties. IFAD has a major role in project management. See "Jahaly-Pacharr Project: A Fact Sheet" (unpublished manuscript, Banjul, n.d.); Patrick Webb, "Of Rice and Men: The Story behind The Gambia's Decision to Dam Its River," in Edward Goldsmith and Nicholas Hildyard, eds., *The Social and Environmental Effects of Large Dams* (Wadebridge, England: Wadebridge Ecological Centre, 1984); Judith Carney, *Contract Farming in Irrigated Rice Production,* Working Paper no. 9, Contract Farming Project (Binghamton, N.Y.: Institute for Development Anthropology, 1987).

32.   See Linares (1985), for a discussion of the origins of rice in Senegambia.

33.   During the eighteenth and nineteenth centuries, Rene Caillie, Richard Jobson, and Frances Moore all documented the complex rice-growing systems among Mandinka and Dyula peoples in the Senegambia. See Watts and Carney (1990).

34.   For a discussion of the groundnut industry, see Gamble (1955), Barrett (1988), and Jeng (1978).

35.   Haswell's (1973) work shows that in the Mandinka village of Genieri, rice accounted for 85 percent of staple foodstuff production.

36.   See Watts (forthcoming) for further discussion. See also Robertson 1987; Swindell 1981.

37.   See Watts and Carney 1991. Haswell's (1963) studies between the late 1940s and 1962 document the growth of labor time (close to 15 percent) per female Mandinka swamp rice worker.

38.   Haswell (1973) did observe the limited participation by men in swamp rice production by the 1970s, largely in the form of assisting women with the transportation of seedlings to and from the swamps and the harvesting of the rice.

39.   Gambian rice imports in 1984 constituted 50 percent of total domestic rice consumption.

40.   The International Fund for Agricultural Development, based in Rome, has favored smallholder development.

41.   The total project area is 1,500 hectares, of which 560 are fully irrigated. Participants in the project include Mandinka, Fulbe, Serrahuli, and Wolof households, four ethnic groups with distinctive social structures and household property relations. The account here refers only to Mandinka peasants, statistically the most numerous in the Jahaly-Pacharr project. I am especially dependent on the research of Dr. Judith Carney on the Jahaly-Pacharr project.

42.   Von Braun and Johm (1987) provided labor allocation data for the 1985 wet season.

43.   As will become clear, the intrahousehold struggles do not exhaust the social and cultural adjustments, but they are particularly important.

44.   In the mid-1970s, Dey (1980) estimated that 165 of 187 acres of the Jahaly swamp had not been returned and remained lease land.

45.   A woman who is resident in her husband's compound loses land rights in her natal unit and cannot remove household land in the event of divorce or death of the husband.

46.   See the BBC documentary *The Lost Harvest* (1987), directed by Sara Hobson.

47.   These periods mark the transition between dry season and wet season irrigation cycles but also correspond to the planting and harvesting periods of upland crops.

48.   Berry 1989. This is also parallel to the point made by Jane Guyer (1989) in her analysis of the recombinations of labor during periods of agrarian intensification.

49.   The International Food Policy Research Institute is based in Washington, D.C.

50.   The literature on the conjugal contract is large, but see Whitehead (1981), Folbre (1986), Guyer (1984, 1988a, 1989), and Roberts (1988).

51.   See Carney 1986, 1988; Carney and Watts 1990, 1991. According to von Braun and Webb (1989:523) these sorts of compensation were equivalent in value to the activities undertaken by women in their least remunerative agricultural activity.

52.   Women are fully cognizant of both the need for skilled paddy field labor, which they can supply, and the grower's dependency on prompt in-field operation to meet the rigorous schedules imposed by project management. The *kafo* groups bid up their collective wage accordingly. Twenty women typically charge eighty dalasis for transplanting one plot. Working as a group, the women are able to transplant two plots a day, the proceeds from which total roughly 60 percent more than the individual daily wage (see Carney 1987).

53.   See Carney and Watts (1990, 1991) for a discussion of other collective adjustments to the new social relations on the scheme.

54.   Unlike the well-organized capitalist growers in northern Mexico, very few peasant growers have formal organizations. Those few schemes with long-

standing grower organizations—for example, the Kenya Tea Development Authority—have little or no impact on prices, policy, and project organization.

55.   Tobacco is three to four times more labor-intensive per unit area than hybrid maize in western Kenya (Shipton 1985); contracted irrigated rice production in The Gambia increased annual farm rice work by 60 percent (Carney and Watts 1990).

56.   For other cases, see Ayako and Glover (1989), Clapp (1988), and Jackson and Cheater (1989).

57.   Kitching points out that the relative bargaining power of women is also shaped by the timing of commodity production: "Where . . . entry into commercial production was a discrete, spatially separated step with a completely different labor process controlled by the household head, his decision-making power might not be challenged to the same extent, and access by wives to . . . the surplus product would be more on a grace and favour basis" (1980:50).

58.   Almost no contracting schemes with smallholders have official grower representation, have institutional means for price determination, or enable growers to own equity in the company. The British American Tobacco Company has recently threatened to withdraw from Kenya if its growers are organized in cooperatives. USAID sees its Guanchias coops, which contract for Standard Fruit in Guatemala, as model democratic institutions, yet they are heavily funded as political showcases. The coops are paternalistic and represent much-publicized alternatives to militant and self-run peasant organizations. See McCommon et al. 1985. For a good discussion of grower organizations in the United States, see Wilson (1986).

CHAPTER 4 *Capitalisms, Crises, and Cultures II*

1.   Note earlier comments on these mutations and the temporal rhythms of capitalist development in Chapter 1. Important discussions of capitalist mutations are provided in Davis (1978), Aglietta (1979), Soja (1989), and Harvey (1982).

2.   Since the late 1970s, a number of pivotal anthropological and related works have appeared, which address the cultural conflicts and resistances resulting from the introduction of new forms of capitalism into specific non-Western settings. In addition to the works of Ong (1987) and Wolf (1990) already cited in Chapter 1, see, for example, Nash (1979), (Taussig 1980), Comaroff (1985), and Scott (1985). Also see Holmes (1989) on the cultural struggles deriving from the insertion of urban industrial activities into the everyday life of peasants in the Friuli region of northeast Italy. Cf. note 22.

3.   Regarding the textual strategy of this chapter, see the "Prefatory Articulations" at the beginning of this book. Complementary and overlapping aphorisms and propositions are to be found in Pred (1989, 1990a, 1990b, 1990c). The bibliographies contained therein include numerous additional references to the literatures of critical human geography, social theory, anthropology, and sociolinguistics, from which this section is complexly derived.

4.   Here *discourse* is employed in Foucault's (1972, 1973, 1979) sense, to refer to a set of interrelated concepts and values.

5.   Hall 1981:26, emphasis added. This insistence on the inseparability of

culture and social practice is in keeping with Hall's "Birmingham school" as well as some of the central writings of E. P. Thompson (1968) and Raymond Williams (1973, 1977). Cf. Brenkman 1987:vii, 8. Also note Ryan's (1989:8–24) constructive critique of Hall and Williams; and contrast with Archer (1988), who rightfully debunks the "image of culture as a coherent pattern, a uniform ethos or a symbolically consistent universe" (pp. xv, 1–21), but insists upon the "relative autonomy of structure and culture" while at the same time conceptualizing some important ways in which they interplay.

6.   Williams 1982:13.

7.   The construction of human geographies, or the production of space and place, at one and the same time refers to the production of an unevenly developed built environment; the shaping of landscape and land use patterns; the appropriation and transformation of nature; the organization and use of specialized locations for the conduct of economic, social, and religious or ritual practices; the generation of patterns of movement and interdependence between such localized activities; and the formation of symbolically laden, ideology-projecting sites and areas (Pred, 1990c).

8.   Thus, as the *Passagen-Werk* and other writings of Benjamin so richly suggest (Buck-Morss 1989), any critical understanding or interpretation of historically and geographically specific forms of society requires a simultaneous interpretation of their culture(s).

9.   Compare Williams (1977:121–127) on the interactions and conflicts occurring among "residual," "dominant," and "emergent" forms of culture.

10.   Marcus and Fischer 1986:78.

11.   Thrift 1983:46, emphasis added.

12.   Scott 1990.

13.   Obviously, locally occurring language usages and symbolic forms are not likely to be confined to those of local origin—especially under modern circumstances. Many, if not most, usages and forms—and their meanings—will be more or less similar over widespread areas as a result of migration, diffusion, or dissemination and reinforcement via the printed and electronic media.

14.   Compare Fantasia (1988) on the cultural interplay of solidarity and acts of opposition.

15.   Cf. Bourdieu 1985, 1987, 1989, 1990; Stedman Jones 1983.

16.   Bourdieu 1987, 1990.

17.   Compare the argumentation developed by Scott (1990) and the observations on symbolic social inversion in Babcock (1978), Bakhtin (1984), and Stallybrass and White (1986).

18.   Olsson 1991.

19.   Cf. Marcus and Fischer 1986:85, 153. Much of the literature on the cultural and ideological terrains of struggle embedded in everyday life is directly or indirectly rooted in Gramsci (1971).

20.   See the argumentation developed by Harvey (1989).

21.   Paraphrased from Jameson 1988:351.

22.   The classic works of Thompson (1963) and Tilly (1986) in different ways attach central importance to the context-dependent, place-specific, everyday-practice-embedded cultural struggles and symbolic discontent that emerged in parts of England and France in conjunction with the factory system and early forms of industrial capitalism. Thompson's work in particular has inspired a vast

literature of related studies regarding class struggle in the realm of cultural production and the production of symbolic meanings, several of which (for example, Sewell [1980], Smail [1987], and Stedman Jones [1983]) focus on language and discourse.

23.   This observation is consistent with the body of theory that insists that "all identity is constructed across difference" (Hall 1987:45), that rejects any notion of a truly autonomously arrived-at identity, and that conceptualizes ethnic or group "identity as a dynamic process of construction and reproduction over time, in direct relation or opposition to specific other groups and interests" (Löfgren 1989:9).

24.   Hegemony should not be conceptualized as something uncontested, as something definitionally strangling resistance, as something existing without a counterhegemony. "Gramsci's notion of hegemony, . . . which names domination by consensus rather than by coercion, through culture rather than through the exercise of force," is—as Hall and others point out—"never stable but instead . . . constantly negotiated through struggle" (Ryan 1989:17–18). Furthermore, Ryan (1989:18) adds: "One could argue . . . that hegemony is in fact itself a kind of [cultural-political] resistance, a means of securing the identities of property and of political power against very real internal threats that are always potentially active in a system of economic subordination founded on a radical difference or inequality."

CHAPTER 5 *Languages of Everyday Practice and Resistance*

This chapter is derived largely from Chapter 4 of Pred (1990b).

1.   The late-nineteenth-century transformation of Stockholm's manufacturing activities, international trade linkages, demography, and physical structure is treated at length in several standard works, the most noteworthy of which are Gustafson (1976), Hammarström (1970), and William-Olsson (1937).

2.   See Pred (1990b: ch. 6) for details.

3.   Compare Harvey 1985:1–35.

4.   The strikes, trade union activities, and political mobilization of Stockholm's working classes during the period considered here are admirably summarized in Cederqvist (1980).

5.   ACM, folio 70 (Mekaniska verkstäder). See bibliography for ACM and other abbreviations.

6.   The languages of production, consumption, social reference, and social address are spelled out in Chapters 3 and 5 of Pred (1990a).

7.   The daily path concept is associated with Torsten Hägerstrand's "time-geography." This framework captures the constant becoming and material continuity of biographies and society in place by depicting individuals in terms of the unbroken "paths" they weave through time-space and depicting society in terms of the time-specific, individual-path-coordinating "projects" generated by its constituent institutions. For key references to the time-geographic literature see Pred (1990c).

8.   Stockholm's local government 1897:16–17, 147–149. The working-class recollections of late-nineteenth-century life contained in ACM and other

sources make virtually no reference to the use of trolleys, although details of their operation are provided by conductors and other employees.

9.   A comparison of speech acts and pedestrian utterances, as well as conventional rhetorics and perambulatory rhetorics, is eloquently developed by de Certeau (1984: 97–102; 1985:129–138).

10.   Jameson 1984:90, commenting on Lynch 1960. Although geographers and others have produced a considerable volume of research on individual spatial cognition and "spatial behavior," relatively little has been done on the communication of popular geographies and other forms of linguistically conveyed knowledge necessary to spatial orientation and getting around in urban environments. See, for example, the literature cited in Gale and Golledge (1982), and note the discussion of "commonsense geographies" and "locally organized knowledge" in Schegloff (1972).

11.   A glossary of roughly three hundred terms and phrases is presented in Chapter 4 of *Lost Words and Lost Worlds* (Pred 1990b). All of the terms and phrases appearing in this chapter are from that glossary, which was compiled primarily from ACM, AINS, Thesleff (1912), and Uhrström (1911), as well as from several published recollections and secondary sources. For a complete list of sources, including the specification of archival folios, see the notes accompanying the glossary in question.

12.   The bourgeoisie and upper classes of Stockholm used this term to designate both the working class and those who were unemployed.

13.   *Söder,* unlike any of the other terms discussed here, remains part of common Stockholm usage today.

14.   The nonsense -*is* and -*an* endings were appended to many Stockholmska (Stockholm dialect) words other than locational designations, and they still remain important in the formation of new slang terms. On the origins of -*is* and -*an* popular geographic names, see Ståhle (1981:138–158).

15.   *Tav* is possibly from a corruption of *tarvlig* (needy, or shabby).

16.   ACM, folio 101 (Ligor).

17.   ACM, folios 101 (Ligor) and 144 (Gatuliv); and Sperlings 1973:47.

18.   The names of some of these establishments actually may have been derived not from the customers who frequented them but from the one-time occupation of the current operator or one of his predecessors.

19.   Compare de Certeau (1984:115–130) on the "spatiality" of stories.

20.   ACM, folios 11 (Krogar), 119 (Toffelmakare), 123 (Diverse uppteckningar), and 148 (Per Ludvig Lindgren).

21.   ACM, folios 11 (Krogar), 81 (Slakterier och slaktare), and 171 (Instrumentmakare).

22.   ACM, folios 130 (Superi) and 171 (Instrumentmakare).

23.   ACM, folios 9 (Tunnbindare), 11 (Krogar), 68 (Porslinfabriker), 70 (Mekaniska verkstäder), and 170 (Vindragare).

24.   ACM, folios 1 (Sömmerskor), 13 (Matställen), and 159 (Kaféer); and Sjöström 1937:76.

25.   See Note 14.

26.   ACM, folio 148 (Per Ludvig Lindgren).

27.   At least a dozen other popular windmill names, most of them deeply sedimented, appear in ACM, folio 207 (Diverse rörande väderkvarnar).

28.   ACM, folio 36 (Kuskar).

29.   ACM, folio 148 (Per Ludvig Lindgren).

30.   ACM, folio 123 (Diverse uppteckningar); Uhrström 1911; Lundin 1890: 206. Given the comic inversions used in this case, it may be assumed that the sermons delivered at the Syrupy Church by no means dripped with sweetness.

31.   Frykman and Löfgren 1987:221. The Swedish counterparts of late Victorians are referred to as Oscarians, after Oscar II, who reigned from 1872 to 1907.

32.   ACM, folio 34 (Husbyggen).

33.   Sjöström 1937:15.

34.   Regarding the physical expansion, spatial reconfiguration, and architectural transformation of Stockholm during this period, see William-Olsson (1937:45–59, 167–170), Gejvall (1954:30 ff.), and Råberg 1985:102–147).

35.   Note the middle-class memoirs cited in Frykman and Löfgren (1985: 24–27) and Tarschys (1982:521–522).

36.   Police station arrest ledgers from the period are filled with accounts of street fights among drunks occurring during morning and afternoon hours as well as evenings and nights. Reports of public urination were less numerous, but occasionally precinctwide campaigns were conducted against such behavior, prompted by, among other reasons, concern for the attire of bypassers. SSA, 1889, vol. 1, Report no. 502 (March 9), vol. 5, no. 3156 (November 3); 1896, vol. 6, nos. 3560, 3573, 3574, 3575 (all November 24), and 3940 (December 31). Arrests also occurred for addressing insulting language to women on the streets. SSA, 1889, vol. 5, Report no. 3327 (December 12).

37.   Such bourgeois fears, like industrial capitalism itself, came much later to Stockholm than to London, Paris, and other northern continental centers. Cf. Franzén 1982:4–7.

38.   For fundamental observations on such joinings of knowledge and power, and on the exercise of "bio-power," see Foucault (1978, 1979) and Rabinow (1984:14–23).

39.   By 1886 nineteen cab stations were subject to control. Brodin and Dahlman 1887:46.

40.   The full details of these rules were publicized in a number of places, including the annually published city directories, the Adress-Kalender för Stockholms Stad (Stockholm, 1880–1900).

41.   Stockholm's local government 1882:91; Stockholm's local government 1902:105. In percentage terms, however, this increase only very slightly exceeded Stockholm's population growth for the period. Whenever crowd control was required, these numbers could be much enhanced by locally garrisoned troops and reserve constables.

42.   NMA, Polisundersökningen, Del 1 (2), item EU 44605, 79–97. Officers are known to have been dismissed for on-the-job drunkenness or falsely reporting illness, taken to task for talking on the beat "to an unidentified male" between 12:03 and 12:11 A.M., and suspended for several days because of excessive familiarizing. SSA, 1889, vol. 3, Report nos. 1342 (June 14) and 1416 (June 21), vol. 4, no. 2498 (October 3), and vol. 5, no. 3231 (December 1). There are also accounts of on-duty patrolmen dropping into breweries in order to drink a few beers. ACM, folio 162 (Poliser).

43.   Selling 1970, 1973; Gejvall-Segar 1982; Gejvall 1954: 28–29 (source of quotes). Albert Lindhagen was the prime mover for the "street regulation" of Stockholm from 1866 until his death in 1887.

44.   Although there was much else motivating Hausmann's plan, Walter Benjamin, among others, has noted that in devising the boulevards his "real aim . . . was the securing of the city against civil war." The width of the boulevards discouraged the erection of barricades, and the lengthy and straight avenues "were to provide the shortest route between the barracks and the working-class areas" (Benjamin 1973:174–175).

45.   There remained, however, considerable emphasis on the catechism and religious knowledge. Cf. Rappe 1973; Sandin 1984:122, 125. The imposition of bourgeois attitudes toward cleanliness and neatness was also an important part of school disciplining. ACM, folio 18 (Skolor).

46.   Löfgren 1984:18–20. Cf. Kern 1983:36 ff., 208; Lowe 1982:40.

47.   This ideological overlapping and transition is alluded to by Frykman and Löfgren (1987:274–276) and is considered at greater length in the literature cited therein.

48.   Ståhle 1981:10–20. Some eventually legitimated street names of popular origin did manage to remain official beyond 1885. For example, the name David Bagares Gata (David [the] Baker's Street) in Norrmalm was a persisting folk usage traceable back to 1667.

49.   Ample evidence of this is given in Chapters 3 and 4 of *Lost Words and Lost Worlds* (Pred 1990b).

50.   Compare Scott (1985:297), on the significance of individual acts of resistance, and Schegloff (1972:113) and Bernstein (1970:174), on forms of speech, including locational designations, and cultural boundary maintenance.

51.   Compare Scott's (1985:314–350) arguments against the views developed by Antonio Gramsci, Georg Lukacs, and certain of their successors regarding symbolic hegemony, the impenetrability of dominant ideology, and false consciousness.

52.   Regarding these practices, see Chapter 3 of *Lost Words and Lost Worlds* (Pred 1990b).

53.   ACM, folio 95 (Mjülkutkörare). Other union-centered street-rule violations are implicit in Cederqvist's (1980) discussion of strike activity during the 1880–1900 period.

54.   ACM, folio 26 (Spårvägen).

55.   ACM, folio 101 (Ligor).

56.   SSA, 1889, vol. 1, Report no. 24 (January 3), vol. 4, nos. 2516 (October 5) and 2589 (October 9); 1896, vol. 2, nos. 798 (April 3) and 1051 (April 22).

57.   ACM, folio 54 (Stenarbetare).

58.   See "No Address," Roland Barthes's artful interpretation of moving about in Tokyo's network of nameless streets, in Barthes (1982:33–36).

59.   Thesleff 1912:125. In a gesture of characteristic Oscarian prudery, Thesleff confined all slang terms with a sexual connotation to a special appendix, in which all definitions were given in Latin rather than Swedish. Hence the hyphenated juxtaposition of slang and "proper (Latin)" terms in the text here.

60.   Compare Stallybrass and White (1986), who argue that high/low

symbolic oppositions in the realms of social order, the human body, and geographical space have structured and invaded one another at certain places and moments in European history.

61.   See the section on streets and alleys earlier in this chapter.

62.   ACM, folio 144 (Gatuliv).

63.   Compare the "Postmodern Geographies or Maps of Meaning?" section of Chapter 1.

CHAPTER 6 *Outside(rs) In and Inside(rs) Out*

I am most thankful to my colleague Dick Walker, who carefully read the initial version of this chapter. As always, his comments were insightful and thought-provoking.

1.   William C. Hogan, of Fordham University, quoted in the *Los Angeles Times,* March 26, 1987.

2.   By no longer obtaining coils from the USX Geneva Works in Provo, Utah, and instead acquiring them from Pohang, where production costs were low because of cheap labor and state-of-the-art technology, the facility in Pittsburg could save fifty dollars per ton (Hoerr 1988:489).

3.   Exports to New Zealand, Guatemala, Japan, South Korea, and India occurred for the first time in 1988. These shipments occurred, however, before the computerized milling equipment had operated in anything other than test mode. *Antioch Daily Ledger,* February 2, 1988; *Contra Costa Times,* March 24, 1989. Other details of the summary contained in this paragraph are derived from several 1985–1989 issues of these same two newspapers, as well as similarly dated issues of the *Pittsburg Post Dispatch* and the business sections of the *Los Angeles Times* and the *San Francisco Chronicle.*

4.   U.S. production climbed back to 83.9 million metric tons in 1984, but by 1986 had fallen back to 74.0 million metric tons (American Iron and Steel Institute 1974–1987).

5.   Howell et al. 1988:503. Local unemployment problems were compounded by negative multiplier effects, derived from both the cessation of factory input purchases and diminished income expenditures on the part of former employees.

6.   The decline of U.S. steel output has propagated a number of book-length studies. In addition to the closely documented, almost 700-page-long, analysis of Hoerr (1988), these include Kiers (1980); Crandall (1981); Barnett and Schorsch (1983); Locker/Abrecht Associates, Inc. (1985); Strohmeyer (1986); Bensman and Lynch (1988); Howell et al. (1988); Reutter (1988); and Tiffany (1988), which, like the Reutter book, focuses primarily on somewhat earlier events and developments.

7.   Global capacity outside of the United States was 100.7 metric tons in 1950 and 578 million metric tons in 1974 (Howell et al. 1988:16).

8.   Between 1974 and 1986, nonsocialist "developing" countries more than doubled their total steelmaking capacity, from 54 to 122 million metric tons (Ibid.:5).

9.   As of July 1984, imports accounted for more than 30 percent of U.S. steel consumption, or more than double the corresponding 1973 level (Bensman

and Lynch 1988:74). Because of gaping loopholes in the Reagan administration's 1984 Voluntary Restraint Agreement, cheap foreign steels continued to flood U.S. markets with impunity. Steel imports still accounted for 27 percent of the domestic market in February 1985 (*Los Angeles Times*, March 30 and June 16, 1985).

10.   Between 1977 and 1987, there was a net increase in U.S. minimill capacity of five million metric tons (Howell et al., 1988:54).

11.   By 1983, half the domestic market for rods and wire had been captured by minimills (Bensman and Lynch 1988:86).

12.   According to a 1988 report, the plant construction costs of a minimill capable of producing five hundred thousand tons per year amounted to $631 per ton of capacity, while the corresponding costs for an integrated mill capable of producing six million tons per year amounted to $1,465 per ton (Howell et al. 1988:24).

13.   Hoerr 1988:15, 22, 315. Until some reforms in late 1983 eliminated at least two layers, workers on the floor of a U.S. Steel plant had ten levels of "operating management" above them, no less than seven of them within the production facility itself.

14.   Bensman and Lynch 1988:78. See also Barnett and Schorsch 1983.

15.   Ibid.:89. Regarding industrial restructuring in general, Reagan's early "zap labor" policy, and the growing boldness with which employers challenged union certification and demanded takebacks, see Harrison and Bluestone (1988). Also note Clark (1989) on the role of the National Labor Relations Board in the decline of organized labor in the United States.

16.   Hourly costs per worker at U.S. Steel were about twenty-three dollars, while Japanese costs were from ten dollars to eleven dollars (Hoerr 1988: 429).

17.   Ibid.:430. Although these actions led to innumerable grievances and some lost arbitration cases, U.S. Steel management thereby "demonstrated to employees that the unions no longer had monopoly control of either labor supply or work practices" (ibid.:435).

18.   Ibid.:425. Regarding the local consequences of a "labor crackdown" climate in other industries, see Clark (1989).

19.   "The government and the government-owned Korean Development Bank held a majority of the equity ownership and the rest of the firm's stock was held by government-controlled Korean banks" (Howell et al. 1988:293–294).

20.   Ibid.:295; Amsden 1989:293–295. Tae Joon Park had earlier made something of a mark for himself by turning around the government-owned Korea Tungsten Corporation. In connection with a major realignment of parties in South Korea during the fall of 1989, Tae Joon Park established himself as one of the country's most powerful political figures.

Except where otherwise documented, the remainder of this section is based upon both the account of the South Korean steel industry provided by Howell et al. (1988:286–307) and Amsden's (1989:291–318) analysis of POSCO's history.

21.   *Los Angeles Times*, May 23, 1988; *Wall Street Journal*, April 29, 1988. Although the state itself directly held only about 30 percent of POSCO, its power over the company was much greater, for another 40 percent was owned by the government-run Korea Development Bank. Although the remaining 30 per-

cent was held by private commercial banks, those institutions are subject to considerable government regulation and influence.

22.   *Los Angeles Times*, February 22, 1985; *Contra Costa Times*, November 7, 1988.

23.   *Contra Costa Times*, November 7, 1988. POSCO's entry in many ways represents a classic case of capital from an outlying new center of growth and innovation moving into a stagnant, mature industrial territory (cf. Storper and Walker 1989).

24.   The Nathan Koburn quote appeared in the *Antioch Daily Ledger* and *Pittsburg Post Dispatch* on September 4, 1988. The narrative account given in the remainder of this chapter rests primarily on reports made in the local press—which covered the entire USS-POSCO modernization story with considerable intensity—rather than on information derived from scattered interviews conducted in the fall of 1989. For all its possible limitations with respect to omitted details, inaccurate quotes, and unintended ideological coloring, the reportage contained in the *Antioch Daily Ledger*, the *Pittsburg Post Dispatch*, and other newspapers for the most part provides participant statements and action descriptions from within the actual flow of struggle events, rather than recollections filtered through the optic of subsequent developments and experiences.

25.   *Antioch Daily Ledger* and *San Francisco Business Times*, July 6, 1987.

26.   *Engineering News Record*, March 19, 1987.

27.   *Kennebek Journal* (Augusta, Maine), June 24, 1987. At one point BE & K was officially condemned by the AFL-CIO as a "strikebreaking service, attractive to companies willing to engage in unfair labor practices" (*San Francisco Chronicle*, March 11, 1988).

28.   Davidson 1989:16, 53–57. As Davidson points out (p. 17), such comparisons may prove deceptive since numerous "studies have found that higher paid union construction workers are more productive than lower paid non-union workers," presumably because the former group is characterized by lower rates of turnover and higher average levels of skill and experience. An analysis conducted by Allen (1984) indicated that nonunion costs were at least 17–22 percent higher when measured by value added per employee and deflated for interregional differences in construction goods prices.

29.   *Antioch Daily Ledger*, January 19, 1987.

30.   *San Francisco Business Times*, July 6, 1987; *Antioch Daily Ledger*, May 21, 1987.

31.   *Antioch Daily Ledger*, January 19, 1987. In order to conduct a continuing defense through the local and regional media, USS-POSCO took on the services of Morrison & Foerster, a San Francisco public affairs consulting firm.

32.   The construction of a portion of Highway 580 originally had been given over to a consortium of nonunion Oregon contractors. Through intensive monitoring activities, the Alameda County Building and Construction Trades Council had been able to reveal several violations of state and federal regulations regarding safety and construction standards. With large fines pending, the Oregon group declared bankruptcy and defaulted on its commitment. This left the door open for a reassignment of the remaining portion of the forty-eight-million-dollar job to a union contractor (*San Francisco Business Times*, July 6, 1987).

33.   *Antioch Daily Ledger* and *Pittsburg Post Dispatch*, March 8, 1987.

34.   The two secondary partners were the Eichleay Corporation, of Pittsburgh, Pennsylvania, and Daelim American, Inc., of New York. Because of its clearly primary role, BE & K remains the term of principal usage throughout the rest of this chapter.

35.   *Antioch Daily Ledger,* March 4 and 8, 1987; *Pittsburg Post Dispatch,* March 8, 1987. The political consulting firms that had been able to bring pressure were the Kamber Group of Washington, D.C., and Cerrell Associates of Los Angeles.

36.   *Antioch Daily Ledger,* February 13, 1987.

37.   *Pittsburg Post Dispatch,* December 1, 1987; *San Francisco Chronicle,* June 7, 1988.

38.   Walker and Bay Area Study Group 1990:27. On the importance of the "politics of place" within the larger-scale processes associated with the nation-state and the modern world economy, see Agnew (1987).

39.   *Antioch Daily Ledger,* January 19, 1987.

40.   Ibid., March 4, 1987. The resulting study (Davidson 1989) is discussed in notes 28 and 108.

41.   *Antioch Daily Ledger,* July 30, 1987; *Contra Costa Times,* August 25, 1987.

42.   *Antioch Daily Ledger,* June 23, 1987.

43.   Ibid., March 29, 1988. The California Highway Patrol recommendation further suggested that local industries should be reminded of the registration law prior to the implementation of a one- to two-week crackdown. *Contra Costa Times,* March 28, 1988.

44.   *Contra Costa Times,* July 15, 1988; *Antioch Daily Ledger,* July 22 and August 17, 1988. Those caught were subject to a fifty-dollar fine unless they registered their vehicles immediately upon leaving the roadblock.

45.   *Pittsburg Post Dispatch,* May 19, 1988.

46.   The Robertson quote appeared in the *Antioch Daily Ledger* on July 30, 1987. The Freere quote appeared in the *Antioch Daily Ledger* and *Pittsburg Post Dispatch* on September 4, 1988.

47.   *Los Angeles Times,* March 26, 1987.

48.   *Antioch Daily Ledger,* July 30, 1987; *Contra Costa Times,* April 11, 1988. The arbitration panel sat in Washington, D.C.

49.   *Antioch Daily Ledger,* March 4, April 18, June 23, and July 30, 1987; *Pittsburg Post Dispatch,* December 13, 1987. Technical experts brought in by the lawyers had failed to convince a majority of the board that, once modernized, the plant would be producing enough toxic waste to fall subject to the ordinance.

50.   *Antioch Daily Ledger,* June 23, 1988.

51.   Ibid., July 26, 1988. Despite the context, the EPA insisted that the inspection was not motivated by the filing of any complaints.

52.   Ibid., May 19, 1988.

53.   Ibid., May 8, 1987.

54.   *Oakland Tribune,* December 3, 1987; *Pittsburg Post Dispatch,* October 28, December 1, and December 13, 1987; *Antioch Daily Ledger,* February 10, May 28, and June 1, 1988; *San Francisco Chronicle,* June 7, 1988. Not surprisingly, AMK International (BE & K) contested the safety citations, thereby bringing about the drawn-out involvement of a judge-led review commission. *Antioch Daily Ledger* and *Pittsburg Post Dispatch,* June 11, 1988.

55.   *Martinez Gazette,* August 9, 1988.

56.   *Contra Costa Times,* January 13, 1988.

57.   *Antioch Daily Ledger,* July 30, 1987.

58.   *San Francisco Chronicle,* March 8, 1988. Demonstrators did not confine themselves to picket carrying and chanting, but in many instances pelted convention delegates with eggs, fruit, and pint cartons of milk.

59.   *Antioch Daily Ledger,* July 30 and December 20, 1987; *Pittsburg Post Dispatch,* September 4, 1988.

60.   See text accompanying note 42.

61.   See text accompanying note 48. Eichleay Corporation, the partner in question, maintained that they were really comprised of two separate firms, only one of which was bound to the collective bargaining agreement. *Antioch Daily Ledger,* June 1, 1987.

62.   Ibid., July 24 and October 9, 1987; *Contra Costa Times,* December 19, 1987; *Pittsburg Post Dispatch,* September 4, 1988.

63.   *Antioch Daily Ledger,* April 8, 1987.

64.   *Contra Costa Times,* April 11, 1988.

65.   *San Francisco Examiner* and *San Francisco Chronicle,* March 20, 1988. The longshoremen's work stoppage was not total, as it did not apply either to vessels carrying mail or perishable goods or to military and passenger ships.

66.   *News-Pilot* (San Pedro, California), March 11, 1988; *Pittsburg Post Dispatch,* March 15, 1988; *San Francisco Chronicle,* March 16, 1988. The port improvements were to occur on eighteen acres of waterfront land, sold by USS-POSCO to a Hong Kong–financed Oakland group, whose chief was openly antagonistic to unions. As of the spring of 1988, steel bound for USS-POSCO was unloaded either from Korean vessels by unionized longshoremen at the ports of Richmond and Oakland or from trains, trucks, and domestic ships at the plant site itself by unionized steelworkers, who did so by virtue of a 1960 ruling of the National Labor Relations Board. In contrast, it was anticipated that once trade restraints were removed, all of the plant's arriving unfinished steel—about one hundred thousand tons monthly—would come from South Korea and be unloaded entirely at the new docking facilities at its doorstep. *Antioch Daily Ledger,* June 20, 1988.

67.   *San Francisco Chronicle,* April 7, 1989; *Antioch Daily Ledger,* April 6, 1989.

68.   In other words, class consciousness is here viewed as an experience-based awareness, or understanding, of the time- and place-specific power relations in which one's everyday production or employment activities are enmeshed, rather than simply an articulated awareness of membership in a widely encompassing, undifferentiated, statically structured workers' or employers' class. Cf. Fantasia 1988:3–19; Walker 1985. Also note Scott and Storper (1986:308–309) on the regional specificity of industrial and employment mixes, of class consciousness, and of consequent political responses.

69.   *Antioch Daily Ledger,* June 25, July 24, July 30, and July 31, 1987.

70.   Ibid., July 24, 1987.

71.   Ibid., October 9, 1987; *Contra Costa Times,* December 19, 1987.

72.   *Los Angeles Times,* March 26, 1987; *Antioch Daily Ledger,* February 13, 1987. An attorney for the Contra Costa Council previously had publicly

asserted: "We don't think some other government ought to be able to undercut wages in this country" (*Antioch Daily Ledger*, January 26, 1987).

73. *Antioch Daily Ledger*, July 24, 1987.

74. *San Francisco Chronicle*, April 7, 1989; *Antioch Daily Ledger*, April 6, 1989. According to the *Daily Ledger* account, a contingent of Korean War veterans also burnt flags.

75. The handbill was not only sponsored by a building trades union, the United Brotherhood of Carpenters and Joiners of America, but also by the United Paperworkers International Union, an organization that had come into conflict with BE & K at several locations elsewhere in the country (see text accompanying note 26).

76. *Waterville Morning Sentinel (Maine)*, June 8, 1988.

77. On the connections between folk, or popular, imagery and identity, see Dundes (1989:1–39), and the literature cited therein.

78. On the social inversion accomplished through hybridization, see Stallybrass and White (1986).

79. *Antioch Daily Ledger*, October 9, 1987; *Pittsburg Post Dispatch*, December 20, 1987; *San Francisco Examiner*, March 8, 1988.

80. *Antioch Daily Ledger* and *Pittsburg Post Dispatch*, December 13, 1987, and September 4, 1988.

81. *Pittsburg Post Dispatch*, December 20, 1987; and *Antioch Daily Ledger*, July 24, 1987.

82. *Oakland Tribune*, August 25, 1987; *Antioch Daily Ledger*, July 29, 1987; *Pittsburg Post Dispatch*, December 13, 1987, and March 20, 1988; *Contra Costa Times*, April 11, 1988.

83. *Antioch Daily Ledger* and *Pittsburg Post Dispatch*, September 4, 1988.

84. *San Francisco Chronicle*, March 11, 1988.

85. *Antioch Daily Ledger*, May 21, 1987. In other instances, union negotiators convinced their members to accept more flexible work rules, the sacrifice of double-time pay, or other concessions in order to win particular contracts.

86. Based on interview remarks. Compare comments by an unionized construction ironworker in the *Antioch Daily Ledger*, July 24, 1987.

87. Two rank and filers who voted for the new contract are quoted above. Both quotes appeared in the *Antioch Daily Ledger* and *Pittsburg Post Dispatch*, the first, on August 9, 1987, and the second, on September 4, 1988.

88. Hoerr 1988:489; *Antioch Daily Ledger* and *Pittsburg Post Dispatch*, March 21, 1987. The Fontana facility, by now out of business, was the old Kaiser Steel plant.

89. On the complex genesis of the six-month work stoppage, which had the attributes of both a strike and a lockout, see Hoerr (1988: esp. 485ff.).

90. Stanton had been financial secretary for the more militant local at the Homestead Works until USX Corp. closed that famous Pennsylvania facility in 1986.

91. *Antioch Daily Ledger*, June 20, 1988.

92. Ibid., December 2, 1988.

93. *Antioch Daily Ledger* and *Pittsburg Post Dispatch*, September 4, 1988.

94.   Ibid. March 1, 1987; *Contra Costa Times,* April 11, 1988. Also note the epigraphs at the beginning of this section.

95.   *Antioch Daily Ledger* and *Pittsburg Post Dispatch,* March 8, 1987; *Contra Costa Times,* April 11, 1988.

96.   *Antioch Daily Ledger* and *Pittsburg Post Dispatch,* August 9, 1987, and September 4, 1988.

97.   Cf. note 68.

98.   Cf. note 16 and accompanying text. In Pittsburg, Local 1440 had accepted some creation of "supercrafts" as early as 1984.

99.   *Local 1440 United Steelworkers Rank & Filer* 2, no. 6 (June 1989).

100.   Pittsburg steelworkers have not been alone in experiencing some negative consequences of flexible production routines. Unlike Piore and Sabel, some have recognized that "the new flexibility of job tasks can mean increased exploitation and job loss or genuine job enrichment" (Lash and Bagguley 1988:323).

101.   Because of the legal secrecy surrounding grievance procedures, and because such procedures were still in motion at the time of this study, more detailed information regarding their content could not be uncovered by way of interview.

102.   Regarding the long-standing nature of this question in the steel industry, see Hoerr (1988: esp. 312–317). For a critical assessment of the literature regarding workplace control and the "employment relation" in general, see Storper and Walker (1983:17–21). Also note Storper and Walker's (1989) observations on the new social relations in production associated with distant, "peripheral" investments made from new industrial centers.

103.   On both "relations in production" and "the labor process as a game" with unintended consequences, see Burawoy (1979).

104.   *Local 1440 United Steelworkers Rank & Filer* 2, nos. 8–10 (August–October 1989).

105.   Ibid., no. 8, August, 1989.

106.   *Local 1440 United Steelworkers Rank & Filer* 2, nos. 8 and 10 (August and October 1989).

107.   For further theoretical and empirical observations on the interplay among the making of histories, the construction of human geographies, and already existing social and spatial structures see, Pred (1990a).

108.   The earlier report (Davidson 1989:i–ii) had drawn the following conclusions: "The employment practices of AMK [BE & K] had substantial negative impacts on Contra Costa County. The payment of wages below prevailing rates and the use of substantial numbers of out-of-state workers resulted in a loss of construction payroll going to local workers of $36.5 million dollars and a loss of spending in the local area of $18.6 million. Through the multiplier effect the lost spending led to an additional loss of local secondary income of $19.9 million and a loss of 933 potential secondary jobs. The combined loss of direct payroll income and secondary income in turn led to a loss of $393,655 in local sales tax revenues. . . . Workers from outside of California added an estimated 150 students to the average daily attendance of Contra Costa County schools at a cost to the state in school revenue limit funding of $365 thousand. . . . Incoming workers without health insurance . . . cost the state health care system an estimated third of a million dollars. And, by hiring out-of-state workers AMK [BE & K] increased local unemployment by 4,842 worker weeks and [thereby] increased state

unemployment insurance costs by an estimated $200,924." Not surprisingly, BE & K has vehemently contested the "Davidson Report."

109.   Former President Gerald Ford, quoted in the *San Francisco Chronicle*, April 7, 1989.

Coda

1.   In this regard, our dependence on the work of Walter Benjamin is considerable. His rabbinical, apocalyptic, and messianic vision leaves us somewhat cold, but his exploration of dialectical images and his interrogation of capitalism through the archaeology of the commodity—his juxtaposition of the very old with the very new—seems to us to be brilliant and original. In this light, we have also benefited substantially from the work of Susan Buck-Morss (1988) and Mick Taussig.

2.   We have relied heavily here on the excellent discussion by Denning (1990) on the end of mass culture and his superb analysis of cultural studies.

3.   "The creative element in a process whereby meanings are attributed to symbols and practices, and where symbols and practices are selected, reselected, highlighted, and recomposed to resonate further appropriated and particularized meanings . . . [g]rounded aesthetics are the yeast of common culture" (Willis 1990:21).

Bibliography

Archival Sources and Abbreviations

ACM. Archives of the Stockholm City Museum (Stockholms Stadsmuseum). All references pertain to *Uppteckningar om olika miljöer, arbetsförhållanden och företeelse i Stockholms stad*, an extensive set of transcribed oral recollections gathered during the 1930s and 1940s.

AINS. Archives of the Division for Stockholm Research, Department of Scandinavian Languages (Institutionen för nordiska språk), University of Stockholm.

NAG. National Archives, The Gambia.

NMA. Archives of the Nordic Museum (Nordiska museet).

SSA. Stockholm Municipal Archives (Stockholms stadsarkiv). All references pertain to *Rapport Bok för första Polisdistriktet*, the record of arrest bookings of the First Police Precinct for the years 1889 and 1896.

Books, Articles, and Papers

Achebe, C. 1988. *Anthills of the Savannas*. New York: Vintage.

———. 1984. *The Trouble with Nigeria*. London: Heinemann.

Adams, W. 1988. Rural protest, land policy and the planning process on the Bakalori Project, Nigeria. *Africa* 58(3):315–335.

Agbonifo, P. 1980. State farms and rural development. Ph.D. diss., University of Wisconsin, Madison.

Aggar, B. 1989. *Fast Capitalism*. Urbana: University of Illinois Press.

Aglietta, M. 1979. *A Theory of Capitalist Regulation*. London: Verso.

Agnew, J. 1987. *Place and Politics: The Geographical Mediation of State and Society*. Boston: Allen & Unwin.

Aho, P. 1983. An economic evaluation of broiler chicken supply organization in Shiawassee County Michigan. Ph.D. diss., Michigan State University.

Akerlof, G. 1980. A theory of social custom. *Quarterly Journal of Economics*, 54:749–775.

Akpan, N. 1976. *The Struggle for Succession*. London: Cass.

Alkali, A. R. 1985. U.S. agribusiness and the proletarianization of the peasantry in Kaduna State. Paper presented to the Seminar on Nigerian Economy and Society, Zaria, Ahmadu Bello University.

Allen, G. 1983. The development of the Mumias Company, Kenya. *Oxford Agrarian Studies* 12:63–93.

Allen, S. G. 1984. Unionized construction workers are more productive. *Quarterly Journal of Economics* 99:251–274.

Alliez, E., and M. Fisher. 1985. The luster of capital. In *Zone I*, 315–359. Cambridge: MIT Press.

American Iron and Steel Institute. 1974–1987. *Annual Statistical Reports*, Washington, D.C.: AISI.

Aminzade, R. 1989. What is historical about historical sociology? Working Papers, History and Society Program, University of Minnesota, Minneapolis.

Amsden, A. H. 1989. *Asia's Next Giant: South Korea and Late Industrialization*. New York: Oxford University Press.

Amuzegar, J. 1982. Oil wealth: A very mixed blessing. *Foreign Affairs*, Spring, 814–835.

Anderson, B. 1983. *Imagined Communities*. London: Verso.

Anderson, P. 1990. A culture in contraflow. II. *New Left Review*, no. 182:85–137.

Andrae, G., and B. Beckman. 1987. *Industry Goes Farming*. Uppsala: Scandinavian Institute of African Studies.

———. 1985. *The Wheat Trap*. London: Zed Press.

Appadurai, A. 1990. Disjuncture and difference in the global cultural economy. *Public Culture* 2(2):1–24.

Archer, M. S. 1988. *Culture and Agency: The Place of Culture in Social Theory*. Cambridge, Cambridge University Press.

Arjomand, S. 1983. The Iranian revolution in comparative perspective. Paper presented to the Centennial in Celebration of Emil Lederer, New School for Social Research, New York.

Aronowitz, S. 1991. An introductory essay on cultural studies. Unpublished manuscript, Sociology Department, Graduate Center, CUNY, New York.

Asano-Tamanoi, M. Farmers. 1988. Industries and the state: The culture of contract farming in Spain and Japan. *Comparative Studies in Society and History* 30(3):432–452.

Awojobi, A. 1982. *Where Our Oil Money Has Gone?*, Lagos: Nigerian Press. Lecture delivered at the University of Ile-Ife, May 11, 1982.

Ayako, A., and D. Glover, eds. 1989. *Contract Farming and Smallholder Outgrower Schemes in Eastern and Southern Africa*. Special issue of *Eastern Africa Economic Review*.

Babcock, B. 1978. *The Reversible World: Symbolic Inversion in Art and Society*. Ithaca, N.Y.: Cornell University Press.

Bakhtin, M. 1984. *Rabelais and His World*. Bloomington: Indiana University Press.

Ball, R. 1987. Agricultural contractors. *Journal of Agricultural Economics* 38(3):481–488.

Bangura, Y., and B. Beckman. 1989. African workers and structural adjustment: A Nigerian case study. Paper prepared for UNRISD/ISER Conference on Economic Crisis and Third World Countries, Jamaica, April.

Bannbers, O. 1944. Arbetaren och språket. In A. Lindblom, ed., *Arbetaren i helg och socken—Kulturhistoriska studier, II Vardag och fest,* 343–375. Stockholm: Tidens Förlag.

Barber, K. 1986. Radical conservatism in Yoruba popular plays. *Bayreuth African Studies Series,* no. 7:5–32.

———. 1982. Popular reactions to the Petro-Naira. *Journal of Modern African Studies,* 20(3):431–450.

Bardhan, P. 1988. Dominant proprietory classes and India's democracy. In A. Kuli, ed., *India's Democracy,* 76–83. Princeton: Princeton University Press.

Barnett, D. F., and Louis Schorsch. 1983. *Steel: Upheaval in a Basic Industry.* Cambridge, Mass.: Ballinger.

Barrett, H. 1988. *The Marketing of Foodstuffs in The Gambia:*1400–1980. Avebury, U.K.: Gower Publishers.

Barthes, R. 1982. *Empire of Signs.* New York: Hill and Wang.

———. 1970–1971. Remarks in *Architecture d'aujourd'hui,* no. 153:11–13.

Bashir, I. 1983. The politics of industrialization in Kano. Ph.D. diss., Boston University.

Bassett, T. 1988. Breaking up the bottlenecks in food crop and cotton cultivation in northern Ivory Coast. *Africa* 58(2):148–173.

Beckman, B. 1985. Bakalori: Peasants versus capital and state. *Nigerian Journal of Political Science* 4(1–2):76–104.

BE & K. 1986. Introduction to BE & K. Circulated document.

Belil, M. 1985. Subcontracting networks. M.A. thesis, University of California, Berkeley.

Beneria, L., and M. Roldan. 1987. *The Crossroads of Class and Gender: Industrial Homework, Subcontracting and Household Dynamics in Mexico City.* Chicago: University of Chicago Press.

Benjamin, W. 1973. *Charles Baudelaire: A Lyric Poet in the Era of High Capitalism.* London: New Left Books.

———. 1969. *Illuminations.* New York: Beacon.

Bensman, D., and R. Lynch. 1988. *Rusted Dreams: Hard Times in a Steel Community.* Berkeley: University of California Press.

Berger, H. 1927. *Drömlandet.* Stockholm: Albert Bonniers Förlag.

Berger, S. 1980. Discontinuity in the politics of industrial society. In S. Berger and M. Piore, eds., *Dualism and Discontinuity in Industrial Societies,* 129–141. Cambridge: Cambridge University Press.

Bergman, G. 1951. *Språket på Söder.* Stockholm: Skolan för Bokhantverk.

Berman, M. 1982. *All That Is Solid Melts into Air: The Experience of Modernity.* New York: Simon and Schuster.

Bernstein, B. 1970. *Class, Codes and Control.* Vol. 1, *Theoretical Studies Towards a Sociology of Language.* London: Routledge & Kegan Paul.

Bernstein, H. 1986. Capitalism and petty commodity production. *Social Analysis* 20:11–28.

Berry, S. 1989. Social institutions and access to resources. *Africa* 59(2):41–55.

———. 1985. *From Fathers to Their Sons.* Berkeley: University of California Press.

Bhabha, H. 1989. Location, intervention, incommensurability. *Emergencies* 1(1):63–88.

Bienen, H. 1983. *Oil Revenues and Public Choice in Nigeria.* Working Paper no. 592. Washington, D.C.: World Bank.

Bierstecker, T. 1988. *Multinationals, the State, and Control of the Nigerian Eocnomy*. Princeton: Princeton University Press.

Bierstecker, T., L. Diamond, T. Callaghy, and P. Lewis. 1987. The prospects for structural adjustment in Nigeria. Manuscript prepared for the Annual Meetings of African Studies, Denver, Colo.

Billings, D. 1990. Religion as opposition. *American Journal of Sociology* 96(1): 1–31.

Binswanger, H., and M. Rosenzweig. 1986. Behavioral and material determinants of production relations in agriculture. *Journal of Development Studies* 22:59–112.

———, eds. 1984. *Contractual Arrangements and Wages in Rural Labor Markets in Asia*. New Haven: Yale University Press.

Björklund, A. 1984. *Hamnens arbetare-En etnologisk undersökning av stuveriarbetet i Göteborg*. Nordiska museets Handlingar, no. 101. Stockholm.

Bourdieu, P. 1990. *In Other Words: Essays towards a Reflexive Sociology*. Stanford: Stanford University Press.

———. 1989. Social space and symbolic power. *Sociological Theory* 14:14–25.

———. 1987. What makes a social class? On the theoretical and practical existence of groups. *Berkeley Journal of Sociology* 22:1–17.

———. 1986. *Distinction*. Cambridge: Harvard University Press.

———. 1985. Social space and the genesis of groups. *Theory and Society* 14: 723–744.

Brass, T. 1986. Unfree labor and capitalist restructuring in the agrarian sector. *Journal of Peasant Studies* 14:50–77.

Brautigam, D. 1987. Chinese agricultural aid to West Africa. Ph.D. diss., Tufts University.

Braverman, H. 1974. *Labor and Monopoly Capital*. New York: Monthly Review.

Brecht, B. 1964. *Brecht on Theatre*. London: Methuen.

Brenkman, J. 1987. *Culture and Domination*. Ithaca, N.Y.: Cornell University Press.

Brodin, R., and C. E. Dahlman. 1887. *Beskrifning till . . . år 1886 ånyo utgifna . . . karta över Stockholm*. Stockholm: privately printed.

Buch-Hansen, M., and H. Marcusen. 1981. Contract farming and the peasantry. *Review of African Political Economy* 23:9–36.

Buck-Morss, S. 1989. *The Dialectics of Seeing: Walter Benjamin and the Arcades Project*. Cambridge: MIT Press.

Burawoy, M. 1989. Two methods in search of science: Skocpol versus Trotsky. *Theory and Society* 18:759–805.

———. 1985. *The Politics of Production*. London: Verso.

———. 1979. *Manufacturing Consent: Changes in the Labor Process under Monopoly Capitalism*. Chicago: University of Chicago Press.

Burke, E. 1986. Understanding Arab protest movements. *Arab Studies Quarterly* 8(4):333–345.

Burke, E., and I. Lapidus, eds. 1988. *Islam, Politics and Social Movements*. Berkeley: University of California Press.

Burke, E., and P. Lubeck. 1987. Explaining social movements in two oil-exporting states. *Comparative Studies in Society and History*, 29(4):643–665.

Callinicos, A. 1988. *Making History*. Ithaca, N.Y.: Cornell University Press.

Carney, J. 1988. Struggles over crop rights and labor within contract farming households in Gambian irrigated rice projects. *Journal of Peasant Studies* 15(3):334–349.

———. 1986. The social history of Gambian rice production. Ph.D. diss., University of California, Berkeley.

Carney, J., and M. Watts. 1991. Disciplining women: Rice, mechanization and the evolution of Mandinka gender relations in Senegambia. *Signs* 16(4): 651–681.

———. 1990. Manufacturing dissent: Work, gender and the politics of meaning. *Africa* 60(2):207–241.

Casals, M. 1983. *L'Economia de Sabadell*. Barcelona: Ajuntament de Sabadell.

Cederqvist, J. 1980. *Arbetare i strejk—Studier rörande arbetarnas politiska mobilisering under industrialsmens genombrott, Stockholm 1850–1909*. Stockholmsmonografier utgivna av Stockholms kommun, no. 41. Stockholm.

Chatelus, M., and Y. Schemeil. 1983. Towards a new Political economy of state industrialization in the Arab Middle East. *International Journal of Middle Eastern Studies*, 16(2):145–168.

Chevalier, J. 1983. There is nothing simple about simple commodity production. *Journal of Peasant Studies* 10:153–186.

Christelow, A. 1987. Three Islamic voices in contemporary Nigeria. In W. Roff, ed., *Islam and the Political Economy of Meaning*. 226–253. London: Croon Helm.

———. 1985. The 'Yan Tatsine disturbances in Kano: A search for perspective. *Muslim World* 75(2):69–84.

———. 1984. Religious protest and dissent in northern Nigeria: From Mahdism to Qu'ranic integralism. *Journal of the Institute of Muslim Minority Affairs* 6(2):375–391.

Clapp, R. 1988. Representing reciprocity, reproducing domination. *Journal of Peasant Studies* 19(1):5–39.

Clark, G. L. 1989. *Unions and Communities under Siege: American Communities and the Crisis of Organized Labor*. Cambridge: Cambridge University Press.

Clark, T. J. 1984. *The Painting of Modern Life: Paris in the Art of Manet and His Followers*. Princeton: Princeton University Press.

Clarke, P. 1987. The Maitatsine movement in northern Nigeria in historical and current perspective. In Rosalind Hackett, ed., *New Religious Movements in Nigeria*, vol. 5, 93–115. Lewiston: Edwin Mellen.

Clifford, J. 1988. *The Predicament of Culture*. Cambridge: Harvard University Press.

Cohen, R. 1974. *Labor and Politics in Nigeria*. London: Heinemann.

Collier, P. 1983. Oil and inequality in Nigeria. In D. Ghai and S. Radwan, eds., *Agrarian Policies and Rural Poverty in Africa*. Geneva: 191–248. Geneva: ILO.

Comaroff, J. 1985. *Body of Power, Spirit of Resistance: The Culture and History of a South African People*. Chicago: University of Chicago Press.

Commander, S., and P. Peek. 1983. *Oil Exports, Agrarian Change and the Rural Labor Process*. Working Paper no. 63. Geneva: ILO.

Commonwealth Development Corporation. 1984. *CDC and The Small Farmer.* London: Commonwealth Development Corporation.

Cooke, P. 1990a. *Back to the Future: Modernity, Postmodernity, and Locality.* London: Allen & Unwin.

———. 1990b. Locality, structure and agency. *Cultural Anthropology* 5(1):3–15.

Cowen, M. 1986. Changes in state power, international conditions and peasant producers: The case of Kenya. *Journal of Development Studies* 22(2):355–384.

Crandall, Robert W. 1981. *The U.S. Steel Industry in Recurrent Crisis: Policy Options in a Competitive World.* Washington, D.C.: Brookings Institute.

Crozier, Michael. 1984. *The Bureaucratic Phenomenon.* Chicago: University of Chicago Press.

Crystal, J. 1985. Coalitions in oil monarchies: Patterns of state building in the Gulf. Unpublished manuscript, Department of Government, Harvard University.

Currie, K., and L. Ray. 1986. On the class location of contract farmers in the Kenyan economy. *Economy and Society* 15:445–475.

Daddieh, C. 1987. Contract farming in the oil palm industry. Working Paper no. 4, Institute for Development Anthropology, Binghamton, N.Y.

Davidson, C. 1989. *The Impact of Out-of-Area Workers in Non-Residential Construction on Contra Costa County: A Case Study of the USS-POSCO Modernization.* Martinez, Calif.: Contra Costa County Board of Supervisors.

Davis, J. 1980. Capitalist agricultural development and the exploitation of the propertied laborer. In F. Buttel and H. Newby, eds., *The Rural Sociology of Advanced Societies,* 133–153. London: Croon Helm.

———. 1979. Property without power: A study of the development of contract farming in the U.S. Ph.D. diss., Cornell University.

Davis, M. 1990. *City of Quartz.* London: Verso.

———. 1987. Chinatown, Part Two? *New Left Review,* no. 164:65–86.

———. 1985. Urban renaissance and the spirit of postmodernism. *New Left Review,* no. 151:106–113.

———. 1978. Fordism in crisis. *Review* 2(2):207–269.

De Certeau, M. 1985. Practices of space. In M. Blonsky, ed., *On Signs,* 122–145. Oxford: Basil Blackwell.

———. 1984. *The Practice of Everyday Life.* Berkeley: University of California Press.

De Gaudemar, Jean-Paul. 1985. The mobile factory. In *Zone I,* 285–291. Cambridge: MIT Press.

Deleuze, G., and F. Gattari. 1977. *The Anti-Oedipus.* New York: Viking.

Denning, M. 1990. The end of mass culture. *International Labor and Working Class History,* no. 37:4–18.

De Treville, D. 1987. *Agribusiness and Contract Farming: An Annotated Bibliography.* Binghamton, N.Y.: Institute for Development Anthropology.

Dey, J. 1980. Women and rice in The Gambia. Ph.D. diss., University of Reading.

Diamond, L. 1983. Class, ethnicity and the democratic state: Nigeria 1950–1966. *Comparative Studies in Society and History* 25(3):457–489.

Dundes, A. 1989. *Folklore Matters*. Knoxville: University of Tennessee Press.
Dwyer, D., and J. Bruce, eds. 1988. *A Home Divided: Women and Income in The Third World*. Stanford: Stanford University Press.

Eagleton, T. 1990. *The Ideology of the Aesthetic*. Oxford: Basil Blackwell.
The Economist. 1984. *The Political Economy of Nigeria*. Cambridge: Cambridge University Press.
Economist Intelligence Unit. 1980–1990. *Quarterly Economic Report for Nigeria*. London: The Economist.
Ellis, F. 1988. Small-farm sugar production in Fiji. *IDS Bulletin* 19(2):47–53.
Elson, D. 1988. Market socialism or the socialization of the market? *New Left Review*, no. 172:3–44.
Emecheta, Buchi. 1982. *Naira Power*. London: Macmillan.
Evans, P., and D. Reutschmeyer. 1985. The state and economic transformation. In P. Evans et al., eds., *Bringing the State Back In*, 44–47. Cambridge: Cambridge University Press.

Fantasia, R. 1988. *Cultures of Solidarity: Consciousness, Action and Contemporary American Workers*. Berkeley: University of California Press.
Fischer, M., and M. Abedi. 1990. *Debating Muslims*. Madison: University of Wisconsin Press.
FitzSimmons, M. 1986. The New industrial agriculture. *Economic Geography* 62(4):334–353.
Folbre, N. 1986. Hearts and spades: Paradigms of household economics. *World Development* 14(2):245–255.
Foucault, M. 1979. *Discipline and Punish: The Birth of the Prison*. New York: Vintage.
———. 1978. *The History of Sexuality*. Vol. 1, New York: Pantheon.
———. 1973. *The Order of Things: An Archeology of the Human Sciences*. New York: Vintage/Random House.
———. 1972. *The Archeology of Knowledge*. New York: Harper Colophon.
Franzén, M. 1982. Gatans disciplinering. *Häften för kritiska studier*, 15(5):3–25.
Freund, W. 1978. Oil boom and crisis in contemporary Nigeria. *Review of African Political Economy* 13:91–101.
Friedland, W. 1984. Commodity systems analysis. In H. Schwarzweller, ed., *Research in Rural Sociology*, vol. 1, 221–253, Greenwich, Conn.: JAI Press.
Friedmann, H. 1987. The family farm and the international food regimes. In T. Shanin, ed., *Peasants and Peasant Society*, 247–258. Oxford: Basil Blackwell.
Froebel, F., J. Heinrichs, and O. Kreye. 1980. *The New International Division of Labor*. Cambridge: Cambridge University Press.
Frykman, J., and O. Löfgren. 1987. *Culture Builders: A Historical Anthropology of Middle-Class Life*. New Brunswick, N.J.: Rutgers University Press.
———. 1985. På väg—bilder av kultur och klass. In J. Frykman, O. Löfgren, G. Alsmark, E. Johansson, M. Lindqvist, M. Stigsdotter, L. Åkesson, and L. Åström, *Modärna tider—Vision och vardag i folkhemmet*. 20–139. Lund: Liber Förlag.
———. 1979. *Den kultiverade människan*. Lund: Liber Läromedel.

Gale, N., and R. Golledge. 1982. On the subjective partitioning of space. *Annals of the Association of American Geographers* 72:60–67.

Gamble, D. P. 1955. *Economic Conditions in Two Mandinka Villages: Kerewan and Keneba.* London: Research Department, Colonial Office.

Geertz, C. 1983. *Local Knowledge: Further Essays in Interpretive Anthropology.* New York: Basic Books.

Gejvall, B. 1954. *1800–talets Stockholmsbostad-En studie över den borgerliga bostadens planlösning i hyreshusen.* Monografier utgivna av Stockholms kommunförvaltning, no. 16. Stockholm.

Gejvall-Seger, B. 1982. Stockholms hyreshusbebyggelse p 1800-talet. In H. Ahnlund, I. Hammarström, and T. Nevéus, eds., *Historia kring Stockholm—Stockholm från förhistorisk tid till sekelskiftet,* 444–474. Stockholm: Wahlström & Widstrand.

Gelb, A. 1981. *Capital Importing Oil-Exporters.* Working Paper no. 375. Washington, D.C.: World Bank.

Gertler, M. 1989. The limits to flexibility. *Trans IBG* 13:413–432.

Giddens, A. 1990. *The Consequences of Modernity.* Stanford: Stanford University Press.

Gilbert, J., and R. Akor. 1988. Increasing structural divergence in U.S. dairying. *Rural Sociology* 53(1):56–72.

Gilsenan, M. 1980. *Recognizing Islam.* London: Pantheon.

Gjerdman, O. 1937. Ett knippe ord ur slang och vulgarspråk. *Nysvenska studier* 17:182–184.

Glover, D. 1987. Increasing the benefits to smallholders from contract farming. *World Development* 15(4):441–448.

———. 1984. Contract farming and smallholder outgrower schemes in LDC's. *World Development* 12:1143–1157.

———. 1983. Contract farming and transnationals. Ph.D. diss., Toronto University.

Gomez-Pena, G. 1987. The conflicts and culture of the borderlands. *Utne Reader,* July, 1.

Goodell, G. 1980. From status to contract. *Archives Européennes de Sociologie* 21(2):285–325.

Goodman, D., J. Sorj, and J. Wilkinson. 1987. *From Farming to Biotechnology.* Oxford: Basil Blackwell.

Graborsky, P. N., and L. Persson. 1977. Stockholm: The politics of crime and conflict, 1750 to the 1970s. In T. R. Gutt, P. N. Graborsky, and R. C. Hula, eds., *The Politics of Crime and Conflict: A Comparative History of Four Cities.* 239–279. Beverly Hills, Calif.: Sage Publications.

Graf, W. 1987. *The Nigerian State.* London: Heinemann.

Graham, E., and I. Floering. 1984. *The Modern Plantation in the Third World.* London: Croon Helm.

Gramsci, A. 1971. *Selections from the Prison Notebooks.* New York: International Publishers.

Gregory, D. 1990. Chinatown, Part Three? Soja and the missing spaces of social theory. *Strategies* 3:40–104.

Gupta, A., and J. Ferguson. 1992. Beyond culture: Space, identity and the politics of difference. *Cultural Anthropology* 7(1):6–23.

Gustafson, U. 1976. *Industrialisms storstad- Studier rörande Stockholms sociala, ekonomiska och demografiska struktur, 1860–1910*. Monografier utgivna av Stockholms kommunalförvaltning, no. 37.

Guyer, J. 1988a. Dynamic approaches to domestic budgeting: Cases and methods from Africa. In Daisy Dwyer and Judith Bruce, eds., *A Home Divided*, 155–172. Stanford: Stanford University Press.

——. 1988b. The Multiplication of labor. *Current Anthropology*, 29:242–272.

——. 1984. Naturalism in models of African production. *Man* 19:371–388.

Guyer, J., and P. Peters, eds. 1987a. *Conceptualizing the Household: Issues of Theory and Policy in Africa*. Special issue of *Development and Change* 18(2).

——. 1987b. Introduction to J. Guyer and P. Peter, eds., *Conceptualizing the Household: Issues of Theory and Policy in Africa*. Special issue of *Development and Change* 18(2).

Hadi, I. 1980. Mutanen 'Yan Awaki sun kai karar Mallam Marwa. *Maganar Kano*, December 19th, 8.

Hall, B. 1989. Chicken empires. *Southern Exposure* 17(2):12–17.

Hall, S. 1989. Imaginary identification and politics. Transcript of talk given at the Institute of Contemporary Arts, London.

——. 1987. Minimal selves. In L. Appignanesi, ed., *Post-Modernism and the Question of Identity*, ICA Document no. 6, 44–46. London: Institute of Contemporary Arts.

——. 1981. Notes on deconstructing the popular. In R. Samuel, ed., *People's History and Socialist Theory*, 256–283. London: Routledge.

——. 1980. Cultural studies in two paradigms. In T. Bennett et al., eds., *Culture, Ideology and Social Process*, 19–37. London: Batsford.

Hammarström, I. 1970. *Stockholm i svensk ekonomi 1850–1914*. Stockholm: Monografier utgivna av Stockholms kommunalförvaltning, 22:II.

Harris, O. 1981. Households as natural Units. In Ann Whitehead et al., eds., *Of Marriage and The Market*, 49–68. London: CSE Books.

Harrison, B., and B. Bluestone. 1988. *The Great U-Turn: Corporate Restructuring and the Polarizing of America*. New York: Basic Books.

Hart, O., and B. Holmstrom. 1987. The theory of contracts. In T. Bewley, ed., *Advances in Economic Theory Fifth World Congress*, Cambridge: Cambridge University Press.

Harvey, D. 1991. Flexibility: Threat or opportunity? *Socialist Review*, 21(1):65–78.

——. 1990. Between space and time: Reflections on the Geographical imagination. *Annals of the Association of American Geographers* 80(3):435–447.

——. 1989. *The Condition of Postmodernity: An Enquiry into the Origins of Cultural Change*. Oxford: Basil Blackwood.

——. 1985. *Consciousness and the Urban Experience*. Oxford: Basil Blackwell.

——. 1982. *The Limits to Capital*. Oxford: Basil Blackwell.

Haswell, M. 1973. *The Nature of Poverty*. London: St. Martin's.

——. 1963. *The Changing Pattern of Economic Activity in a Gambian Village*. Research Publication no. 2. London: HMSO.

Hausman, R. 1981. State landed property, oil rent and accumulation in Venezuela. Ph.D. diss., Cornell University, Ithaca, N.Y.

Hayes, D. 1989. *Behind the Silicon Valley.* Boston: South End Press.

Heald, S. 1991. Tobacco, time and the household economy in two Kenyan societies: The Teso and Kuria. *Comparative Studies in Society and History* 33(1):130–157.

———. 1988. Tobacco, time and the household economy in two Kenyan societies. Unpublished manuscript, Department of Anthropology, Lancaster University.

———. 1985. Problems of theory and research. *Review of African Political Economy,* 34:89–94.

Hebdige, D. 1979. *Subculture.* London: Methuen.

Henderson, J., and M. Castells. 1987. Introduction to J. Henderson and M. Castells, eds., *Global Restructuring and Territorial Development,* 1–17. London: Sage.

Herbst, J. 1990. Migration, the politics of protest and state consolidation in Africa. *African Affairs* 89(355):183–203.

Hickey, R. 1984. The 1982 Maitatsine uprising in Nigeria: A note. *African Affairs* 83(331):251–256.

Hirschmann, A. 1976. A generalised linkage approach to economic development with special reference to staples. *Economic Development and Cultural Change* 56:134–159.

Hiskett, M. 1987. The Maitatsine riots in Kano, 1980. *Journal of Religion in Africa* 17:209–223.

Hoerr, J. P. 1988. *And the Wolf Finally Came: The Decline of the American Steel Industry.* Pittsburgh: University of Pittsburgh Press.

Holmes, D. R. 1989. *Cultural Disenchantments: Worker Peasantries in Northeastern Italy.* Princeton: Princeton University Press.

Horton, J. 1987. Characteristics of horticultural export enterprises utilizing contract farming in Senegal. Working Paper no. 5, Institute for Development Anthropology, Binghamton, N.Y.

Howell, Thomas R., William A. Noellert, Jesse G. Kreier, and Alan William Wolff. 1988. *Steel and the State: Government Intervention and Steel's Structural Crisis.* Boulder, Colo.: Westview Press.

Hughes, R. 1980. *The Shock of the New.* London: BBC Publications.

IBRD. 1988. *The Nigerian Structural Adjustment Program.* Washington, D.C.: World Bank.

———. 1985a. *Nigeria: Agricultural Pricing Policy.* Washington D.C.: World Bank.

———. 1985b. *Nigeria: Agricultural Sector Memorandum.* Washington, D.C.: World Bank.

———. 1981. *Nigeria: Basic Economic Report.* 3 vols. Washington, D.C.: World Bank.

———. 1980. *Accelerated Development in Sub-Saharan Africa.* Washington, D.C.: World Bank.

———. 1979. *Nigeria Agriculutural Sector.* 3 vols. Washington, D.C.: World Bank.

Ihimodu, A. 1983. External loans and debt servicing problems in the Nigerian economy. Unpublished manuscript, Nigerian Institute for Social and Economic Research, Ibadan.

Iliya, M. 1988. Induced agricultural change in Northwest Nigeria. Ph.D. diss., University of Birmingham.

ILO. 1981. *First Things First*. Geneva: ILO.

Imam-Jomeh, I. 1985. Petroleum-based accumulation and state form. Ph.D. diss., University of California, Los Angeles.

International Bank for Rural Development. *See* IBRD.

International Labor Organization. *See* ILO.

Isichei, E. 1987. The Maitatsine risings in Nigeria 1980–1985: A revolt of the disinherited. *Journal of Religion in Africa* 17:194–208.

Jackson, J., and A. Cheater. 1989. Contract farming: Sugar, tea and cotton in Zimbabwe. *Eastern Africa Economic Review*, special issue, 97–107.

Jacques, M., and S. Hall, eds. (1989). *New Times*. London: Lawrence and Wishart.

Jaffee, S. 1987. Case studies of contract farming in the horticultural sector in Kenya. Working Paper no. 7, Institute for Development Anthropology, Binghamton, N.Y.

Jakobsson, S. 1977. Rotemansinstitutionen i Stockholm för folkbokförning och mantalskrivning m.m., 1878–1926. Uppsala. Mimeo.

Jamal, V. 1981. Rural-urban gap and inequality in nigeria. Working Paper JASPA/ILO, Addis Ababa.

Jameson, F. 1989. Marxism and postmodernism. *New Left Review*, no. 176:31–46.

———. 1988. Cognitive mapping. In Cary Nelson and Lawrence Grossberg, eds., *Marxism and the Interpretation of Culture*, 347–360. Urbana: University of Illinois Press.

———. 1984. Postmodernism, or the cultural logic of late capitalism. *New Left Review*, no. 141:53–92.

———. 1979. Reification and utopia in mass culture. *Social Text* 1:134–146.

Jega, A. 1985. The state, peasants and rural transformation in Nigeria: A case study of the Bakalori irrigation project, Sokoto State. Ph.D. diss., Northwestern University, Evanston, Ill.

Jeng, A. 1978. An economic history of the Gambian groundnut industry, 1830–1924. Ph.D. diss., Birmingham University.

Jessop, B. 1988. Regulation theories in retrospect and prospect. Working Paper no. 1, Universitat Bielefeld, Zentrum fur interdisziplinare Forschung, Bielefeld.

Jones, C. 1983. The mobilization of women's labor for crop production. Ph.D. diss., Harvard University.

Joseph, R. 1987. *Democracy and Prebendal Politics in Nigeria*. Cambridge: Cambridge University Press.

Kaduna State. 1981. *Report of the Land Investigation Committee*. 12 vols. and General Findings and Recommendations. Kaduna: Government Printer.

Kano State Government. 1981. *The Views and Comments of the Kano State Government on the Report of the Kano Disturbances Tribunal of Inquiry*. Kano: Kano State Government.

Kargbo, A. 1983. An economic analysis of rice production systems and production organization of rice farmers in The Gambia. Ph.D. diss., Michigan State University.

Karl, T. 1982. The political economy of petro-dollars: Oil and democracy in Venezuela. Ph.D. diss., Stanford University, Palo Alto, Calif.

Kasfelt, N. 1989. Rumours of Maitatsine. *African Affairs*, 88(350):83–90.

Katouzian, H. 1981. *The Political Economy of Modern Iran*. New York: New York University Press.

Keller, J. 1981. The production worker in electronics. Ph.D. diss., University of Michigan.

Kenny, M., J. Curry, and W. Goe. 1987. Contextualizing agriculture with postwar U.S. society. Working Paper no. 15, Technology, Innovation and Social Change Project, Ohio State University.

Kern, S. 1983. *The Culture of Time and Space, 1880–1918*. Cambridge: Harvard University Press.

Key-Åberg, K. 1902. Stockholmsutskänkningsbolag—dess organisation och tjugofemåriga verksamhet. Stockholm: P. A. Norstedt and Söner.

Kiers, Luc. 1980. *The American Steel Industry: Problems, Challenges, Perspectives*. Boulder, Colo.: Westview Press.

Kimmage, K. 1989. The evolution of the wheat trap: The great Nigerian wheat rush. Unpublished manuscript, Department of Geography, Cambridge University.

Kirk-Greene, A. 1971. *Crisis and Conflict in Nigeria*. London: Oxford University Press.

Kirk-Greene, A., and D. Rimmer. 1981. *Nigeria since 1970*. London: Hodder and Stoughton.

Kitching, G. 1980. *Class and Economic Change in Kenya*. New Haven: Yale University Press.

Kondo, D. 1990. *Crafting Selves: Power, Gender and Discourses of Identity in a Japanese Workplace*. Chicago: University of Chicago Press.

Kuru National Institute for Policy and Strategic Studies. *See* NIPSS.

Kusterer, K., M. de Batres, and J. Cuxil. 1981. *The Social Impact of Agribusiness*. USAID Evaluation Study no. 4. Washington, D.C.: USAID.

Lagerstedt, S. 1963. *Drömmaren från Norrlandsgatan—En studie i Henning Bergers liv och författarskap*. Monografier utgivna av Stockholms kommunalförvaltning, no. 25. Stockholm.

Laitin, D. 1986. *Hegemony and Culture*. Chicago: University of Chicago Press.

Lambek, M. 1990. Certain knowledge, contestable authority. *American Ethnologist* 17(1):23–40.

Lapidus, I. 1983. *Contemporary Islamic Movements in Historical Perspective*. Berkeley: Institute of International Studies.

Lash, S., and P. Bagguley. 1988. Labour relations in disorganized capitalism: A five-nation comparison. *Society and Space* 6:321–338.

Lavers, J. 1982. Popular Islam and unpopular dissent: Religious disturbances in northern Nigeria. Paper delivered to the African Studies Conference, University of Illinois, Urbana-Champaign.

Levin, R. 1986. Uneven development in Swaziland. *GeoForum* 17:239–250.

Linares, O. 1985. Cash crops and gender constructs: The Jola of Senegal. *Ethnology* 24(2):83–94.

Lipietz, A. 1987. *Mirages and Miracles*. London: Verso.

Little, P. 1991. Anthropology, policy and contract farming. *Institute for Development Anthropology Newsletter* 9(1):14–20.

Local 1440 1988–1989. *United Steelworkers Rank & Filer.*

Locker/Abrecht Associates, Inc. 1985. *Confronting the Crisis: The Challenge for Labor.* Pittsburgh, Pa.: United Steelworkers of America.

Löfgren, O. 1989. The nationalization of culture. *Ethnologia Europaea* 19:5–24.

———. 1985. Wish you were here! Holiday images and picture postcards. *Ethnologia Scandinavica*, 90–107.

———. 1984. Hur tillverka man ett kulturarv? In O. Löfgren, and D. Gaunt, eds., *Myten om Svensken*, 11–27. Stockholm: Liber Förlag.

Lovering, J. 1989. The restructuring debate. In R. Peet and N. Thrift, eds., *New Models in Geography*, vol. 1, 198–223. London: Unwin.

Lowe, D. M. 1982. *History of Bourgeois Perception.* Chicago: University of Chicago Press.

Lubeck, P. 1987. Islamic protest and oil-based capitalism. In M. Watts, ed., *State, Oil and Agriculture*, 268–290. Berkeley: Institute of International Studies.

———. 1986. *Islam and Urban Labor in Northern Nigeria.* Cambridge: Cambridge University Press.

———. 1985. Islamic protest under semi-industrial capitalism. *Africa* 55(4): 369–389.

———. 1984. Islamic networks and urban capitalism: An instance of articulation from northern Nigeria. *Cahiers d'etudes africaines*, nos. 81–82:67–78.

———. 1981. Conscience de classe et nationalisme Islamique à Kano. *Politique Africaine* 1(4):31–68.

Lundgren, A. R. 1886. *Atlas över Stockholm, 1885.* Stockholm: privately printed.

Lundin, C. 1890. *Nya Stockholm*, Stockholm: privately printed.

Lynch, K. 1960. *The Image of the City.* Cambridge: MIT Press.

Mackintosh, M. 1989. *Gender, Class and Rural Transition.* London: Zed Press.

———. 1977. Fruit and vegetables as an international commodity. *Food Policy* 2:277–292.

Main, H. 1989. Workers, retrenchment and urban-rural linkages in Kano, Nigeria. In K. Swindell et al., eds., *Inequality and Development*, 223–242. London: Macmillan.

Makanda, D. 1984. The utilization of Kenya's irrigation potential: A case study of Kibirigwe. M.A. thesis, University of Nairobi.

Malkki, L. 1990. Context and consciousness. In R. Fox, ed., *Nationalist Ideologies and the Production of National Cultures*, American Ethnological Society Monograph Series, no. 2, 32–62.

Mann, S., and J. Dickenson. 1978. Obstacles to the development of a capitalist agriculture. *Journal of Peasant Studies* 5:446–481.

Marcus, G. E., and M. J. Fischer. 1986. *Anthropology as Cultural Critique: An Experimental Moment in the Human Sciences.* Chicago: University of Chicago Press.

Marsden, T., S. Whatmore, R. Munton, and J. Little. 1988. The restructuring process and economic centrality in capitalist agriculture. *Journal of Rural Studies* 2(4):271–280.

Maruf, B. 1986. Yan Awaki redevelopment scheme Kano. M.Sc. thesis, Architecture, Ahmadu Bello University.

Marx, K. [1894] 1982. *Capital.* Vol. 3. Reprint. New York: International Publishers.

———. [1859] 1970. *Contributions to the Critique of Political Economy.* Reprint. New York: International Publishers.

———. [1852] 1963. *The Eighteenth Brumaire of Louis Bonaparte.* Reprint. New York: International Publishers.

Marx, K., and F. Engels. [1848] 1952. *The Communist Manifesto.* Reprint. Moscow: Progress Publishers.

Massey, D. 1991. A global sense of place. *Marxism Today,* June, 4–29.

———. 1984. *Spatial Divisions of Labour.* London: Macmillan.

Matovic, M. R. 1984. *Stockholmsäktenskap—Familjebildning och partnerval i Stockholm, 1850–1890.* Monografier utgivna av Stockholms kommun, no. 57. Stockholm.

Mayer, M. 1991. Politics in the post-Fordist city. *Socialist Review* 21(1):105–124.

Mblinyi, M. 1988. Agribusiness and women peasants in Tanzania. *Development and Change* 19(4):549–583.

McCommon, C., N. Rueschoff, L. Tavis, and J. Wilkowski. 1985. *Guanchias Limitada: A Case Study of Agrarian Reform Co-operatives in Honduras.* Washington, D.C.: USAID.

Mead, D. 1984. Of contracts and subcontractors. *World Development* 12:1095–1106.

Mead, W. 1990. The world economic order. *Dissent,* Summer, 383–393.

Mighell, R., and M. Jones. 1963. *Vertical Co-ordinations and Contract Farming,* Report no. 19. Research Papers, U.S. Department of Agriculture. Washington, D.C.: GPO.

Miles, R. 1987. *Capitalism and Unfree Labor.* London: Tavistock.

Minn. legislature panel calls for study on impact of hiring out-of-state workers. 1989. *Construction Labor Report* 35:912–914.

Minot, R. 1986. Contract farming and its impact on small farmers in LDC'S. Working Paper, Department of Agricultural Economics, Michigan State University.

Moghadam, V. 1988. Oil, the state and limits to autonomy. *Arab Studies Quarterly* 10(2):225–238.

Moore, H. 1986. *Space, Text and Gender.* Cambridge: Cambridge University Press.

Morrissy, D. 1974. *Agricultural Modernization and Production Contracting.* New York: Praeger.

Munoz, C. 1989. *Youth, Identity, Power.* London: Verso.

Na-Ayuba, A. 1986. Yantatsine: An analysis of the Gardawa uprising in Kano, Nigeria 1980–1985. M.Sc. diss., Bayero University, Kano.

Nabuguzi, E. 1987. L'agriculture sous contrat et la paysannerie au Nigeria. *Politique Africaine,* no. 27:107–113.

Nash, J. 1979. *We Eat the Mines and the Mines Eat Us: Dependency and Exploitation in Bolivian Tin Mines.* New York: Columbia University Press, 1979.

Nicolas, G. 1981. Guerre sainte a Kano. *Politique Africaine* 1(4):73–81.

Nigerian Federal Government. 1982. *Report of the Commission of Inquiry into Religious Disturbance in Bulum Kutu Area of Maiduguri.* Lagos: Federal Government Press.

———. 1981a. *Report of Tribunal of Inquiry on Kano Disturbances.* (Aniagolu Report). Lagos: Federal Government Press.

———. 1981b. *Views of the Government of the Federation on the Report of the Kano Disturbances Tribunal of Inquiry.* Lagos: National Assembly Press.

NIPSS, 1986. *Religious Disturbances in Nigeria.* Kuru: Research Department, National Institute for Policy and Strategic Studies.

Nolutshungu, S. 1990. Fragments of a democracy. *Third World Quarterly* 12(1):86–115.

O'Connor, J. 1984. *The Accumulation Crisis.* Oxford: Basil Blackwell.

Oil, Debts and Democracy in Nigeria. 1986. Special issue of *Review of African Political Economy*, no. 37.

Olsson, G. 1991. *Lines of Power, Limits of Language.* Minneapolis: University of Minnesota Press.

Omoniwa, M., and J. Abu. 1986. *The Maitatsine Riots in Nigeria 1980–1984.* Zaria: Kashim Ibrahim Library.

Ong, A. 1990. State versus Islam. *American Ethnologist* 17(2):258–276.

———. 1987. *Spirits of Resistance and Capitalist Discipline: Factory Women in Malaysia.* Albany: State University Press of New York.

Onoh, J. 1983. *The Nigerian Oil Economy.* New York: St. Martin's Press.

Othman, S. 1984. Classes, crises and Coup. *African Affairs* 27:441–461.

Paden, J. 1973. *Religion and Political Culture in Kano.* Berkeley: University of California Press.

Palmer-Jones, R. 1987. Buying time and staggering along: The smallholder tea authority in Malawi. Working Paper, Institute for Development Anthropology, Binghamton.

Patton, A. 1987. An Islamic frontier polity. In I. Kopytoff, ed., *The African Frontier: The Reproduction of Traditional African Societies*, 187–203. Bloomington: University of Indiana Press.

Paz, O. 1990. *In Search of the Present.* New York: Harcourt.

Pearce, R. 1983. Sharecropping: Toward a Marxist view. *Journal of Peasant Studies* 16:42–70.

Peet, R., and N. Thrift, eds. 1989. *New Models in Geography.* 2 vols. London: Unwin Hyman.

People's Redemption Party (Kaduna). *See* PRP.

Pesaran, M. 1982. The system of dependent capitalism in pre- and post-revolutionary Iran. *International Journal of Middle Eastern Studies* 14:501–522.

Peters, P. Forthcoming. *Dividing The Commons: Politics, Policy and Culture in Botswana.* London: International African Institute.

Petras, J., and M. Morley. 1983. Petro-dollars and the state. *Third World Quarterly* 5:8–27.

Pfeffer, M. 1985. Contracting peas, corn and beans in the United States. Working Paper, Department of Rural Sociology, University of Wisconsin.

Piore, Michael J., and Charles F. Sabel. 1984. *The Second Industrial Divide: Possibilities for Prosperity.* New York: Basic Books.

Pipes, D. 1980. *In The Path of God.* New York: Basic Books.

Pollard, H. 1985. The erosion of agriculture in an oil economy. *World Development* 13(7):819–835.

Post, K., and M. Vickers, eds. 1973. *Structure and Conflict in Nigeria.* London: Heinemann.

Pred, A. 1990a. In other worlds: Fragmented and integrated observations on gendered languages, gendered spaces and local transformation. *Antipode* 22:33–52.

———. 1990b. *Lost Words and Lost Worlds: Modernity and the Language of Everyday Life in Late Nineteenth-Century Stockholm.* Cambridge: Cambridge University Press.

———. 1990c. *Making Histories and Constructing Human Geographies: The Local Transformation of Practice, Power Relations, and Consciousness.* Boulder, Colo.: Westview.

———. 1989. The locally spoken word and local struggle. *Society and Space* 7:211–233.

PRP. 1982. *The Struggle for a New Social Order.* Kaduna: People's Redemption Party.

Pynchon, T. 1966. *The Crying of Lot 49.* New York: Bantam.

Råberg, M. 1985. *Husen på Malmarna-En bok om Stockholm.* Stockholm: Prisma.

Rabinow, P. 1989. *French Modern: Norms and Forms of the Social Environment.* Cambridge: MIT Press.

———. , ed. 1984. *The Foucault Reader.* New York: Pantheon.

———. 1983. Ordonnance, discipline, regulation: Some reflections on modernity. *Humanities in Society* 5:267–278.

Radway, J. 1990. Response. *International Labor and Working Class History,* no. 37:19–26.

Rama, R. 1985. Do transnational agribusiness firms encourage the agriculture of developing countries? *International Social Science Journal* 37:331–343.

Rappe, E. 1973 Från katekes till "social fostran"—Om folkundervisningen i Sverige från 1842 till 1906. *Häften för kritiska studier* 6(5–6):6–32.

Rebel, H. 1989. Cultural hegemony and class experience. *American Ethnologist* 16(1):117–136.

Rehnberg, M. 1967. *Vad skall vi göra med de blanka gevär?* Stockholm: Nordiska museet.

Reidmund, D., J. Martin, and C. Moore. 1981. *Structural Change in Agriculture.* USDA Economics and Statistical Service Technical Bulletin no. 1968. Washington, D.C.: GPO.

Reutter, M. 1988. *Sparrows Point: Making Steel—The Rise and Fall of American Industrial Might.* New York: Summit Books.

Robertson, A. 1987. *The Dynamics of Productive Relationships.* Cambridge: Cambridge University Press.

Roemer, M. 1983. The Dutch disease in developing countries. Working Paper no. 156, Harvard Institute of International Studies.

Roff, W., ed. 1987. *Islam and the Political Economy of Meaning.* London: Croon Helm.

Rosaldo, R. 1989. *Culture and Truth: The Remaking of Social Analysis.* New York: Basic Books.

Roseberry, W. 1989. *Anthropologies and Histories.* New Brunswick, N.J.: Rutgers University Press.

Ross, K. 1988. *The Emergence of Social Space: Rimbaud and the Paris Commune.* Minneapolis: University of Minnesota Press.

Rouse, R. 1991. Mexican migration and the social space of postmodernism. *Diaspora* 1(1):Forthcoming.

Roy, E. 1972. *Contract Farming and Economic Integration.* Danville, Ill.: Interstate Press.

Runstan, D., and S. Archibald. 1986. Technology and labor intensive agriculture. Paper presented to the Conference on Binational Labor Market Interdependence, Mexico City.

Ryan, M. 1989. *Politics and Culture: Working Hypotheses for a Post-Revolutionary Society.* Baltimore: Johns Hopkins University Press.

Rydberg, O. 1986. Så gick det till på Per Froms Velocipedfabrick—Ur Fredrik Rydbergs dagbok från 1890–talet. *Sankt Eriks Årsbok,* 113–132.

Saad, H. 1988. Urban blight and religious uprising in northern Nigeria. *Habitat International* 12(2):111–128.

Sajau, J. P., and J. von Muralt. (1987). *Plantations and Plantation Workers.* Geneva: ILO.

Sanderson, S., ed. 1986a. *The Americas in the International Division of Labor.* New York: Holmes-Meier.

———. 1986b. *The Transformation of Mexican Agriculture.* Princeton: Princeton University Press.

Sandin, B. 1984. Familjen, gatan, fabriken eller skolan? In K. Aronsson, M. Cederblad, G. Dahl, L. Olsson, and B. Sandin, *Barn i tid och rum,* 107–127. Malmö: Liber Förlag.

Sanusi, H. 1982. State and capitalist development in Nigeria. Ph.D. diss., Northwestern University, Evanston, Ill.

Saxenian, A. 1990. The origins and dynamics of production networks in Silicon Valley. Working Paper no. 516, City and Regional Planning, University of California, Berkeley.

Sayer, A. 1989a. Postfordism in question. *International Journal of Urban and Regional Research* 13(4):666–695.

Schatz, P. 1984. The inert economy. *Journal of Modern African Studies* 22(1): 45–57.

Schegloff, E. A. 1972. Notes on a conversational practice: Formulating place. In P. P. Giglioli, ed., *Language and Social Context,* 95–135. Harmondsworth: Penguin.

Schoenberger, E. 1989. Multinational corporations and the new international division of labor. In S. Wood, ed., *The Transformation of Work,* 91–101. London: Unwin.

Scott, A. 1984. Industrial organization and the logic of intra-metropolitan location. *Economic Geography* 60:1–26.

Scott, Allen J., and M. Storper, eds., 1986. *Production, Work, Territory: The Geographical Anatomy of Industrial Capitalism,* Boston: Allen & Unwin.

Scott, C. 1984. Transnational corporations and asymmetries in the Latin American food system. *Bulletin of Latin American Research* 3:63–80.

Scott, J. C. 1990. *Domination and the Arts of Resistance: The Hidden Transcript.* New Haven: Yale University Press.

———. 1985. *Weapons of the Weak: Everyday Forms of Peasant Resistance.* New Haven: Yale University Press.

Seers, D. 1964. The mechanism of an open petroleum economy. *Social and Economic Studies* 13(2):233–242.

Selling, G. 1973. *Hur Gamla stan överlevde.* Stockholm: Stockholms Stadsmuseum.

———. 1970. *Esplanadsystemet och Albert Lindhagen—Stadsplanering i Stockholm åren 1857–1887.* Monografier utgivna av Stockholms kommunalförvaltning, Stockholm.

Sennett, R. 1991. Fragments against the ruin. *Times Literary Supplement,* February 8, 6–7.

Sewell, W. H., Jr. 1980. *Work and Revolution in France: The Language of Labor from the Old Regime to 1848.* Cambridge: Cambridge University Press.

Shipton, P. 1989. *Bitter Money: Cultural Economy and Some African Meanings of Forbidden Commodities.* American Ethnological Society Monograph Series, no. 1. Washington; D.C.

———. 1985. Land, credit and crop transitions in Kenya. Ph.D. diss., Harvard University.

Simmel, G. 1978. *The Philosophy of Money.* London: Routledge.

Sivanandan, A. 1989. All that melts into air is solid. *Race and Class* 31(3):1–30.

Sjöström, C. 1937. *En Stockholmares minnen, 1880–1900.* Studier utgivna av Arbetarnas kulturhistoriska sällskap, no. 6. Stockholm.

Sklar, R. 1963. *Nigerian Political Parties.* Princeton: Princeton University Press.

Smail, J. 1987. New languages for labour and capital: The transformation of discourse in the early years of the Industrial Revolution. *Social History* 12:49–71.

Soja, E. 1989. *Postmodern Geographies: The Reassertion of Space in Critical Social Theory.* London: Verso.

Sperlings, S. 1973. Kriminalitetsutvecklingen i Stockholm. 1840–1965. Kriminalvetenskapliga Institutet vid Stockholms Universitet. Stockholm. Mimeo.

Spivak, G. 1990. Gayatri Spivak on the politics of the postcolonial subject. *Socialist Review* 20(3):81–90.

Sporleder, T. 1983. Emerging information technologies and agricultural structure. *American Journal of Agricultural Economics* 65:388–394.

Stacey, J. 1990. *The Postmodern Family.* New York: Basic Books.

———. 1987. Sexism by a subtler name. *Socialist Review,* 17(6):7–30.

Ståhle, C. I. 1981. *Stockholmsnamn och Stockholmspråk.* Stockholm, P.A.: Norstedt & Söner.

Stahre, N. F., P. A. Fogelström, J. Ferenius, and G. Lundqvist. 1984. *Stockholms gatunamn.* Monografier utgivna av Stockholms kommun, no. 50. Stockholm.

Stallybrass, P., and A. White, 1986. *The Politics and Poetics of Transgression.* Ithaca, N.Y.: Cornell University Press.

Stavrianos, G. 1981. *Global Rift.* New York: William Morrow.

Stedman-Jones, J. G. 1983. *Languages of Class: Studies in English Working Class History, 1832–1982.* Cambridge: Cambridge University Press.

Stinchcombe, A. 1978. *Theoretical Methods in Social History*. New York: Academic.

Stock, R. 1985. The rise and fall of universal primary education in northern Nigeria. *TESG*, 71:274–287.

Stockholm City Council. 1886. *Stockholms Stadsfullmäktiges Beredningsutskottets utlåtande och memorial år 1885*. "N:r 146. Utlåtande med anledning af dels återförvisning i vissa delar af utlåtandet n:o 218 för år 1884 angående nya och ändrade namn å gator, dels ytterligare förslag om sådana ändrade namn."

———. 1885. *Stockholms Stadsfullmäktiges Beredningsutskottets utlåtande och memorial år 1884*. "N:r 218. Utlåtande med förslag till nya och ändrade namn å gator."

Stockholm's local government. 1902. *Berättelse angående Stockholms kommunalförvaltning—År 1900*.

———. 1897. *Berättelse angående Stockholms kommunalförvaltning—År 1895*.

———. 1887. *Berättelse angående Stockholms kommunalförvaltning—År 1885*.

———. 1882. *Berättelse angående Stockholms kommunalförvaltning—År 1881*.

Storper, M. 1987. The post-Enlightment challenge to Marxist urban studies. *Society and Space* 5:418–426.

Storper, M., and A. Scott. 1989. The geographical foundations and social regulation of flexible production spaces. In J. Wolch and M. Dear, eds., *The Power of Geography*, 21–40. London: Unwin.

Storper, M., and R. Walker. 1989. *The Capitalist Imperative: Territory, Technology and Industrial Growth*. Oxford: Basil Blackwell.

———. 1984. The spatial division of labor: Labor and the location of industries. In Larry Sawers and William K. Tabb, eds., *Sunbelt/Snowbelt: Urban Development and Regional Restructuring*, 19–47. New York: Oxford University Press.

———. 1983. The theory of labour and the theory of location. *International Journal of Urban and Regional Research* 7:1–43.

Strohmeyer, J. 1986. *Crisis in Bethlehem: Steel's Struggle to Survive*. Bethesda, Md.: Adler & Adler.

Swainson, N. 1986. Public policy in the development of export crops. *IDS Bulletin* 17(1):57–61.

Swindell, K. 1986. Urban peripheries in Africa. Unpublished manuscript, University of Birmingham.

———. 1981. *Strange Farmers of The Gambia*. Centre for Development Studies, Swansea University, Monograph no. 15. Swansea.

Sydow, H. von. 1897. Stockholms polis. In E.W. Dahlgren, ed., *Stockholm, Sveriges hufvudstad skildrad med anledning af allmänna konst-och industriutställningen*. Stockholm.

Tahir, I. 1975. Scholars, Sufis, saints and capitalists in Kano 1904–1974. Ph.D. diss., Cambridge University.

Tarschys, B. 1982. Perspketiv på åttiotalet. In H. Ahnlund, I. Hammarström, and T. Nevéus, eds., *Historia kring Stockholm—Stockholm från förhistorisk tid till sekelskiftet*, 511–522. Stockholm: Wahlström & Widstrand.

Taussig, M. 1990. Violence and resistance in the Americas. *Journal of Historical Sociology* 3(3):209–224.

————. 1980. *The Devil and Commodity Fetishism in South America.* Chapel Hill: University of North Carolina Press.

Tchala-Abina, F. 1982. The state, bureaucracy and farmers in rural development. Ph.D. diss., Cornell University.

Terdiman, R. 1987. *Discourse/Counter Discourse.* Baltimore: Johns Hopkins University Press.

Thesleff, A. 1912. *Stockholms förbryttarspråk och lägre slang, 1910–1912.* Stockholm: Albert Bonniers Förlag.

Thompson, E. P. 1968. *The Making of the English Working Classes.* Harmondsworth: Penguin.

Thompson, J. B. 1984. *Studies in the Theory of Ideology.* Berkeley: University of California Press.

Thrift, N. J. 1983. On the determination of social action in time and space. *Society and Space* 1:23–57.

Tiffany, Paul. 1988. *The Decline of American Steel: How Management, Labor and Government Went Wrong.* New York: Oxford University Press.

Tilly, C. 1986. *The Contentious French: Four Centuries of Popular Struggle.* Cambridge: Harvard University Press.

Trotsky, L. [1932] 1977. *The History of the Russian Revolution.* Reprint. New York: Pathfinder.

————. 1969 [rpt.]. *The Permanent Revolution.* Reprint. New York: Pathfinder.

Tucket, J. 1977. Vuvulane irrigated farms, Swaziland. *Agricultural Administration* 4:79–97.

Uhrström, W. 1911. *Stockholmska slang, vulgarismer och skämtord.* Stockholm: P. A. Norstedt och Söners förlag.

Ukpolo, V. 1983. An economic evaluation of the Yobe River Irrigation Project in Nigeria. Ph.D. diss., The American University, Washington, D.C.

USDA. 1976. *People on the Farm: Broiler Growers.* U.S. Department of Agriculture Technical Report. Washington, D.C.: GPO.

Usman, Y. B. 1986. *Nigeria against the IMF.* Kaduna: Vanguard Press.

————. ed. 1982. *Political Repression in Nigeria.* Zaria: Gaskiya.

Usman, Y. B. 1980. *For the Liberation of Nigeria: Essays and Lectures 1969–1978.* London: New Beacon Books.

Van de Laar, A. 1980. *The World Bank and the Poor.* Boston: Nijhoff.

Vandeman, A. 1988. Labor contracting in California agriculture. Ph.D. diss., University of California, Davis.

Vergopolous, K. 1985. The end of agribusiness or the emergence of biotechnology? *International Journal of Social Science* 37:389–400.

Virilio, P. 1988. *Speed and Politics.* New York: Semiotexte.

Vlaverde, L. 1980. Analysis comparative des enterprises banaieres de Costa Rica. Ph.D. diss., University of Paris X, Nanterre.

Volosinov, V. [1929] 1986. *Marxism and the Philosophy of Language.* Reprint. Cambridge: Harvard University Press.

Von Braun, J., D. Hotchkiss, and M. Immink. 1989. *Non-Traditional Export Crops in Guatemala.* International Food Policy Research Institute Research Report no. 3. Washington, D.C.: IFPRI.

Von Braun, J., and K. Johm. 1987. Tradeoffs in the rapid expansion of small-holder rice production in The Gambia. Unpublished report, International Food Policy Research Institute (IFPRI), Washington, D.C.

Von Braun, J., and P. Webb. 1989. The impacts of a new crop technology on the agricultural division of labor in a West African setting. *Economic Development and Cultural Change* 37(3):513–534.

Von Bulow, D., and A. Sorensen. 1988. *Gender Dynamics in Contract Farming*. CDR Project Report no. 88.1. Copenhagen: Centre for Development Research.

Walker, R. 1989. Regulation, flexible specialization and the forces of production in capitalist development. Unpublished paper, Department of Geography, University of California, Berkeley.

———. 1985. Class, division of labour and employment in space. In Derek Gregory and John Urry, eds., *Social Relations and Spatial Structures*. London: Macmillan.

Walker, R., and Bay Area Study Group. 1990. The playground of U.S. capitalism? The political economy of the San Francisco Bay Area in the 1980s. In Mike Davis, Steven Hiatt, Marie Kennedy, Susan Ruddick, and Michael Sprinker, eds., *Fire in the Hearth: The Radical Politics of Place in America*, 3–80. London: Verso.

Wallerstein, I. 1983. *Historical Capitalism*, London: Verso.

Watts, M. Forthcoming. *Manufacturing Discontent: Production Politics in a Peasant Society*. London: Heinemann.

———. 1992. The devil's excrement: Oil money and the spectacle of black gold. In N. Thrift, ed., *Money, Power and Space*. Oxford: Basil Blackwell. Forthcoming.

———. 1991. Geography and struggles over nature. In F. Buttel and Lori-Ann Thrupp, eds., *Sustainable Development*. Ithaca, N.Y.: Cornell University Press.

———. 1990a. Peasants under contract. In B. Crow, H. Berstein, and M. Mackintosh, eds., *The Food Question*, 149–63. London: Earthscan.

———. 1990b. Visions of excess: African development in an age of market idolatry. *Transition*, no. 151:124–141

———. 1989. The agrarian question in Africa. *Progress in Human Geography* 13(1):1–41.

———. , ed. 1987. *State, Oil and Agriculture in Nigeria*. Berkeley: Institute of International Studies.

———. 1986. Contract farming in Africa. Working Paper, Institute of Development Anthropology, Binghamton, N.Y.

———. 1984. State, oil and accumulation: From boom to crisis. *Society and Space* 2:403–428.

———. 1983. *Silent Violence: Food, Famine and Peasantry in Northern Nigeria*. Berkeley: University of California Press.

Watts, M., and O. P. Little, eds. Forthcoming. *Contract Farming in Africa*. Ithaca, N.Y.: Cornell University Press.

Watts, M., and P. Lubeck. 1983. The popular classes and the oil boom. In W. Zartman, ed., *The Political Economy of Nigeria*, 105–144. New York: Praeger.

Weil, P. 1973. Wet rice, women and adaptation in The Gambia. *Rural Africana* 19:20–29.

Wellford, H. 1972. *Sowing the Wind*. New York: Grossman.

Wells, M. 1987. Commodity systems and family farms. Working Paper, Department of Applied Behavioral Sciences, University of California, Davis.

West, C. 1990. The new cultural politics of difference. *October*, no. 53:93–109.

Whitehead, A. 1984. "I'm hungry, Mum": The Politics of Domestic Budgeting. In Kate Young et al., ed., *Of Marriage and the Market*, 88–111. London: CSE Books.

William, S., and R. Karen, eds. 1985. *Agribusiness and the Small Farmer*. Boulder, Colo.: Westview.

William-Olsson, W. 1937. *Huvuddragen av Stockholms geografiska utveckling, 1850–1930*. Stadskollegiets utlåtanden och memorial, bihang no. 11. Stockholm.

Williams, G. 1980. *Inequality in Nigeria*. Geneva: International Labor Office.

———. 1988. Why is there no agrarian capitalism in Nigeria? *Journal of Historical Sociology* 1(4):345–398.

Williams, R. 1982. *The Sociology of Culture*. New York: Schocken Books.

———. 1977. *Marxism and Literature*. Oxford: Oxford University Press.

———. 1973. *The Country and the City*. New York: Oxford University Press.

———. 1961. *The Long Revolution*. London: Chatto and Windus.

Williamson, O. 1985. *The Economic Institutions of Capitalism*. New York: Free Press.

Willis, P. 1990. *Common Culture*. Boulder, Colo.: Westview.

———. 1977. *Learning to Labor*. London: Gower Publishers.

Wilson, J. 1987. The political economy of contract farming. *Review of Radical Political Economics* 18:47–70.

Wolf, D. 1990. *Gender, Households and Rural Industrialization: Factory Daughters and Their Families in Java*. Berkeley: University of California Press.

Wood, E. 1988. Capitalism and human emancipation. *New Left Review*, no. 167:1–21.

World agriculture, contractors and bargaining in Agriculture. 1976. *World Agriculture* 25(1):3–9.

Wright, S. 1986. *Nigeria: The Dilemmas Ahead*. Economist Intelligence Unit Special Report no. 1072. London.

Yeoman, B. 1989. Don't count your chickens. *Southern Exposure* 17(2):20–26.

Young, L. 1987. Internationalization of the labor process in agriculture. Ph.D. diss., University of California, Berkeley.

Yusuf, A. 1988. *Maitatsine: Peddler of Epidemics*. Syneco: Kano.

Zeno, C. Mabbs 1986. *Nigeria: An Export Profile*. Foreign Agriculture Report no. 218, Washington, D.C.: USDA.

Newspapers, Magazines, and News Services

Africa Confidential. 1982.

Africa News. 1984, 1985.

Antioch Daily Ledger. 1985–1989.
Contra Costa Times. 1985–1989.
Engineering News Record. 1987.
Guardian. 1984.
Kano Annals. 1988.
Kennebek Journal. (Augusta, Me.) 1987.
Los Angeles Times. 1985–1989.
Martinez Gazette. 1988.
New Nigerian. 1980, 1981, 1984.
News-Pilot. (San Pedro, Calif.) 1988.
New York Times. 1981, 1982, 1988.
Nigerian Standard. 1982, 1985.
Nigerian Herald. 1981.
Nigerian Tribune. 1984.
Oakland Tribune. 1987–1989.
Pittsburg Post Dispatch. 1985–1989.
Punch. 1982, 1984.
San Francisco Business Times. 1987.
San Francisco Chronicle. 1985–1989.
San Francisco Examiner. 1988.
Sunday Sketch. 1982.
Worker. 1980.
Radio Nigeria Kaduna Domestic Service. 1982.
Wall Street Journal. 1988.
Waterville Morning Sentinel (Maine). 1988.
West Africa. 1981–1982, 1984.

Name Index